Partnerships in Urban Property Development

Nigel Dubben
School of Surveying and Planning
Kingston University

Brendan Williams
School of Geography, Planning and Environmental Policy
University College Dublin

WILEY-BLACKWELL
A John Wiley & Sons, Ltd., Publication

This edition first published 2009
© 2009 N. Dubben and B. Williams

Blackwell Publishing was acquired by John Wiley & Sons in February 2007. Blackwell's publishing programme has been merged with Wiley's global Scientific, Technical, and Medical business to form Wiley-Blackwell.

Registered office
John Wiley & Sons Ltd, The Atrium, Southern Gate, Chichester, West Sussex, PO19 8SQ, United Kingdom

Editorial office
9600 Garsington Road, Oxford, OX4 2DQ, United Kingdom
2121 State Avenue, Ames, Iowa 50014-8300, USA

For details of our global editorial offices, for customer services and for information about how to apply for permission to reuse the copyright material in this book please see our website at www.wiley.com/wiley-blackwell.

Library of Congress Cataloging-in-Publication Data

Dubben, Nigel, 1949–
    Partnerships in urban property development / Nigel Dubben, Brendan Williams. – 1st ed.
        p. cm.
    Includes bibliographical references and index.
    ISBN 978-1-4051-1179-9 (pbk. : alk. paper) 1. Real estate development 2. Partnership.
3. Cities and towns – Growth. I. Williams, Brendan. II. Title.

    HD1390.D83 2009
    333.77′15 – dc22

                                                                                          2009001747

A catalogue record for this book is available from the British Library.

Set in 10/12pt Sabon by Laserwords Private Limited, Chennai, India
Printed and bound in Malaysia by KHL Printing Co Sdn Bhd

1 2009

Contents

Preface

In this book we have written about partnerships in the broadest sense of the word. Virtually any property development scheme can be regarded as some sort of partnership as there will be a provider of finance, perhaps many, a developer who sees the opportunity, and a landowner who may also benefit from the development profits realised. The emphasis in this book is placed on the relationship between developers and landowners, developers and funders and the provision of public services through the use of private finance. Throughout the book, reference is made to practical examples many of which stem from our professional experience although it is not appropriate to identify some of the examples in the text. We do not deal with tax or legal matters in any great depth as these areas are subject to constant change and any book on these subjects is out of date even before publication.

The major change in world financial markets occurring through 2009/2010 will have profound consequences for future public/private partnership arrangements in urban development projects. The expansion in this sector internationally was largely based on the easy availability of credit over the preceding decade. In the coming years it is clear that credit will be greatly restricted. In addition the recent necessary role of the state as the final line of support to the entire financial system will have major implications for the conduct of all large-scale financial transactions in the future. A particular change that will be evident is in the transparency threshold required in major financial issues which will be set much higher than in the past. It is now clear also that the borrowing ability of construction and property interests will be subject to a greater level of scrutiny and control. The previous lack of regulation has been a major contributor to the problems of banking and financial interest in the UK, Ireland and internationally which are unravelling in the current market turmoil.

In another sense the recovery from the current recession will also have consequences for public private partnerships in development activities. The emerging recovery strategies in both the USA and Europe will be reliant on state investment projects to kick start economies and avoid a depression. This in turn will create a major need to fund many infrastructure and other development projects. The necessity to find every available mechanism to fund such investment programmes will involve examination of public private mechanisms anew. In turn investors may find such projects a more efficient use of funds as speculative asset investment markets unwind. It is therefore opportune that this book examines the experiences of recent decades with a view to contributing to and improving debate in this important policy area.

The book chapters are summarised as follows:

Chapter 1: The Public and Private Sectors
The ideas of public and private are considered from basic principles and the community power theories are summarised and debated. The practical relationships between the various parties involved with property partnerships are compared with the theoretical concepts and previous literature identifying power relationships in urban areas.

Chapter 2: The Property Development Process
Property Development is discussed in terms of the stages of a typical partnership project and the roles of the parties are identified.

Chapter 3: Partnership Negotiations Using Development Appraisal Techniques
Examples of development appraisals are used to illustrate development appraisal including the use of discounted cash flow.

Chapter 4: The Private Finance Initiative
The PFI is discussed and debated and a wealth of references are drawn on to examine this controversial area. A case study derived from personal experience and procured before PFI is compared with a similar project procured under PFI.

Chapter 5: Public Private Partnerships: the Urban Experience of Dublin
Dublin is used as the basis of a discussion which traces the use of private public partnerships in the modern development of the City.

Chapter 6: Property Funding Partnerships
The ways in which developers negotiate short- and long-term funding are examined using many numerical examples. The forms of agreement between the funder and developer are discussed in some depth.

Chapter 7: Development Partnerships and Landowners
The relationship between developer and landowner is discussed and examples are used to illustrate the many ways in which landowners can benefit from partnerships. Two case studies of department stores benefiting from development profits are both drawn from personal experience.

Chapter 8: International Trends and Public Private Partnerships
The methods used in public private partnerships in other parts of Europe and the world are discussed and comparisons drawn with those in the United Kingdom and Ireland.

Chapter 9: Economic Background and Future Trends
At the time of writing, the UK economy is undergoing a process of read-justment as the consequences of unwise bank lending works through the financial system. The current situation is summarised and the way in which property reacts to macro economic conditions is discussed.

Nigel Dubben
Brendan Williams

About the Authors

Nigel Dubben, MSc, BSc (Econ), MRICS, is Postgraduate Course Director in the School of Surveying at Kingston University. He was Development Surveyor for Slough Estates in the 1970s, a Partner in Conspectus Project Management in the 1980s and a Director of Grosvenor Waterside plc in the 1990s. He was also a Director of Hall, Pain and Foster before its takeover by Chesterton, now Atis Real, where he was Associate Director. He has been responsible for many development schemes, particularly in the retail sector and has managed major public and private sector projects.

Dr Brendan Williams lectures in Urban Development and Urban Economics at University College Dublin and is also Deputy Head of the School of Geography, Planning and Environmental Policy at UCD. In addition, he is a Chartered Planning and Development Surveyor who has worked on urban development projects in both a research and consultancy capacity in Ireland and internationally.

Acknowledgements

The work on the evolution of partnerships in Dublin development activity evolved from unpublished Ph.D. research by B. Williams in the 1990s and the authors' UCD working paper and journal article on 'Urban Regeneration in Dublin from 1986 to 2005' published in the *Journal of Property Investment and Finance* in 2006. Some of the material in Chapter 4 evolved from a journal article published in the final edition of the Kingston University publication *Environments by Design*.

Thanks to Stephen Hannon at UCD for assistance with graphs in the chapters on property development process and public private partnerships. Photos used are from a UCD project on Urban Development Policy in Dublin by Brendan Williams and Ian Boyle.

Thanks to Paul Sanderson of DTZ and Louise Ellison of IPF for the use of the graphs in Chapter 9. Thanks also to Emma Neal for typing the manuscript and to Madeleine Metcalfe of Wiley-Blackwell for her constant support.

Chapter 1
The Public and Private Sectors

The nature of partnership

In this chapter the nature of the relationship between public and private sectors is explored. State and community power were the subjects of a protracted debate in the 1990s as the implications of the Conservative government's policies of deregulation and privatisation were examined. The election of the Labour government in 1997 also attracted comments but these have been directed more at the practicalities of policy implementation including public–private partnerships. This chapter examines arguments concerning the interface of the state and the private sector, which were made by many commentators throughout the 1990s and the community power debate of the same period. This evolves into the practical implementation of policy by the incumbent Labour administration.

Procurement of public sector facilities to provide public goods increasingly involves the private sector through the private finance initiative (PFI), which is dealt with in detail in Chapter 4. Public goods are usually considered to have three main characteristics (Sloman 1992):

1. In a free market the private sector would underproduce a good or not produce it at all.
2. The consumption of a good by one person does not prevent others from enjoying it.
3. It is not possible to provide a good to one person without it being available for others to enjoy.

Public goods may therefore encompass bridges, national health hospitals, government buildings of all types, law courts and other facilities of a public nature. Although the free market would not provide the goods, the government increasingly involves private companies in their provision through the PFI. The PFI is a means of procurement that involves the private sector (typically) in financing, constructing and managing public facilities in return for a yearly payment by the public sector that will use the building. The private and public sectors can therefore be said to be in partnership. Both have incentives and responsibilities and the distinction between the two seems clear. On occasions, however, this is not quite so clear cut. For example, Local Improvement Finance Trust (LIFT) involves agencies of the public sector investing directly in the PFI consortium, which will provide health care facilities. It is difficult in these circumstances to clearly define where the public sector ends and the private sector begins. The lines demarcating the state and state agencies become blurred, and it is therefore important to be able to define the roles and power of the actors in partnerships.

Some commentators see the public sector, in the role of sovereign states, as powerless in the face of global forces (Ohmae 1995). It is believed that transnational and multinational companies will invest in those countries that maintain low corporate taxation and weak regulatory policies. The footloose nature of unregulated capital is believed to negate the traditional power of the state. However, property partnerships are designed and contracted on a micro basis and require commitment from all parties, at least until the buildings and facilities are completed when refinancing can take place.

The influence of global forces on public sector power is further considered in the following section.

The public sector

The public sector is usually taken to refer to a range of organisations collectively seen as part of 'the state'. These will include government departments such as the Treasury, the Home Office, County and District Councils and the Regional Development Agencies, together with other agencies concerned with land management and development, such as the Welsh Development Agency. Property partnerships may involve arrangements by any, and more, of these organisations with the private sector. Some Quasi Autonomous Non-Governmental Organisations (QUANGOs) may be difficult to categorise as part of the state although their functions may be considered to be part of the public sector. It is important to establish a clear definition of what exactly constitutes the public sector and what distinguishes it from the private sector before the relationship between public and private sectors can be discussed.

The state can be defined in the way it functions or by the means that it uses to fulfil its functions. The German historian Max Weber (1864–1920) believed that the state could only be defined as something that could legitimately use the means of violence to achieve its ends. Pierson (1996) helpfully lists what he regards as the most important features of the mechanisms of the modern state. These are as follows:

1. control of the means of violence
2. territoriality

3. sovereignty
4. constitutionality
5. impersonal power
6. the public bureaucracy
7. authority/legitimacy
8. citizenship
9. taxation

Of these, the way in which the state uses the public bureaucracy and impersonal power are particularly relevant when property partnerships are considered.

Other commentators see the state more directly in terms of functions. Greenberg (1990) collectively refers to the bureaucracy, the government, and the body of law, precedent and custom as 'the rules of the game', whereas Skocpol (1985) emphasises the importance of organisations in defining the state: 'administrative, legal, extractive and coercive organisations are the core of any state'. Dunleavy and O'Leary (1987) distinguish organisational definitions of the state from functional ones. They see the latter taking two forms, either defining the state in terms of goals or by consequences. They define the state as 'that set of institutions which carries out particular goals, purposes or objectives' and they extend this further by defining 'any organisation whose goals or purposes overlap with "state functions" automatically becomes part of the state'. This is interesting as it proposes a definition based on function, which may encompass utility companies, for example, as part of the state.

Although some commentators see the state merging into the private sector on the basis of function, most see a distinct identity for the state as a form of centralised power over a geographical area. David Held (1995) extends this concept to a number of other characteristics of the state. A monopoly of the means of violence, an impersonal structure of power and an acceptance by citizens of the legitimacy of the state are all seen as defining characteristics. The idea of legitimacy is closely linked to that of sovereignty defined by Held as 'a determinate structure of laws and institutions with a life and standing of its own'. In this context, the power of the state in comparison with private corporations can be tested by considering to what extent society is influenced by corporations that do not profess the legitimacy accorded to the state by public consent.

The principle of consent is important for it provides one method of separating state activity from that of a private corporation. Cole *et al.* (1993) also considers the principle of consent and sees the state representing the 'logical development' of this principle. He distinguishes the principle of the despotic state and the democratic state with the former justifying its legitimacy on the basis of the 'metaphysical conception of real wills whereas the latter has legitimacy resting on the actual wills of the ruled'. The validity of this argument is perhaps doubtful when considered in the circumstances of modern Western democracies with low turnouts and effective choice limited to one of two parties. Poggi (1990) takes the argument a stage further when he considers the sovereignty of the state, which is prepared to claim 'and if necessary is willing to prove, that it owes to no other power its control over the population in question; that it responds to no other organisation for the modalities and the outcomes of that control. It exercises that control on its own account activating its own resources, unconditionally, does not derive or share it with any other reality'. This extreme view of the power of the modern state can be compared with the reality of the 'hollowed out' state of the current millennium. This is further dealt with under the heading 'State and private sector power'.

Cole sees the state in different terms and puts forward the idea that the state is not the unlimited source of power but just another association, together with many others in society. He also distinguishes the concepts of nation and state and implies that nation is a subjective concept derived from the perception, habits and beliefs of the population. 'A nation may be a community but it cannot be, though it may possess a state. A nation is not an association; a state is'.

In the case of property partnerships, the relationship between state and private organisations is given legal weight by means of various contracts, usually a development agreement and a ground lease. In the case of arrangements where services are to be performed, such as with contracts under the PFI, the contract takes the form of a service agreement. The contracting parties are thus legally distinct although some commentators may see them as functionally indistinct. Usually, the state freehold ownership of land and buildings is combined with private sector expertise and finance to create new buildings and facilities. In this way the state, or the state agency, is distinctive. On a wider basis, the state underpins the market economy and allows it to function by maintaining the rule of law. John Kay sees the function of the state changing from waging war, adjudicating disputes and levying taxes to the provision of goods and services such as education, transport infrastructure, collection of rubbish and provision of essential services (Kay 1994). The present government increasingly involves the private sector in providing these functions in partnership (however defined) with the state or state agencies. This is not inconsistent with the state maintaining supreme power justified by democratic consent as this is necessary for the state to provide the rule of law for its citizens.

A further distinctive feature of state activity is the power of the state to regulate the private sector where public goods are provided and to levy taxation to provide public goods. Norman Barry (2004) identifies two further activities that define the function of the state – the way in which the state deals with a form of market failure in the provision of public goods and treatment of externalities. In the provision of public goods, the state is active and Barry identifies two features that define a public good: 'it is non-rival in consumption and non-payers cannot be excluded from its enjoyment'. Property partnership schemes are often devised to supply public goods through private means. Where the action of a private or public agency results in adverse effects to a third party, and the third party is not compensated by the original agency, there is said to be a negative externality and the state is charged with taking action to correct the problem. Dunleavy and O'Leary define the nature and activities of the functional state in a useful summary that can be related to the state's activities in property partnerships:

1. The state is a recognisably separate institution or a set of institutions so differentiated from the rest of society as to create identifiable public and private spheres.
2. The state is sovereign, or is the supreme power, within its territory, and by definition, the ultimate authority for all law, that is, binding rules supported by coercive sanctions. Public law is made by state officials and backed by a formal monopoly of force.
3. The state's sovereignty extends to all the individuals within a given territory and applies equally even to those in formal positions of government or rule making. Thus, sovereignty is distinct from the personnel who at any given time occupy a particular role within the state.
4. The modern state's personnel are mostly recruited and trained for management in a bureaucratic manner.
5. The state has the capacity to extract monetary revenues (taxation) to finance its activities from its subject population (Dunleavy and O'Leary, 1987, p. 2).

Many of the terms used above require further discussion and perhaps the most important one is the urban power of the state in terms of its nature, the way in which it is exercised, and how it relates to the power of the private sector.

The state and private sector power

In discussing state power it is appropriate to commence with Hobbes' *Leviathan*. Hobbes wrote his enduring account of state power in the mid-seventeenth century and in writing it, he was much influenced by his views of the English civil war. Hobbes' view of the state is of an entity, comprising the citizens of the state, which has supreme power and is able to order stable relations among all citizens of the state. The idea that the state actually comprises its citizens does not feature in Hobbes' work. It was left to John Locke to explain what modern man would recognise as democratic principles. '... supreme power was the inalienable right of the people; that governmental supremacy was a delegated supremacy held on trust; that government enjoyed full political authority so long as this trust was sustained; and that a government's legitimacy or right to rule could be withdrawn if the people judged this necessary and appropriate, that is, if the rights of individuals and the ends of society were systematically flouted' (Held 1995, p. 44).

Where the state contracts with the private sector to produce buildings and facilities for public use there is clearly a power relationship. Dowding (1996) identifies two types of power, which he calls 'outcome' power and 'social' power. The former is the ability to bring about or help to bring about outcomes, whereas the latter implies a change in the incentive structure of another party to bring about outcomes. In terms of property partnerships where a District Council owns the freehold interest in a site that it wants to see developed, it can be said that the council has the outcome power to legally make the land available by way of a ground lease. It also has the social power to frame the development agreement in such a way as to produce a scheme that accords with the planning brief and carries public benefits by incentivising the developer. The two types of power considered here are sometimes referred to as *power to* and *power over*.

The two types of power considered above can be further divided into the way in which power is exercised and by whom. Theories of social and business power can be categorised under three main headings: elitism, pluralism and regime theory. Elitism derives from the classical world and proposes a hierarchical view of social power, where a small privileged group of people rule a society comprising persons with little power 'to' or power 'over'. It therefore owes much to the Greek model, particularly the Athenian state, where a sizeable elite was involved with political matters. 'Athens in her great days governed and defended herself by the service of over 7,000 citizens, out of a total resident citizen population of about 40,000' (Barker 1967). Dahl (1957) takes a slightly different view and believes that the reality of ancient Greece was that only a small minority of citizens attended meetings of the assembly and it was the rich and powerful who held sway. This feature of Athenian politics strikes similarities with elitism but the relevance of the Greek model is seen to an even stronger extent with the normative views of Plato, who believed that democratic politics could only lead to a failure of social cohesion. His well-known belief in the value of rule by philosophers has common features with later elitist theories.

Harding (1995, p.35) identifies three positions that encapsulate the approach to elite theory. Firstly, the presence of a powerful elite may be regarded as the best way in which benefits to society may be realised. This pragmatic view can be argued on the basis of efficiency. Secondly, it may be possible to demonstrate that problems only appear when rule by a few is either resisted or overthrown. Thirdly, the elite rule may be regarded as a 'necessary evil' for society to function at all and this is called the 'techno-cratic' approach by Harding. The maintenance of the elite is seen to be the only way in which modern industrialised society can be organised. Power is therefore concentrated in the hands of the few who occupy commanding positions within society's leading bureaucracies.

Harding believes that the normative approach adopted by the Italian theorists Mosca and Pareto can be regarded as truly elitist in the sense that elitism is seen as superior to other forms of rule. Dunleavy and O'Leary make a similar point when they describe the most important developments in elite theory commencing with the Italian school. 'Pareto defined an elite at its simplest as those individuals who have the highest indices of excellence in any particular activity, whether it be train-robbing, fishing, political science, or big business' (Dunleavy and O'Leary 1987, p. 136). Elite theory in the context of the modern industrial state therefore moves logically into urban politics and it is in the study of urban politics that Harding sees a further development that he calls critical elite theory. 'Critical elite theorists . . . see the "power elite" as neither natural nor desirable but as the worrying product of historical trends' (Harding 1995). In this analysis, it is the capacity to act, only available to those who have control over vast industrial or bureaucratic organisations, which is the important factor. Elitism is a fact of modern industrialised society.

The involvement of later elite theorists in urban politics opened up what Harding describes as 'a methodological can of worms' (Harding 1995). The application of empiricism was a departure from earlier elite theory, but serious problems were encountered with its application. As Dunleavy and O'Leary put it, 'A . . . fundamental problem for empirical work in the elite theory tradition is the difficulty of demonstrating that a power relationship exists' (Dunleavy and O'Leary 1987). One reaction of elite theorists to this problem was to adopt reputational analysis that sought to identify the reputations of supposedly powerful individuals. Those people who can be shown to be believed to have power can also be assumed to have power relationships in urban society. The most famous work was that of Hunter (1953) in his study of Atlanta where he identified a business-dominated elite, but this precipitated a sustained critique, mainly from pluralists, who criticised his methodological approach. Some commentators believed that he commenced his study with pre-formed ideas about where power would lie and only investigated the reputations of those people who fell into this pre-empted list. It was also believed that Hunter ignored the functional context in which power was assumed to be exercised because, in his analysis, power was concentrated on individuals outside of, for example, the jobs they might perform. A further, fairly obvious, point to make was that Hunter, in concentrating on reputation, had failed to prove that power was actually exercised in the way he stated.

The pluralist challenge to elite theory is given impetus by elite theorists attempting to empirically prove their theories by researching urban communities. Although there are other theoretical areas that are important, the community power debate has focused around the elitist and pluralist views and on whether either theory can be proved. Before considering the importance and influence of regime theory to the debate, it is necessary to consider the pluralist position.

David Judge (1995) defines pluralism, not necessarily within an urban context. Power is decentralised with many focus points; all groups in society are able to make themselves heard in some way; dispersion of power is normatively seen to be 'a good thing'; political outcomes will vary according to the myriad distributions of power, processes and actors; political power is exercised outside the accepted political institutions of liberal democracy; legitimate authority would result from interaction of interests rather than any interpretation of the 'general will'. Finally, the process is underpinned by the commitment of the actors to a system that is both uncertain and dispersed throughout society. The inference is that some power can be exercised by all groups in society and therefore no group will be powerless. In attempting to define the pluralist position, therefore, it appears imprecise in comparison with the definite statements of the elitists but, as many commentators have pointed out, pluralism comes to life when it is used to criticise other theories of community power. 'In fact, perhaps the central defining feature of pluralism is what it sets itself against. In this sense . . . it is no more than an anti theory' (Judge 1995).

One of the most important publications that address pluralism is Dahl's *Who Governs?* (1961). In this book, Dahl investigates positivistic and behaviourist theories and attempts to define the power structure in New Haven, particularly from the competing theories of oligarchy (elitist) versus polyarchy (pluralist). Positivists believe that all political statements are evidently logical, can be tested by empirical methods or are meaningless, in which case they cannot be researched. Behaviourism, which flows from positivism, concentrates on people's behaviour patterns, which can be observed and measured, rather than their covert incentives, which cannot be subject to scientific investigation. Dahl's approach first of all defines power as 'a successful attempt by A to get B to do something he would not otherwise do' (Dahl 1957). By investigating decision-making where there was a conflict of interests, Dahl seeks to define who is successful in either initiating or vetoing policy changes. He concludes that power is not exercised by a discrete ruling elite, but is disseminated throughout the community with different groups enjoying success at varying times and for varying reasons.

Dahl sees New Haven (Connecticut, USA), the subject of his research, changing from oligarchy to pluralism, but he also identifies a stratification in society where certain individuals are much more involved in political policy and action than the rest of the population. Dahl sees stratification from a number of standpoints. The political strata are 'relatively rational human beings', whereas in the apolitical strata choices are influenced by 'inertia habit, unexamined loyalties, personal attachments, emotions, transient impulses' (Dahl, 1961, p. 90). The apolitical strata are also seen to be uninformed with all this translating into a predictable lack of direct influence in politics. Dahl here seems to be approaching common ground with the elitists, but this is, in fact, not the case for he believes that the political stratum is easily penetrated by anyone with an interest in being involved. The incentive for this in terms of the political strata, Dahl believes, lies in the nature of the democratic system with politicians having a direct incentive to increase the strength of their coalitions and their political support.

In the urban context, some commentators see pluralism increasing as city size increases as in the studies of New York and New Haven (Judge 1995). In contrast, Dahl identifies a political apathy in New Haven. He sees New Haven's government being dominated by the 'various petty sovereignties that made up the official and unofficial government of New Haven' (Dahl 1961) and this system is underpinned by three factors: the indifference of the citizenry towards matters that did not immediately affect them; the fragmentation of political resources and the non-involvement of the Mayor that results in government agencies being largely autonomous. In contrast, the works of Thomas and Savitch (1991) identify a distinct growth in the number and power of political groups in cities. The result of this is to make cities virtually ungovernable with chaotic political systems. These views are not accepted by all commentators, but they are collectively known as *hyperpluralism* as they represent one extreme of the pluralist spectrum.

A feature of pluralist theory that is distinctive is cited by Dunleavy and O'Leary (1987) as the way in which pluralism ascribes far more importance to input politics than other theories. 'Pluralists insist that large size does not prevent modern nation-states from being effective polyarchies. Electoral accountability provides the binding chain' (Dunleavy and O'Leary 1987, pp. 23–24). Pluralism is, however, a theory with a wide base of application and can have a range of meanings. It does not even have to be shown that there is any distinct change of policy resulting from the influence of different groups in society. As Keith Dowding writes, 'I do not even need to persuade policy-makers to do what I want, as long as they have to take my views into account. As long as they are forced to hear "legitimate groups" and spend time and effort doing what they ask, then we have a pluralist system' (Dowding 1996).

Regime theory can be argued to have developed from pluralist research and shares much common ground with it. It is uncontroversial in the sense that it recognises a range of government institutions that are, to varying degrees, subject to some form of popular control. It also recognises the presence of an economy heavily, but not exclusively, influenced by private investment decisions. The essence of regime theory is that regimes are formed to ease the implementation of a range of policy outcomes that could not be accomplished autonomously either by government or business interests. Moreover, the true regime theorist recognises the long-lasting nature of regimes. Dowding sums up the nature of regimes succinctly, although he does not see regimes resulting from a conscious decision by certain actors, but from the 'systematic luck' of capitalists in which their interests fortunately coincide with those of ruling politicians. 'Regimes are coordinating devices which provide opportunities for bargaining with the different sides in controversies and, importantly, establish the parameters through which bargaining takes place' (Dowding 1996).

A criticism of regime theory is that it adds little to the study of urban politics as it is essentially nothing more than a further variant of pluralist theory. Clarence Stone addresses this in his study of Atlanta (Stone 1989), which is a cornerstone of regime theory. In this work, Stone writes about the systematic power of the business elite in forming a sustained regime with government so that policy could be implemented. Stone's often-quoted definition of a regime is 'an informal yet relatively stable group with access to institutional resources that enable it to have a sustained role in making governing decisions' (Stone 1989). The difference from Dowding's definition (Dowding 1996 quoted above) is significant in that Stone's regime comprises a (relatively) stable group and this emphasises the importance he places on its long-lasting nature. Dowding's view is clearly pluralist in that he uses the word 'bargaining' and implies that bargains will be struck between the myriad organisations envisaged by the pluralist model. The reference to setting parameters is important, however, and is a subject that is an important feature of regime theory.

Regime theory therefore has an essentially pragmatic focus in the sense that actors are assumed to realise that policies cannot be implemented unless cooperation is ensured among those who hold power in society. No one group can exercise enough control to implement policy on its own and regime theory here shows a distinct difference from elite theory, which assumes that the elite will possess power over society. Stone himself, in writing about Atlanta, emphasises the pragmatic nature of regime theory when he states, 'What is at issue is not so much domination and subordination as a capacity to act and accomplish goals. The power struggle concerns not control and resistance, but gaining and fusing a capacity to act – power to, not power over' (Stone 1989; also quoted in Stoker and Mossberger 1994).

The distinction between regime theorists and pluralists is sometimes blurred by the common ground between the two, notably the acceptance of the diffusion and changing nature of power in society. However, pluralists emphasise the ever-changing nature of the power relationship with governments 'likely to respond to groups on the basis of their electoral power or the intensity of their preferences' (Stoker and Mossberger 1994, p. 197). Regime theorists, in contrast, emphasise the tendency of powerful groups to form coalitions with others that are long lasting over a range of policy issues. There are strong differences between regime theorists and pluralists also in the way in which they perceive the nature of government. Pluralists and elitists emphasise the incentive for government to control society and this is backed up by the normative idea that if government is accessible to all, this is acceptable. In contrast, regime theorists see power as organised through coalitions so that certain outcomes may be achieved, although some common ground can be seen with elite and regime theories in terms of agenda setting.

Elite theorists recognise the capacity of elites to set agendas and regime theorists recognise similar features. 'Regimes may also practice a politics of exclusion, seeking to ensure that certain interests are not provided with access to decision-making' (Stoker and Mossberger 1994). Stone (1989), in reconsidering the work of Floyd Hunter (1953), believes that Hunter's work has relevance in the study of regimes. Hunter's argument falls into three areas. Firstly, power is formally divided between government and business; secondly, the policy setting role is a necessary function in society; and thirdly, the policy setting powers of major business actors (considered as 'prestige' figures) extend to the government and civic sectors.

Although Hunter did not use the term 'pre-emptive power', Stone believes that this concept 'is embedded in his work' (Stone 1989). Pre-emptive power, as defined by Stone, is 'power as a capacity to occupy, hold, and make use of a strategic position' (Stone 1989, p. 83). Hunter's view is that the policy-making function is performed by those who hold a form of pre-emptive power and do not see this in terms of individual actors but in a more complex form. 'Community context, a strategic role within that context, and complex entities – those are the ingredients for a pre-emptive power relationship' (ibid.). Stone's views of community power derive from Hunter's work and also that of Bachrach and Baratz (1970) who first used the phrase 'non-decision making'. Elites 'expend their resources strategically by preventing unfriendly issues from gaining access to the decision making agenda' (Stone 1989).

In developing Hunter's and Bachrach and Baratz's (1970) theories of power, Stone describes how policy-setting coalitions can maintain their power by controlling the agenda. Of itself, this activity generates resources to counter resistance and the only way forward for a challenging group is to construct an even more powerful coalition. Stone concedes that orthodox pluralists would point out that the incentive to challenge an established coalition is strengthened by the presence of pre-emptive power in the coalition. However, while acknowledging the merits of the pluralist argument, Stone emphasises the difficult task of challenging an established coalition: 'the challenge group must be able to bear the cost, not only of resistance, but also of bringing together a viable policy coalition'. The pluralist position is that power in society is diffused with large numbers of groups being able to influence the policy agenda. The elitist position does not challenge this view but contends that elites exist and dominate society to achieve their ends. In contrast, Stone's view of pre-emptive power developed from Hunter's work puts forward a different argument. Pre-emptive power has two main dimensions: 'the power advantage of holding a strategic position and . . ., the capacity to occupy that position'. Regime theory describes the setting up and maintenance of a regime as the most effective way for policy to be implemented, and the long-lasting nature of the regime operating across a range of initiatives is underpinned by the presence of pre-emptive power.

Regime theory has common themes with elements of the classic community power debate but has developed a discrete research base. Stoker and Mossberger (1994) offer a typology of urban regimes as a major part of this research. Types of regime are classified under three main headings: organic, instrumental and symbolic. 'The instrumental regime – is typified by Stone's description of Atlanta'. This type of regime is one which achieves goals that would be difficult to achieve by one actor. A regime is necessary to deliver results. The organic regime derives from a cohesive urban settlement with 'a tightly knit social fabric'. Although they do not quite say as much, this form of regime is described by Stoker and Mossberger as a pre-existing regime. It is therefore interesting, as it appears to be a regime that is not consciously formed by its members. Symbolic regimes are characteristic of cities in the process of change in governance and image. Stoker and Mossberger build on the general purpose of regimes by offering a classification of the mechanisms by which community action problems are solved. These are concerned with mobilising participation, the development of a common sense of purpose, the way in which interests come together in coalitions and the interface between regimes and the wider political environment.

Stoker and Mossberger regard their initial four categories as valuable only in very general ways. In illustrating and explaining their research, they identify a number of subtypes that can be seen in a practical sense. The focus is on the purpose for which the regime is formed and the authors describe a number of types of regime that seek to maintain the status quo. This is a departure from the usual way in which regimes are envisaged, for in this type the emphasis is on preventing change rather than affecting it. Similarly, exclusive regimes involve distinct groups (such as a certain class) maintaining the status quo (more accurately their status) by a rigid politics of exclusion. Traditional regimes are also proposed as a type that derives from 'the maintenance of prestige as defined by the city's position in a regional hierarchy' (Stoker and Mossberger 1994). These can all be recognised as passive regimes in comparison with regimes that are formed to achieve an identifiable positive goal. The project realisation regime is an example of this type, where the regime functions to achieve a particular short-term goal. The obvious example would be in the field of property development and the attraction of investment into an urban area.

Further classification is offered in the ways in which regimes form and maintain a common sense of purpose, either by the use of selective incentives (offering distinct rewards to members of the regime), tradition and social cohesion (deriving from shared civic community and pride) or by the strategic use of symbols where political language is used to maintain support even though concrete action may be lacking. The quality of the regime that is formed will result from the way in which the incentives of the parties are brought together to maintain a cohesive strength. Some regimes will require major compromises by the members, whereas in others a pre-existing commonality of interest or motivation may be present. For Stoker and Mossberger, a congruence of interest in terms of political outlook and political partnership results in issues being resolved by discussion and compromise. Finally, regimes may display competitive agreement where there is considerable political discord but the regime sustains through the parties recognising its value above their political differences.

Regime theory has developed both in depth and complexity and it has attracted its own critique. David Imbroscio (1998) believes regime theory is the 'dominant paradigm for the analysis of local politics', but argues that it suffers from a 'flawed conceptualisation of the division of labor (sic) between state and market within cities – a conceptualisation that tends to be overly rigid and largely static or fixed'. The argument here is that although regime theory is valuable in that it recognises the interface between the state and the market, it is wrong to portray this relationship in a fixed way. Imbroscio proposes 'a richer range of possible urban regimes than recognized by established regime typologies'. The example of the involvement of the City of Hull in telecommunications may be an illustration of the first of Imbroscio's models which he identifies as 'the local state as urban accumulator'.

The city is capable of involving itself in what was hitherto private business, and in this way the concept of a strict public/private division breaks down. Imbroscio also identifies the rise of the 'new community economics movement' as an example of a third force, which is neither public nor private but is influential in urban politics. Often run on a non-profit basis, these organisations may have a significant influence on economic regeneration and as such should be recognised in regime theory. Imbroscio quotes a number of examples from the United States, but in a British context, the Training and Enterprise Councils may serve as an example together with Housing Associations and Housing Action Trusts. Similarly, there is a weakness in the way in which regime theorists concentrate on the power of major companies rather than studying the activities of small-scale entrepreneurs. 'For example, rather than being dominated by large, multinational corporations, the city's private sector might be more diversified – driven to a greater extent by an array of small, independent businesses' (ibid.).

Imbroscio proposes further regime typologies to address the flaw in regime theory in assuming a rigid division between state and market. This classification focuses on community-based regimes (deriving from the new economics movement), petty bourgeois regimes (based on small businesses) and local statist regimes where the local state becomes directly involved in public profit-making activities.

Regime theory is therefore a developing area of the study of urban politics. Its concept of community power seeks a classification, which is in many ways derived from pluralist theory drawing on an examination of the incentives and power relationships of various actors. It moves away from normative statements by the use of empiricism, and as a result, the research is given a sharper focus. One feature that is lacking in much of the published research is, however, an in-depth view of the way in which regimes come into existence and the true intentions of the actors. These may not be as one dimensional as some classifications envisage. The complexity of relationships envisaged by regime theory is recognised by a number of commentators. What appears to be lacking is the recognition that a similar complexity might be present within the organisations and actors involved with urban politics. In a sense, of course, this is of no importance as the policy outcome will be the power focus, but in another way, a study of subjective motivation might reveal more accurately why and how a regime comes to form. Dunleavy and O'Leary consider this point when they write about behaviourism: '... behaviourism, the doctrine that social science should focus only on people's objective behaviour patterns – since their subjective intentions, wants and motives are private states which cannot be observed scientifically' (Dunleavy and O'Leary 1987).

Regime theorists appear to adopt a behaviourist approach when writing about motivation and presumably the main reason for this is that subjective wants are regarded as not researchable. Stoker and Mossberger (1994) write about motivation of businesses by focusing on the type of business rather than its internal components. The emphasis is placed on external factors: 'Are the dominant players from the same business sector, or managers in large corporations? What sectors of business are most dominant: property, retail, manufacturers, utilities, finance or service?' The importance of these factors in motivation is clear but an investigation into subjective factors should be possible with business actors and may reveal more. Especially with large business corporations, the strength of the regime may be influenced by the power relationships within the major actors. This might explain, for example, how Associated British Ports plc (as it then was) came to promote a major port extension at Dibden Bay, Hampshire, no more than 6 years after the company made representations to the Hampshire County Structure Plan public enquiry and launched an expensive publicity campaign in favour of a housing scheme on the site.

The question remains as to which, if any, of the theories of community power stated earlier and summarised in Figure 1.1 represent the relationship of the parties involved with property partnerships?

Chapter 1

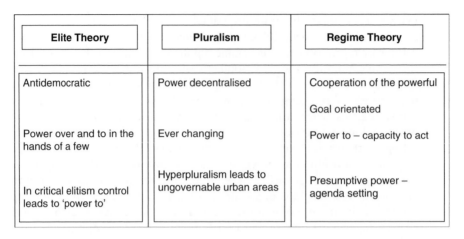

Elite Theory	Pluralism	Regime Theory
Antidemocratic	Power decentralised	Cooperation of the powerful
		Goal orientated
Power over and to in the hands of a few	Ever changing	Power to – capacity to act
In critical elitism control leads to 'power to'	Hyperpluralism leads to ungovernable urban areas	Presumptive power – agenda setting

Figure 1.1   Theories of community power summarised.

Centralisation of power by government

The roles of the various parties involved with a central area development are considered here, but overarching this whole process is the role of central government. Stephen Lukes (1974) first analyses three dimensions of power commencing with decision-making power. Agenda shaping is the second dimension, whereas the third is the power to influence people to such an extent that their desires are changed to accord with the power source, which may be central government, a private consortium or some other body. Lukes' conception of power develops into attempts by central government to bring power into the centre so that decisions made locally are controlled centrally or at least regionally.

An example of this can be seen in the 2004 Planning and Compulsory Purchase Act, where Section 38/6 requires that all planning applications must be determined in accordance with the development plan unless material considerations indicate otherwise. Regional Spatial Strategies and the London Plan form part of the definition of the 'development plan' and the plans of local authorities, such as Local Development Frameworks, have to follow the decisions set by the regional plan. Under the previous legislation, the 1990 Town and Country Planning Act, the predecessor of Regional Spatial Strategies, Regional Guidance, did not come under the equivalent of Section 38/6 (Section 54A of the 1990 Act) and was therefore only advisory, whereas the new plans are mandatory. In this way, central government pulls power into the centre by the use of unelected regional authorities rather than allow power to rest with local authorities such as District Councils. It is true that the 2004 Act introduces Statements of Community Involvement, which oblige local planning authorities to set out proposals for the involvement of the local community in plan making and development control, but this may be an attempt by the central government to reduce the power of local councils by involving the public directly. A recent White

Paper (Communities and Local Government 2008) *Communities in control; real people, real power* states the same message more explicitly: 'We want to shift power, influence and responsibility away from existing centres of power into the hands of communities and individual citizens'. Although the White Paper states that direct participation by citizens will strengthen and not undermine local government, it does not state exactly how this will be achieved without taking considerable power away from democratically elected local authorities; many commentators see the proposals as an attempt at setting the government agenda at the expense of true local representation in the traditional way.

Chapter 1

Power relationships with central area redevelopment

The relationships between the local authority and developer with a typical central urban retail development scheme are now summarised. The actors involved are as follows:

1. local authority (District Council or Metropolitan Borough)
2. developer
3. developer's short-term funder (usually a bank)
4. developer's long-term funder (usually an institution or a bank)
5. tenants
6. the public
7. other public authorities (County Council)
8. pressure groups (civic societies)
9. central government

The incentives of the various parties involved with a typical scheme vary according to the nature of the organisation and its financial stake in the scheme. The Local Authority landowner wishes to see a scheme that accords with its planning and development brief and offers a financial return that represents value for money in terms of the asset it has in the scheme. It will have a long-term interest and will therefore wish to see a firm prospect of competent management that fits in with its aspirations for the remainder of the town centre. The developer is motivated by the prospect of profit and this is usually a short-term profit as it is usual for the developer to assign its interest in the scheme to a long-term funder upon completion; however, this is defined in the financing document. The short-term funder requires loan repayment with accrued interest and the long-term funder a scheme that is well and fully let out, and which will command an investment yield reflecting its quality, value and prospects for future rental growth. The Local Authority, as an elected body, can be expected to pay close regard to the views of the public, although in reality this sometimes does not appear to be the case. The anchor tenants for the scheme will have been committed by means of agreements to lease and should have similar incentives to the long-term funder. Both have a direct interest in the success of the centre and both will wish to see the centre popular with the general public. Pressure groups are sometimes consulted as part of the planning process but may also be influential as a result of the established business contacts of their members. The process for organising the development is dealt with later in detail, but, in summary, it often consists of the Local Authority resolving to dispose of the site to a developer and then seeking bids for a long-term ground lease from between four and six developers, each of which will have pre-qualified. The Local Authority landowner produces a development and planning brief against which tenders will be submitted and will accept (although it will not be obliged to do so) one tender by analysing the design and financial offer against its criteria. A question that arises from this summary of a lengthy process is 'does this typical partnership arrangement accord with any of the established theories of community power?'

An example may be taken of the WestQuay shopping centre in Southampton, which resulted from a long-standing commitment by the City Council to establish the city as one of the major retail centres in the United Kingdom. George Monbiot is unequivocal that this major shopping scheme is the result of an elitist initiative for the benefit of private companies (Monbiot 2000). Yet, as Michelle Lowe points out (Lowe 2005), the initiative to develop WestQuay came about because the City Council fortuitously owned 35 acres of land in the middle of Southampton. The leader of the Council at that time, Alan Whitehead, was ambitious to make the city a regional centre with WestQuay as its retail core. The presence of the John Lewis department store in a relatively poor location in the city was a further incentive, as this store had indicated that it wished to move from the area if it could not relocate to a better location within the city. Michelle Lowe identifies a 'close collaboration' with parties involved with the scheme, but the relationship falls short of what political theorists would describe as a regime. Imry, the developer proposed for the scheme, failed in the harsh economic conditions of the early 1990s and was replaced by Hammerson, with Barclays Bank as the funder. The impetus for the scheme originally rested with the City Council and primarily with John Arnold, Chair of Economic Development (and eventually the leader) and the then leader, Alan Whitehead. Their vision for the city rested on their long-term ambitions and their commitment to Southampton as a place where people would wish to visit and live. The opening of the centre in 2000 had the effect of placing Southampton in the 12th place in the accepted city retail ranking index (Experian 2001). These tables rank cities according to the quality of the retail experience, but the ranking is very much based on the number of multiple retail outlets available in terms of both variety and type. Investors in retail development would find the tables useful as those cities with the highest number of multiple tenants will probably also have the highest retail rents.

The City Council, as the promoter of the scheme, completed the necessary land acquisition so that WestQuay could proceed as the developers wished. Imry had originally been selected as the developer for WestQuay, as it had developed the first phase of retail warehouses. These had let well but also attracted considerable architectural criticism. When this company was no longer viable, its bankers, Barclays, sold the interest to Hammerson. Therefore, the City Council was not the main actor in selecting the developer for the site. In Imry's time, efforts were made to complete the site acquisition by the use of compulsory purchase orders on the necessary areas including a piece of land that would allow a mall to be built to link the centre with the traditional retail core of Southampton, Above Bar. According to John Bywater, the Managing Director of Hammerson, this acquisition was crucial to the success of the scheme. (Interview with John Bywater (5/3/06)) and Lowe (p. 10) describes it as a 'fundamental breakthrough'.

The example of WestQuay does not fit neatly into any theory of community power. The City Council displayed considerable 'power to' by providing most of the land for the scheme and promoting a compulsory purchase order, but the city had no means of bringing the scheme to fruition without a funded developer in partnership. The main component of the scheme, the creation of a major shopping centre let out to the highest paying tenants (multiples based on lady's fashions), was not an issue between the parties. Those representing the Council were concerned with pragmatic issues and, to enable the city to establish itself in the front rank of shopping destinations, a scheme of this nature had to be built. Planning policy followed the market imperatives.

A similar factor is seen in the power of urban governance in Dublin with the implementation of various initiatives to regenerate the city centre (McGuirk and MacLaran 2001), except that some dissension is noted between the planning and market requirements. 'Governing power was socially produced in a collection of cross-sectoral networks which operated across a range of scales and blurred the boundaries of the public and private sectors ... local government planners were sidelined'.

The WestQuay scheme was not the product of a 'regime' in the sense that Clarence Stone defines it, but there is certainly a strong element of agenda setting within and beyond the local community. Private sector profit requirements were paramount in the way the two main parties, the City Council and the developer, perceived the success of the scheme. A more recognisable example of elitism has been reported in the regeneration of Manchester city centre; 'Implicit in this was the emergence of new power brokers, in effect reconstituting the "Manchester Men" of earlier generations, with such elite networks typically spanning the public-private sector divide' (Williams 2006). Other commentators have questioned the benefits that flow from such projects and imply that agenda setting produces buildings that may be profitable for developers and, through ground lease payments, for Councils, but do not provide softer benefits for those excluded from the policy discussion.

In writing about the Paradise Street regeneration of Liverpool city centre, a partnership between Grosvenor as developer and the City Council, Anna Minton describes the new scheme creating private space from what was once the public realm with all its democratic implications: 'in terms of public space the key issue is that while local government has previously controlled, managed, and maintained all streets and public squares the creation of these new "private public" spaces means that, as in the early Victorian period, they will be owned and managed by individual private landlords who have the power to restrict access and control activities' (Minton 2002). The New Economics Foundation (NEF) identifies what it calls a 'clone town', which is defined as 'a place that has had the individuality of its high street shops replaced by a monochrome strip of global and national chains that means its retail heart could easily be mistaken for dozens of other bland town centres across the country' (NEF 2005). The report calls for public sector action to maintain the diversity of the town centres and control free market forces to the benefit of communities that do not choose the urban fabric produced by development partnerships and the dominance of the profit-maximising motive. Apologists for regeneration policies of the type described may well point out that the value of all property depends on the utility enjoyed by the end user, often a rent-paying tenant. If the schemes created were not viable for the retail tenants and popular with the public, they would not be built. It is also true, however, that property development is, for developers, a short-term profit-generating exercise and there is often no incentive to consider longer term implications of major town centre projects.

The state and the private sector – the 'hollowed out' state

David Held (1996) categorises states into various categories over time, culminating in what he refers to as the 'modern state'. His account moves from empires to feudalism, to the polity of estates and absolutist states to the modern state. Pierson refines his original list of features characteristic of the modern state (see the earlier text) into five main areas (1996, p. 52):

1. monopoly control of the means of violence
2. territoriality
3. sovereignty
4. bureaucracy
5. taxation

Although the above features can be applied to the state, at least in Great Britain if not in the United Kingdom, since 1945, there have been more recent changes to the way in which the state relates to the private sector. This has causal effects with the way in which the state organises property partnerships and the cause is rooted in the government's macroeconomic policy. The major change in the nature of the state since 1945 has been the move towards the enabling and regulatory state rather than the state directly providing goods and services including property facilities. Colin Crouch (2004) contrasts 'old government' with 'new governance'. The former is characterised by 'command and control, hierarchy and authority, institutions and organisational structures', whereas the latter is based on 'facilitating, collaborating, bargaining, networks, partnerships, processes, policies, outputs and outcomes'.

George Monbiot (2007) makes a similar point, but far more strongly, when he charts the rise of 'neoliberalism' from 1947, when the founder of the Mont Pelerin Society, Friedrich von Hayek, proposed the philosophy that became known as *neoliberalism*. Monbiot sums it up as follows: 'Neoliberalism claims that we are best served by maximum market freedom and minimum intervention by the state. The role of government should be confined to creating and defending markets, protecting private property and defending the realm. All other functions are better discharged by private enterprise, which will be prompted by the profit motive to supply essential services'. Monbiot here describes the 'hollowed out' state where 'power over' remains (arguably) but 'power to' is passed to the private sector. His definition is, however, subjective, but the way in which the state addresses forces that influence the power it can wield can now be investigated. These forces encompass globalisation, corporate power and the policy of UK governments, in adopting a neoliberal agenda.

The state, globalisation and the corporations

Poggi (1990) defines globalisation as '... a complex of economic, technological, ecological and cultural structures and processes (that) display their effects on the scale of the planet, or at any rate, have a radius of action that ignores, or denies relevance to, any state's territory'. For David Held it is '... a multi-dimensional phenomenon involving diverse domains of activity and interaction including the economic, political, technological, military, legal, cultural and environmental' (Held 1996). The inference to be drawn from Poggi's definition is that global forces render states powerless to successfully achieve domestic policy outcomes, unless they accord with the interests of those who control global corporations. Globalisation is, however, seen to extend beyond the field of economic policy and industrial production. The references to culture imply that globalisation is an enveloping force that has an influence on the whole of society, not just those matters that normally concern the state. Hirst and Thompson (1999) emphasise the importance of studying economic globalisation as all other factors are seen as a consequence of global forces and unsustainable without them. They do not deny that there is an international economy, but they dismiss the views of the extreme globalisers such as Ohmae (1995). They see globalisation as 'largely a myth' and their argument rests on five main tenets.

Firstly, Hirst and Thompson draw comparisons between the present international economy and that of previous periods in history from the industrial revolution onwards. They believe that the current economy in many areas is less open than previously. Secondly, they draw the distinction between transnational companies and national companies that trade internationally. The latter are seen to have a committed economic base in one country, whereas the former are able to locate freely around the globe. Hirst and Thompson believe that true transnational companies, analogous to 'hot' money in financial terms, are rare. Thirdly, there is no discernible shift of capital from the advanced Western countries to the developing economies with foreign direct investment (FDI) concentrated in the former. Fourth, trade and financial movements are concentrated in the Western economies and fifth, governments, by cooperation, are able to control and regulate private global forces if they so wish.

Hirst and Thompson develop their arguments, and other commentators support their views. Linda Weiss (1997) believes that the effect of economic globalisation has been exaggerated. She compares historical international trade and capital flows with those of the present day and concludes that 'As late as 1991 the OECD shares of exports on GDP (17.9%) did not enormously outweigh those estimated for 1913 (16%)'. Also, as manufacturing has declined as a percentage of economic activity within the Organisation for Economic Cooperation and Development (OECD), there has been weaker trade integration and she points to the ratio of world trade to output, which has declined from 1.65 in 1965–1980 to 1.34 in 1980–1990. She also notes that FDI has declined as a proportion of long-term investment flows and is concentrated in merger and acquisition activity with the major part in nonmanufacturing. She concludes that the importance of economic linkages in these areas, which may have an influence on state policy, has been overemphasised. Hirst and Thompson (1999) also consider the development of world trade but from the standpoint of trade to gross domestic product (GDP) ratios. Here again they record that GDP ratios were 'consistently higher in 1913 than they were in 1973' with the exception of Germany where they were roughly equal. They also state that in 1995, Japan, the Netherlands and the United Kingdom were less open than in 1913. There is therefore a weight of evidence to suggest that a global economy, at least by the measurements of FDI and trade, is not a recent phenomenon.

It can be argued that there is historical precedent for a global system of trade and investment flows, but the picture is somewhat different if the time perspective is reduced. Many commentators see distinct differences in the ability of states to pursue unilateral economic policies stemming from the collapse of the Bretton Woods system in 1971. Under this system, which was agreed on by the allied countries in 1944, a fixed dollar/gold exchange rate of $35 per ounce of gold was set and the United States guaranteed that it would freely convert dollars into gold. The United Kingdom pegged its exchange rate to other currencies, and domestic central banks could intervene on the foreign exchange markets. It was also expected that countries would pursue deflationary or inflationary policies in the case of disequilibrium. The International Monetary Fund (IMF), set up at the time, was able to lend money where countries had insufficient reserves to maintain their exchange rates. Only in exceptional circumstances were countries able to devalue their currencies.

The policy objective of the Bretton Woods system was to prevent competitive devaluations and to enable some stability to underpin international trade. Sloman (1995) identifies three consequences of the Bretton Woods system. Firstly, uncertainty was reduced and trade encouraged by the stability of exchange rates over a long period. Secondly, the system of rates pegged to the dollar acted to dissuade governments from pursuing irresponsible economic policies that kept world inflation stable. Thirdly, in the case of severe deficit, a country could devalue, thus avoiding a major recession. Hirst and Thompson (1999) believe that the stability provided by Bretton Woods resulted in 'A period of prolonged economic growth and full employment in the advanced countries, sustained by strategies of active national state intervention and a managed multilateral regime for trade and monetary policy under United States hegemony' (ibid.). The inference is that the system increased the ability of states to pursue domestic economic policies on the Keynesian model as they were able to increase debt on a short-term basis without precipitating a run on the currency, higher interest rates and recession.

A number of factors contributed to the collapse of the Bretton Woods system in 1971. The UK government did not find devaluation an attractive option as it was difficult to assess whether a monetary deficit was a long- or short-term feature of the domestic economy. Also, if devaluation was made, this would have the effect of disrupting domestic business, causing uncertainty and a reluctance to invest. This was compounded by the 'J curve effect', which resulted in an initial deterioration in the balance of payments immediately following a devaluation. The position of the United States as a reserve currency encouraged this government to run large balance of payments deficits, largely as a result of the Vietnam War, and this had the effect of increasing world inflation (Sloman 1995, p. 1003). The result was the breakdown of the Bretton Woods system in 1971, as US gold reserves became so depleted that convertibility could not be ensured. After 1971, states were compelled to adjust their ratios of debt to GDP and 'From the 1970s onwards, then, restrictive policies were called upon to secure the stability of international exchange and the global flow of capital' (Kerr 1998, p. 2281). Each state was compelled, in Kerr's opinion, to protect the value of its own currency in the face of an unregulated international monetary regime and was thus unable to pursue policies that would result in increasing levels of indebtedness. The power of the state to intervene in the economy was thus reduced.

Statistics confirm that the UK Public Sector Borrowing Requirement (PSBR) did indeed increase in the 1960s and 1970s, particularly following the election of the Labour government in 1966. It doubled between 1966 and 1967 from £949m to £1844m, but its most dramatic increase took place between 1972 and 1975, when it went from £1950m in 1972 to £4093m in 1973, and thence to £6452m in 1974 and £10 161m in 1975 (Sloman 1995, p. 678). Contrary to Kerr's opinion, the collapse of Bretton Woods did not result in an immediate curtailing of government borrowing. The state continued its interventionist policies even in the face of an unregulated international financial system. Hirst and Thompson point to this and other factors as contributing to what they call 'the myth of the globalisation of economic activity' (Hirst and Thompson 1999). They believe that there were a number of main changes to the international economy after 1971, which did not amount to economic globalisation, but which in some way contributed to governments believing that they were powerless in the face of insurmountable global forces. 'If the widespread consensus of the 1950s and 1960s was that the future belonged to a capitalism without losers, securely managed by national governments acting in concert, then the later 1980s and 1990s have been dominated by a consensus based on contrary assumptions, that global markets are uncontrollable and that the only way to avoid becoming a loser – whether as nation, firm or individual – is to be as competitive as possible' (Hirst and Thompson 1999).

The factors cited by Hirst and Thompson are the oil price increases of 1973 and 1979, which resulted in rapid cost push inflation compounded by the US involvement in the Vietnam War. Although the increase in oil price was in part a result of the dramatic economic growth that occurred in 1972–1973, Harry Shutt (1998) points out that it was also politically motivated by the Yom Kippur War of October 1973. As a result of inflationary pressures, financial institutions and manufacturers sought opportunities for capital investment in the Third World, the Eurodollar market grew and ratios of foreign trade to GDP grew in domestic economies. Hirst and Thompson also cite the abandonment of exchange controls and market deregulation in the late 1970s and 1980s, and the tendency of Western economies to move from industrial to service economies coupled with the rapid growth of newly industrialising countries (NICs). These factors were joined by the tendency for Western industry to organise itself on the post-Fordist model of more flexible production methods. Hirst and Thompson believe that none of these factors are representative of unstoppable global power and they are of the opinion that the state can still pursue 'radical goals . . . with a modest change of attitude on the part of key elites' (Hirst and Thompson 1998).

Government policy

In terms of government expenditure, it is clear that if power to act is identified with government expenditure as a percentage of GDP the state maintains its position. As a percentage of GDP, government expenditure was greater than 40% in the years 1981–1987 and 39% in the year 2007–2008. The lowest figure, 36%, was recorded in 1989–1990 just before the economic collapse of the early 1990s (Public Sector Statistical Analyses 2007).

There is little evidence that those currently (and recently) charged with running the UK state are inclined to the change of attitude suggested by Hirst and Thompson. Speaking in South Africa in 1996, Tony Blair said 'Globalisation has destroyed any notion of countries cutting themselves off from world markets. Go-it-alone inflation or spending policies will be mercilessly and immediately punished by capital markets that can overwhelm a nation's currency' (Wickham-Jones 2000, p. 2). At the same time, Gordon Brown stated: 'World interdependence shows that true national sovereignty will have to be sought within the realities of the international economy'.

Further evidence of the present government's stance on market forces was provided in Tony Blair's attitude towards the closure of a factory operated by Fujitsu in his Sedgefield constituency. He stated: 'It would be totally dishonest to pretend that government can prevent such decisions' and 'We can't, as Government, do much about the twists and turns of world markets in an increasingly globalised economy' (Wickham-Jones 2000). Government publications illustrate both its belief in the power of global capital and its support for it. A government White Paper on global poverty produced by the Department for International Development defends the activities of the World Trade Organisation (WTO) and 'makes a strong intellectual case for global capitalism' (HM Treasury 2000a).

The government White Paper 'Stability and Investment for the Long Term' (Economic and Fiscal Strategy Report, The Treasury 1998) also provides an indication (*albeit* a broad-brush one) of the thinking behind Labour government policy. The central objective is stated to be the achievement of high and stable economic growth and employment. Low inflation and sound public finances (undefined but assumed to mean the control of government debt) are fundamental objectives and the government is committed to 'pressing for further liberalisation of trade and investment and for competition policies which ensure free and open markets' (Economic and Fiscal Strategy Report 1998, p. 11). In many areas, there is little to choose between the policies of the present Labour government as evidenced by the White Paper and its Conservative predecessor. The 1996 White Paper *Creating the Enterprise Centre of Europe* states that 'the government has an important role to play' (p. 4) in providing a stable macroeconomic framework, deregulation, lowering of marginal tax rates, liberalisation of markets and privatisation, with the provision of business support services. The White Paper also states that government will seek to ensure that 'those services which remain within the public sector achieve higher standards and are provided cost effectively' (p. 4). Both the current government and its predecessor are clear in their commitments to supporting business and trade liberalisation, which, it is assumed, will lead to higher economic growth. It is noticeable that there is an implication in the 1996 White Paper, as evidenced in the earlier quote, that public sector provision is both of poor quality and expensive.

The policies of the mid-1990s, as evidenced by the government publications at the time, have been translated into policy implementation in the new millennium but it is noticeable that globalisation no longer appears to be an issue. The reality of the power of the global capital markets seems to be a self-evident truth to government. The Treasury publication *Globalisation and the UK: Strength and Opportunity to Meet the Economic Challenge* provides an account of government policy by listing six 'key policy challenges' to respond to globalisation. These emphasise the need to achieve macroeconomic stability and build an enterprising and flexible business sector, and make the United Kingdom 'as attractive a place as possible for international business' (HM Treasury 2005). The role of government is that of an enabler and a catalyst. Although the state continues its regulatory role, this is to be accomplished by continuing 'to strive to minimise undue regulatory burdens by ensuring that regulation is used only where absolutely necessary and that administrative burdens ... are as low as possible' (HM Treasury 2005). The policy framework is clear. The role of the state in terms of property facilities is to provide the conditions where the private sector can function efficiently with minimal regulation. 'Power over' is maintained but 'power to' will be increasingly constrained by agreements and contracts with the private sector and this is the subject of positive policy rather than the state accepting a *fait accompli* by default.

The present Labour administration accepts that global forces mean that there is no alternative to pursuing policies that make the United Kingdom an attractive place for private investment. It is clear that certain interventionist policies that might have been followed in the past, such as nationalisation, are only options when private sector solutions are exhausted. Thus the power of the state, at least in terms of policy options, has been curtailed. A number of questions remain, however. Why has the present government accepted this position so wholeheartedly and is there in reality a wider range of policies available that would not result in the economic meltdown foreseen by Tony Blair and Gordon Brown? Why has government policy moved dramatically away from those areas which in the past would have been regarded as entirely appropriate?

Development of government policy

Writing shortly after the Second World War, R H Tawney summarised the policy objectives espoused by the Labour Party after 1918, which to a large extent informed its actions in government from 1945 until 1951: '...the legal enforcement of minimum standards of life and work; the expansion of different forms of communal provision designed to make accessible to all advantages previously confined to the minority with the means to buy them, the use of financial measures to reduce economic inequalities; and the transference of certain foundation services to public ownership' (Tawney 1964). These objectives, particularly the final one, did not commend themselves to the Conservative government that took power in 1951 (*albeit* with a lower popular vote than Labour) and, to an even lesser extent, to the Thatcher government from 1979 onwards.

For most of the late twentieth century, government policy concerning the provision of public goods was highly interventionist, whichever of the two main parties were in power. This is evidenced by the New Towns Act 1946, which was promoted by a Labour government and maintained on the statute book by the next Conservative administration, although this government did not augment Labour's proposals by designating any further towns. Each new town was built by a development corporation that acted as a 'statutory speculative builder with the job of building a town, attracting customers, selling and letting real estate and services and showing a return on capital just like any commercial undertaking' (Harvey 2000, p. 263). The state here, through the agency of a development corporation, regards commercial building as a 'public good' as it was widely believed at the time that the market would not provide a satisfactory solution to the need for new settlements and, if it did, would not satisfy the strategic planning criteria that flowed from the 1947 Town and Country Planning Act. There was a widespread belief in the necessity to use direct state power if the correct type of development was to be provided. The provision of public facilities showed the same belief. War destruction meant that in the immediate post-war period housing and education were the priorities for government, but there was also a need to renew health facilities. The 1946 National Health Service Act resulted in the nationalisation of the health service estate, and renewal was to be financed by central government grants, taxation and national insurance contributions. This finance proved to be inadequate and even when the principle of major hospital investment was adopted in 1962 the rate of completion was poor. This problem has been a continuing one, 'Between 1980 and 1997, only seven public schemes costing more than

£25m were completed' (Gaffney and Pollock 1999) and of the 224 schemes proposed in the 1962 hospital plan, only a third were completed, a third partially completed and a third not started (ibid). The turn in government policy towards the enabling state rather than the interventionist state may be informed by this poor delivery but also by bitter electoral experience.

Some of the reasons for the present government's acceptance of the dominance of global forces stem from Labour's experience in office between 1974 and 1979. Labour came to power following the miners' strike that precipitated the fall of Heath's Conservative administration. In the opinion of Tom Ling (1998), 'the Labour Party came to office with its most radical programme since 1945'. This is perhaps not surprising as Labour had not had the opportunity to implement a programme as a government since 1945. The incoming government was unequivocal; it would engineer a fundamental shift of power and wealth by setting up a National Enterprise Board with a remit to invest in growing sectors of the economy by means of a £1000m budget.

It promised to repeal the 1971 Industrial Relations Act and replace it with the *Social Contract*. A new Industrial Development Unit and a new Industrial Policy Department at the Treasury were set up. Implementation of this strong interventionist programme was curtailed by worsening economic conditions resulting from the oil price increase and the reaction to the pre-1973 speculative boom. The reaction of government to these problems was in line with the prevailing Keynesian orthodoxy. 'This meant seeking to soften the blow of falling output by increasing government borrowing rather than by the orthodox approach of bringing reduced state revenues into line with expenditure – through either big tax increases or corresponding cuts in public spending' (Shutt 1998). Steven Fielding (2000) believes that the cause of the subsequent reduction in public spending and rising unemployment was 'international currency speculation . . . which might be seen as early evidence of globalisation'. Indeed, general government expenditure as a percentage of GDP fell from 49.3% in 1975–1976 to 46.7% in 1976–1977, and thence to 43.0% in 1977–1978 and 44.0% in 1978–1979 (Public Expenditure – Statistical Analyses 1998–1999). Subsequent defeat at the polls in 1979, and a further defeat in 1983 when Labour campaigned on a broadly interventionist programme, led to Neil Kinnock's policy review that made the achievement of low inflation a major policy objective. 'He also recognized that taxing and spending had to remain at "prudent" levels' (Fielding 2000). 'Prudent' in this context is a word much used in the immediate past by the current Prime Minister and can be broadly interpreted to mean economic policies that do not result in inflationary pressures or a run on the currency.

It would appear therefore that bitter electoral experience has had an influence on current Labour economic policy and has helped to convince the present government that the state can no longer increase its indebtedness to pay for direct interventionist programmes. Labour's primary macroeconomic objectives are the control of inflation and the promotion of GDP growth. The former responsibility is the remit of the Monetary Policy Committee (MPC), which uses the manipulation of interest rates to maintain the government's inflation target. Since 1997, the MPC has presided over a downward trend in inflation, which has varied between just over 3 and 2% per annum, although at the time of writing, inflationary pressures have re-emerged as a result of a boom in oil prices and world demand for commodities. The handing over of monetary policy to a reconstituted Bank of England and the setting up of a range of tight fiscal policy rules is seen by Colin Thain (2000) as one of four paradoxes at the heart of Labour's management of the economy, with the key to government strategy lying in the policies established in the early years of the new millennium, which are continued today.

Thain believes that it is paradoxical that the then Chancellor should behave as 'the perfect model of an orthodox Minister of Finance – prudent and cautious' (Thain 2000) while presiding over income redistribution 'by stealth'. At the 1997 election, Blair made a policy commitment not to raise income tax. It can be reasonably surmised that Labour had identified income tax rates as an issue that contributed to the loss of the 1992 General Election. Although Blair was true to his words, the overall burden of tax as a proportion of GDP rose from 35.3% when Labour took office to 37% in 2000 (Thain 2000). Higher indirect taxation and higher social security payments were the main causes of this rise. Higher than predicted economic growth has also resulted in a greater accumulation from corporation tax and indirect taxes. It also had the effect of promoting employment, thus lowering unemployment benefit payments.

The government's Comprehensive Spending Review announced on 18 July 2000 predicted a dramatic increase in spending from £371bn in 2000–2001 to £392bn in 2001–2002 to £440bn in 2003–2004 (Anon 2000b). The major areas of increased expenditure were transport (annual increase of 20%), the home office (6%), the national health service (5.6%) and education (5.4%). Little increase was planned for defence (0.3%), and the foreign and commonwealth budget was predicted to rise by only 1.9% per year (Anon 2000b). The appearance is of a government committed to increasing spending in those areas that are in its direct control and that have a profound influence on the lives of its citizens. It is then perhaps surprising to reflect that public spending as a percentage of GDP was just below 40% in the second quarter of 2000, which was the lowest it had been since 1967, apart from 1989 when it was again, briefly, just under 40% (Anon 2000b). Gordon Brown was able to predict increased public investment between 2000 and 2003 as a result of the government's ability to accumulate capital since 1997. At the same time, he intended to manage government debt to ensure that the British economy displayed low interest rates and competitiveness.

The Labour government's belief in, and acceptance of, global finance have resulted in rigid treasury control over spending. Colin Thain's view is that treasury control contrasts paradoxically with 'an administration committed in some policy areas to decentralisation and devolution' (Thain 2000). He also sees a paradox in Labour's concentration on supply side economic policy in contrast to the demand side Keynesian policies of the past. 'Under Brown, the Treasury has been a leading advocate of increased labour market flexibility and deregulation in an EU dominated by Social Democrat led governments still committed to the Rhine Social Market Model'. Government policy is placed between a liberal transatlantic model and the social market model typified by French labour policy. Keynesian policies that targeted full employment as a major policy goal are no longer of interest to the UK government, it would appear. Bank of England independence emphasises the control of inflation as the target and a major role of the state is to maintain economic conditions favourable to business and enterprise.

Christopher Hood (1994) considers three possible explanations for the decline of Keynesian policies. These are political incumbency, the political business cycle and the effect of entrenched institutional arrangements. Political incumbency assumes that the party in power will make a political value judgement about the importance of certain policy goals with the result that right-wing governments should target inflation control over maintaining employment, whereas left-wing governments will take the opposite view. Hood identifies a number of problems with this approach as the evidence from the history of UK politics is far from clear. James Callaghan's Labour government from 1975 to 1979, for example, clearly adopted monetarist policies in the face of increasing inflation, whereas Thatcher's government after 1979 proceeded very cautiously towards privatisation and was only convinced to do so after the surprisingly successful British Telecom privatisation in the mid-1980s. Also, as Hood says, 'small open economies' may be forced to follow policies dictated by strong trading partners. Ireland may be a good example here.

The political business cycle argument seeks to rationalise policy by focusing on the timing of policy decisions depending on the timing of the next general election. By this logic a government will be willing to allow unemployment to rise immediately after an election to achieve low inflation, whereas in the years just before an election, inflation can be allowed to rise and unemployment to reduce. Hood sees a number of problems with this approach (first proposed by Michael Kalecki in 1943). Voters are unlikely to be as naïve as the theory supposes, and policy switches are far from clean and predictable in terms of results and it is difficult for politicians to be sure that they are promoting policies that will appeal to the correct section of the electorate. Also, it can be said that the theory places an unjustified reliance on the theory first put forward by AW Philips in 1958, which showed an inverse relationship between the rate of unemployment and inflation. The relationship is far more unpredictable than the smooth curve that appears in most economic textbooks.

Entrenched institutional arrangement theory has two main sub-theories. Some states are seen to have developed certain structures that will naturally lead them to reject Keynesian policies. Hood uses the example of the United Kingdom where Keynes, as an academic, had no clear pathway into government decision-making in contrast with Sweden, which quickly adopted Keynesian policies, with easy access provided by the structure of the state. The second strand of arrangement theory is based on the degree of corporatism in a particular state. Hood defines corporatism as the 'extent to which there are tripartite institutional arrangements linking the state with peak associations of labour and capital'. Closeness with other strong economic interests, particularly organised business interests, is assumed to lead to adoption of policies opposed to Keynesianism. Hood

Chapter 1

believes that corporatism only explains changes of style rather than anything more fundamental, but it appears to have some resonance with the business friendly policies pursued by the present government.

Exercise of state power

The state in the United Kingdom therefore exercises considerable influence over society, but the way in which it exercises power is difficult to analyse within existing models. In terms of those areas where the state directly funds and manages, the dominant power is held by the Treasury, although the power it exercises is far from the Weberian model. In other areas, the state uses private agencies to achieve policy goals, typically with the PFI, which is dealt with in Chapter 4. Regime theorists and pluralists concentrate on the analysis of how the state exercises power within its territorial boundaries but in the words of Andrew Gamble (2000) 'For Britain most constituent issues are now decided at supranational level in the various treaties and agreements on security, trade, currency and the environment, which British governments have signed'. There does appear, however, to be a distinct difference in the way in which the freedom of global capital can influence domestic policy. There are high-profile examples of firms appearing to be footloose and relocating from the high labour costs of the West to take advantage of low labour costs in the Third World, but the bulk of FDI remains with the developed Western economies (Weiss 1997; Hirst and Thompson 1999). Plant and buildings for industrial production require substantial amounts of capital which, once invested, becomes relatively illiquid in comparison with capital invested in currency speculation. Many commentators cite the level of commitment that comes with substantial investment in land and buildings (Hutton 1996), but there is a contrast with the attitude of government towards this type of investment and the more volatile type of currency speculation that was typified by the problems of the European Monetary System (EMS) in 1993.

In essence, EMS is a system designed to ensure stable currencies within Europe. Business is able to undertake reliable short- and medium-term financial planning as it is protected from wild fluctuations in currency values. It has much in common with the Bretton Woods system and claims many of its advantages. The United Kingdom was part of the system in the 1990s as an attempt to control inflation where strict monetarism had failed. As a result of German reunification, the non-competitiveness of most of East German industry, and the inflationary pressures that resulted, the Bundesbank raised its interest rates (Martin and Schumann 1997). The United Kingdom subsequently followed this move in an attempt to stave off currency speculation that was driving the value of the pound downwards. The eventual collapse of the EMS, and the United Kingdom's exit from it, demonstrated in stark reality the weakness of states in the face of global monetary forces and, it is reasonable to assume, confirmed the views of Blair and Brown that state policy is heavily constrained by the global financial system.

Although domestic government may accept that there are tight constraints on macroeconomic policy, state power is an essential component to allow international business to function. There is nothing new in this. As Will Hutton points out, the UK state had a substantial role in promoting the development of industry from the time of the industrial revolution: '... protecting the domestic market; guaranteeing traffic in British vessels; developing the London banking system through government deposits; issuing government stock, and underwriting loans and using the power of public procurement to develop key industries' (Hutton 1996). State support remains necessary where financial institutions fail and serious financial instability would result. Shutt (1998) provides the example of US Savings and Loans Corporation, but there are many others such as the rescue of the fringe banking sector at the time of the 1974 crash in the United Kingdom (Fraser 1993).

In spite of the action that might be forced on the state, the nature of the way it promotes and supports industry has changed. It may be true that, in the short term, it is not in private companies' interests to make investments in land, plant and machinery, but only to disinvest and relocate. However, the reality appears to be that states compete with each other to make economic conditions more suitable for private profitability. In terms of taxation, Martin and Schumann see this commencing in 1986 'when the US government set a new standard by reducing the tax on profits for joint-stock companies from 46% to 34%' (Martin and Schumann 1997). This policy has been followed by many other Western states, notably Ireland and Belgium. Companies are able to channel profits through low tax economies, to take advantage of competitive tax rates, but the benefits that result from such state generosity are often obscure: 'BMW supposedly made a third of its total profits in the Belgian branch, without a single car being produced there' (Martin and Schumann 1997).

Martin and Schumann conclude that 'it is no longer democratically elected governments which decide the level of taxes; rather, the people who direct the flow of capital and goods themselves establish what contribution they wish to make to state expenditure' (1997). This view is perhaps extreme as it can be reasonably assumed that business would not regard any level of taxation as attractive. As Monbiot points out, directors of private companies have a 'fiduciary duty' towards their shareholders (Monbiot 2000), which can be translated as 'the obligation to exercise powers bona fide and for the benefit of the company' (Ellison *et al.* 1997). The Confederation of British Industry (CBI) consistently lobbies to reduce taxation and government administrative requirements.

Government therefore has accepted the power of private capital to influence policy, but still retains considerable freedom within overall constraints. This is also seen in the behaviour of the UK government in its involvement with international agencies such as the WTO. The WTO was founded in Geneva in 1994 essentially to promote the liberalisation of trade throughout the world. The justification for this policy owes much to the theory of 'comparative cost advantage' developed by David Ricardo in the nineteenth century (Straffa 1951). The theory states that international trade will benefit both highly productive and less productive countries, but Martin and Schumann (1997) believe that the theory rests on the idea that capital and private business are immobile and remain in their countries of origin. Their view is that the theory is 'completely out of date . . . it is no longer relative differences in cost that are the engine of business. What counts is absolute advantage in all markets and countries at once' (ibid.). When international companies move to an area of low wages the result is that both wages and goods fall, as cost levels fall, as there is no need for firms to be concerned with social or environmental costs. Nevertheless, those countries who are members of the WTO (including the United Kingdom) support the promotion of free trade and it is proposed by the WTO Secretary General that governments should agree that by 2020, all custom barriers and regional agreements should be dismantled and the whole world should be turned into a free trade area (Martin and Schumann 1997).

The policy of the UK government towards the WTO is unequivocal in its support. 'Exposure to competition and trade sharpens incentives, encourages the diffusion of technology and opens up opportunities to catch up with the world's leading firms . . . . Increased market size allows greater . . . exploitation of comparative advantage. Episodes of trade liberalisation are, almost without exception, associated with rapid growth in trade and an increase in economic growth' (Economic and Fiscal Strategy Report 1998, Chapter 2). This is repeated in the Treasury paper *Globalisation and the UK* (2005): 'Globalisation means that economies and markets will become ever more interlinked and interdependent, through increased cross-border trade and investment and more integrated financial markets'. The theory of comparative advantage is accepted as an unequivocal economic truth and increased trade is predicted to bring substantial economic benefits to the United Kingdom if it continues to adopt trade liberalisation policies.

Other commentators disagree with the smooth logic of government policy expressed in the above report. Harry Shutt (1998), for example, believes the impact of the Marshall Plan was far more influential in promoting growth in the post-war world and he also cites the failure of tariff reductions to prevent the end of the economic boom in the 1970s. 'It is thus utterly implausible to suggest that the lowering of tariffs under GATT (General Agreement on Tariffs and Trade, predecessor of WTO) acted as a significant stimulus to the rapid economic growth that occurred in the OECD countries between 1950 and 1973' (Shutt 1998). George Monbiot (2000) sees the WTO and more particularly the failed Multilateral Agreement on Investment (MAI), as representing direct threats to the power of the state to legislate within its territorial boundaries. 'The MAI would have allowed corporations directly to challenge laws passed by national or local governments, through a special tribunal' (Monbiot 2000).

UK government policy, whether justified by statistical fact or not, is geared towards increases in prosperity and it is this that underpins its attitude towards government action and regulation. Prosperity is often regarded by government as synonymous with economic growth, in other words, consistent rises in GDP. Long-term growth in GDP does indeed show a consistent, if unspectacular rise, in the United Kingdom throughout the late twentieth century (IMF 1998). The wages of the top 10% of male earners have risen from 1.67 times the median wage in 1979, to twice the median in 1993, but distribution is more unequal as, over the same period, the wages of the poorest paid 10% fell from 68.5 to 58.2% of the median (Hutton 1996, p. 172). Inward and outward FDI shows that the United Kingdom has a much more open economy than Germany, France, the United States or Japan in the period 1981–1994 (Competitiveness – Creating the Enterprise Centre of Europe, Chart 1.3, 1996). The government contents itself with the promotion of economic growth, but many commentators regard this as a very narrow view of prosperity. Firstly, GDP growth does not deal with inequality and, secondly, it does not provide a reliable index of standards of life. This is indicated by Scitovsky's (1992) work in defining an index of human happiness. This is given the title of the 'Index of Sustainable Economic Welfare' (ISEW) and takes into account such matters as noise pollution and the depletion of natural resources. The conclusion is that, whereas per capita GDP rose by 44% in the period 1976–1996, the ISEW fell by 25%.

Government and private companies

British government policy towards domestic, transnational and multinational companies justifies itself on three main grounds. Firstly, global forces are impossible to resist without courting economic disaster; secondly, minimal barriers must be placed in the way of the operation of private business in the United Kingdom; and thirdly, greater benefit will result to society. Economic policies that curtail the power of the corporations to an unacceptable extent are not regarded as an option for government. What is acceptable or unacceptable is, of course, a matter of degree and judgement as government policy is formed on the assumption that the United Kingdom competes directly with other countries for private investment. In this way, the UK state relies on the private corporations but, in turn, the private corporations rely on the state maintaining their rights to run businesses within an established and enforced legal background. Yet it appears that the effective power of the state to act directly for the benefit of its citizens is curtailed, as it is assumed that prosperity will only result from the activities of private business with minimal regulation. This position is put succinctly by Robert Kuttner: '... one true path to the efficient allocation of goods and services. It includes, above all, the dismantling of barriers to free commerce and free flows of financial capital. To the extent that there is a remnant regulatory role, it is to protect property, both tangible and intellectual; to assure open, non-discriminatory access; to allow any investor to purchase or sell any asset or repatriate any profit anywhere in the world; to remove and prevent subsidies and other distortions of the laissez-faire pricing system; to dismantle what remains of government-industry alliances' (Kuttner 2000).

Both in the macro and the micro sense, government policy is focused on allowing and incentivising the private sector to produce goods and services required by the public. Direct action by the public sector in terms of nationalisation is no longer required or promoted except in special circumstances. The case of Northern Rock, for example, is one area where government found that it was obliged to act to protect the collapse of the bank. The government operates as a catalyst for the maintenance of a buoyant private sector, and as a lender of last resort, to prevent unwanted consequences when a private enterprise accepts too much risk. At a local level, market forces are largely allowed to operate and are assumed to be sensitive to consumer preference although there is clearly a strong element of agenda setting in the way policy emerges.

References

HM Treasury (2000a) *Eliminating World Poverty*. White Paper, Department for International Development.

HM Treasury (2000b) *Comprehensive Spending Review 2000*.

Bachrach P and Baratz MS (1970) *Power and Poverty: Theory and Practice*, OUP, Oxford.

Barker G (1967) *Greek Political Theory*, Oxford University Press, Oxford.

Barry N (2004) The rationale of the minimal state. In: *Restating the State*, (eds A Gamble and T Wright), Blackwell, Oxford.

Cole GDH, Figgis JN and Laski HJ (1993) *The Pluralist Theory of the State*, Routledge, London.

Crouch C (2004) *Post Democracy (Themes for the 21st Century)*, Polity Press, London.

Dahl RA (1957) In: *Journal of Applied Behavioral Science*, NTL Institute for Applied Behavioral Science, 2.3, A and M University, Texas.

Dahl RA (1961) *Who Governs? Democracy and Power in an American City*, Yale University Press, New Haven.

Dept. for Communities and Local Government (2008) *Communities in Control: Real People, Real Power*, Stationery Office, Norwich.

Dowding K (1996) *Power*, Open University Press, Buckingham.

Dunleavy P and O'Leary P (1987) *Theories of the State*, Macmillan, London.

Ellison J *et al.* (1997) *Business Law*, Business Education Publishers, Sunderland.

Experian (2001) *Retail Report*, Experian.

Fielding S (2000) A new politics? In: *Developments in British Politics*, (eds P Dunleavy *et al.*), Macmillan, London.

Fraser W (1993) *Principles of Property Investment and Pricing*, Macmillan, Basingstoke.

Gaffney D and Pollock AM (1999) *Pump Priming the PFI: Why are Privately Financed Hospital Schemes Being Subsidised?* Public Policy and Management January–March 1999.

Gamble A (2000) *The Free Economy and the Strong State*, Macmillan, London.

Greenberg ES (1990) State change: approaches and concepts. In: *Changes in the State, Causes and Consequences*, (eds ES Greenberg and TF Mayer), Sage, London.

Harding A (1995) Elite theory and growth machines. In: *Theories of Urban Politics*, (eds D Judge, G Stoker and H Wolman), Sage, London.

Harvey J (2000) *Urban Land Economics*, Palgrave Macmillan, Basingstoke.

Held D (1995) *Democracy and the Global Order*, Polity Press, Cambridge.

Held D (1996) *Models of Democracy*, Polity Press, Cambridge.

Hirst D and Thompson G (1998) *Globalisation in Question*, Polity Press, Cambridge.

Hirst P and Thompson P (1999) *Globalisation in Question*, Polity Press, Cambridge.

The Treasury (1996) *Creating the Enterprise Centre of Europe*, White Paper, The Treasury.

Hobbes T (1909) *Leviathan*, Clarendon Press, Oxford.

Hood C (1994) *Explaining Economic Policy Reversals*, Open University Press, Buckingham.

Hunter F (1953) *Community Power Structure: A Study of Decision Makers*, University of North Carolina Press, Chapel Hill.

Hutton W (1996) *The State We're In*, Vintage, London.

Imbroscio DL (1998) Reformulating urban regime theory: the division of labour between state and market reconsidered. *Journal of Urban Affairs*, **20**, (3), 233–248.

IMF (1996) *Competitiveness – Creating the Enterprise Centre of Europe*, IMF, London.

Judge D (ed.) (1995) *Theories of Urban Politics*, Sage, London.

Kay J (1994) *Privatisation and Economic Performance*, (ed. M Bishop), OUP, Oxford.

Kerr D (1998) The private finance initiative and the changing governance of the built environment, *Urban Studies*, **35**, (12), 2277–2306.

Kuttner R (2000) The role of governments in the global economy. In: *On the Edge*, (eds W Hutton and A Giddens), Jonathan Cape, London.

Ling T (1998) *The British State Since 1945*, Polity Press, Cambridge.

Lowe M (2005) The Regional Shopping Centre in the inner city: a study of urban-led regeneration. *Urban Studies*, **42**, 449–470.

Lukes S (1974) *Power, a Radical View*, Macmillan Education, London.

Martin HP and Schumann H (1997) *The Global Trap: Globalisation and the Assault on Democracy and Prosperity*, Zed Books Ltd, London.

McGuirk P and MacLaran A (2001) Changing approaches to urban planning in an entrepreneurial city: the case of Dublin. *European Planning Studies*, **9**, (4), 437–457.

Minton A (2002) *The Privatisation of Public Space*, Royal Institution of Chartered Surveyors, London.

Monbiot G (2000) *Captive State: The Corporate Takeover of Britain*, Macmillan, London.

Monbiot G (2007) How did we get into this mess? *The Guardian*, 28/8/07.

NEF (2005) *Clone Town Britain*, New Economics Foundation, London.

Ohmae K (1995) *The End of the Nation State: The Rise of Regional Economies*, Harper Collins, London.

Pierson C (1996) *The Modern State*, Routledge, London.

Poggi G (1990) *The State: Its Nature, Development and Prospects*, Polity Press, Cambridge.

Anon, The Treasury, *Public Sector Statistical Analyses 2007*, HM Treasury.

Scitovsky T (1992) *The Joyless Economy: The Psychology of Human Satisfaction*, Oxford University Press, New York.

Shutt H (1998) *The Trouble with Capitalism: An Enquiry into the Causes of Global Economic Failure*, Zed Books Ltd, London.

Skocpol T (1985) Bringing the state back in: strategies of analysis in current research. In: *Bringing the State Back*, (eds. PB Evans, D Rueschemeyer and T Skocpol), Cambridge University Press, Cambridge.

Sloman J (1995) *Economics*, Prentice Hall, London.

Stoker G and Mossberger K (1994) Urban Regime Theory in comparative perspective. *Environment and Planning C: Government and Policy*, **12**, (2), 195–212.

Chapter 1

Stone N.C. (1989) *Regime Politics: Governing Atlanta 1946–1988*, University Press of Kansas, Kansas.

Straffa P (1951) *The Works and Correspondence of David Ricardo*, Cambridge University Press, Cambridge.

Tawney RH (1964) *Religion and the Rise of Capitalism*, Penguin, Harmondsworth.

Thain C (2000) Economic policy. In: *Developments in British Politics*, (eds P Dunleavy *et al.*), Macmillan, London.

Thomas and Savitch (1991) *Big City Politics in Transition*, Urban Affairs Annual Review, London.

The Treasury (1998) *Economic and Fiscal Strategy Report*, Stationery Office, London.

The Treasury, *Economic and Fiscal Strategy Report 1998*, HM Treasury.

The Treasury (2005) *Globalisation and the UK: Strengths and Opportunities to Meet the Economic Challenges*, White Paper, HM Treasury.

Weber M (1997) *The Theory of Social and Economic Organisation*, The Free Press, New York.

Weiss L (1997) Globalisation and the myth of the powerless state. *New Left Review*, **225**, 3–27.

Wickham-Jones M (2000) New labour in the global economy: partisan politics and the social democratic model. *British Journal of Politics and International Relations*, **2** (1), 1–25.

Williams G (2006) Collaborative partnerships and urban change management. *International Journal of Sociology and Social Policy*, **26** (5/6), 194–206.

Chapter 2
The Property Development Process

Introduction

The object of this chapter is to place the experience of partnerships in development activity in the context of the property development process. Evaluation of the role of property partnerships between the public and private sectors can only have validity within the context of an understanding of fundamental factors and dynamics at work within the development process. Critical to the understanding is an appreciation of decision-making in property development. As a first step, relationships within the private sector need to be understood. Development activity in urban areas is now largely dependent on inputs of private sector investment as public funding for such schemes has been reducing. This trend is accelerated by the increasing role allocated to public–private partnerships in a broad range of development areas previously dealt with by the public sector including health and education infrastructure. The relationship between construction activity, general economy, property investment, development and decision-making provides the essential background against which policy initiatives can be assessed. Policies that improve the functioning of these various activities and their participants can form an important part of development approaches. Equally, policies that make an already complicated process more complex may be inefficient, inequitable or both.

Partnerships in property development have developed as a specialised area of the property market and require an understanding of the essential features of that market and the processes by which development decisions take place and are implemented. The nature of supply and demand for the various sectors of the property market and the interplay between investors, developers, financiers, consumers and policy makers would seem fundamental to success if such partnerships are to benefit all participants. In particular, such understanding would be a requisite for those involved in complex negotiations that surround such schemes.

The property market

The role of property in the urban environment is to provide for the economic functions of modern society. Housing, industrial space, offices, roads and infrastructure are built as functional space for essential urban and regional requirements (Evans 2003). A modern industrial and services economy depends on the built environment for the continuation and development of its economic activities. Improvements and additions to the urban environment are generated by and paid for by such economic activity (O'Sullivan 2006). As the urban or regional economy grows, the built environment grows to provide for the increased levels of production distribution and exchange. Similarly, as the urban labour force or population increases, demand for housing leisure and other activities will be represented by the increasing demand on the urban built environment. Increased pressure for built space results in construction activity and property development to cater for increased demand and such activity is accurately described as a derived demand.

Public policy and governance issues play an important role in urban development, both in the provision of appropriate urban space, infrastructure and services for economic and business functions and in public policy in all fields of urban infrastructure and restructuring. As far as public financial support is concerned, these can range from indirect tax incentives to direct public share holding in development projects. Historically, the state in many European countries has been instrumental in economic development activities (Albrechts et al. 2003). In particular, the state has been the main provider of infrastructure upon which all development and economic activity depends. Public regional or city banks in many areas of Germany provide an important and active role in city development activities. In other European countries, many regional development agencies have been providing capital, buildings and other support to new enterprises.

It is evident that both the level and type of state intervention differ widely across Europe in particular (Cheshire and Magri 2002). This is particularly evident while examining the differing state responses to managing urban development processes in the public interest (Gemaca II Project 2002).

In the United Kingdom, land-use planning system can be characterised as being reliant on indirect development control, in contrast to the direct master planning system most commonly used in continental Europe. It is evident that in Ireland and the United Kingdom, the planning system has some inbuilt flexibility and allows for ongoing negotiation processes between public and private actors. It is considered as an important factor of relatively higher prices and more pronounced cyclical trends of the British property markets compared to other European regions.

By contrast, in other EU continental approaches, the land uses as well as the obligations of the land owners are more clearly defined in urban planning documents. The continental system can be illustrated by the case of the Netherlands, where the government has historically a direct strategic influence on the urban land market, assisted in particular by spatial planning policies. In general, the urban management and planning system decides on the locations that will be developed for housing, businesses and infrastructure. A developer has to make certain that his plans comply with and do not conflict with the local land-use plan once adopted. If the plans do not conform to the designated use and to building regulations, applications for the necessary building permit are refused. The building permit and land-use plan are powerful instruments for the state sector to structure and guide infrastructure provision and the resulting urban development. The Netherlands planning system has resulted in a less cyclical market than many other European markets. Historically, Amsterdam, for example, has also been characterised by high level of supply to meet demand and moderate rental and price growth.

The general economy, therefore, is the generator of demand for increased development and construction activity (Wyatt 2007). Such activity is directly linked to the performance of the real economy, and periods of buoyant output and growth generally coincide with those of high economic growth in the regional and national economy. The logic of this correlation is that increases in disposable incomes lead to increased demand and retail sales, leading to increases in demand for retail space. Similarly, growth in employment leads to increased demand for industrial and office space. The overall increase in economic wealth results in increased investment in social and economic infrastructure. The resultant demands for built space can both increase the exchequer tax flows and provide funds for such development.

The greater volatility represented in construction activity over the gross domestic product (GDP) experienced represents the effects of factors other than economic performance influencing the system. Related factors such as population movement, sector-specific issues and the impact of taxation incentives and disincentives can result in significant changes in patterns of construction activity. Additionally, although the funding of a major part of all property development is private, the significance of public sector investment in both infrastructure and public building programmes is of major importance. Often the linkages are considerably weaker or counter-cyclical as the state may attempt to fund and initiate such activities in times of economic downturn and indeed often, during such times, will attempt to maintain or increase its activity to maintain or stimulate growth.

Within the commercial development sector, the linkage with economic activity is most evident within the speculative element of the market. Anticipating changes in demand or supplying where sector demand appears undersupplied involves an awareness of movements in the real economy along with the resultant sector movements in the property markets (Guy and Henneberry 2002). Structural changes within the economy may similarly result in significant changes in sector demand, which will result in increased development activity. For public sector development projects, the decision-making process for development is heavily influenced by socioeconomic factors. The nature of decision-making processes by the public sector can entail the prioritisation of certain projects or sectors based on cost/benefit analysis and conditioned by the administrative and political context in which such decisions are taken.

Demand and activity generated by owner occupiers is not as strongly linked to the GDP movement. Investment and speculative development can be seen to expand as a region's economy grows and contract as expectations of slower growth become established. However, as land prices and construction costs may tend to be lower during a recessionary period or trough in the pattern of development activity, owner occupiers tend to develop and lift the rate of output during these periods. As the bulk of commercial development is carried out and financed by private development interests within the UK markets, the pattern of boom and bust has tended to dominate the commercial sectors in particular.

The contributory elements of property development, investment and real demand tend to result in surges of development and oversupply, causing effectively the next correction or depression in the property market. This is caused by imperfections within the market processes producing the built environment, with the public sector development activities often tending to parallel private sector development activity, as might be expected, acting rather as a stabilising influence on the process. With the public sector financing a large share of total output in the construction industry, it is perhaps surprising that the state does not, instead, adopt a role of counter-cyclical stabilisation of the industry. Funding and assisting development activity during economic downturns, it can be argued, would prevent markets overheating, remove instability in labour markets and result in a more even development pattern. Evidence over time and regions would suggest, however, that this pattern tends to be repeated internationally (Barras 1994). Building cycles, associated with periodic large expansions in investment in property development, have been accepted as a feature of many economies and linked with international movements of population and capital, as well as with other economic features such as interest rates, commodity price and resource price.

Demand for construction activity and completed development space is therefore the key element in understanding this cyclical process of development and construction activity. This demand arises from two potential pools, the user market for such property that will either own or rent and the property investment market. These two markets evolve from the ability to separate ownership and the occupation rights, allowing separate interests to develop in the same property. Occupiers, particularly the commercial sector operating in central areas, frequently find the capital costs of purchasing a property high relative to current income. Acquisition may therefore involve commitment of substantial capital resources that could be more profitably invested in the occupier's core business activity. Costs of interest on capital borrowed, management and maintenance costs and the management resources needed to acquire and maintain a property will often be regarded as substantially higher than the rental costs.

The result is a market for property on a rented basis. The property investment market exists to supply property at an adequate return to this market. The basis for adequate returns on property investments is generally regarded as stability of income in real terms and rising capital values (Baum and Crosby 2007). These two separate markets for property, occupier demand and investment demand are most obviously prevalent in central areas of major cities, where the preponderance of business users results in high capital values, making the ownership of property sufficiently attractive for major investment interests. Its operation is particularly noted in the office development market in London, where the relative scale of capital values and investment required is highest.

This market for urban space is similar to economic markets of other types in that supply/demand relationships, as expressed through price mechanisms, tend to regulate levels of activity. However, the concept of the perfect market as formulated in basic economic doctrine developed by Adam Smith and others since the eighteenth century is not always appropriate for the property market. The imperfections and uncertainties of the real property market and the complexity of the multiple variables that tend to influence its movement take analysis of the market beyond conventional economic theory. While investment in property, whether for utility or market return, is but one part of the overall investment market, there are numerous factors that make this form of investment unique.

Investment in general terms can be defined as the giving up of the present use of capital for future income return or capital gain. This return can be by way of rent for investors or by way of rent foregone and occupational benefits for occupiers. In central city areas, long-term investment capital seeks to purchase properties for leasing purposes to receive long-term flows of income. In doing so, such interests may develop a dominant role in the market. Differences between property and other commodities available for investment purposes begin with the heterogeneous nature of each individual property investment. Unique factors such as its location, design, function and other characteristics have positive and negative investment consequences. Positively, this uniqueness can contribute to fixity in supply in that in general terms the purchaser of a prime investment property at a key location in a central city expects a high level of continuing demand for this property. As most buildings have a long life and additions to the stock are relatively small, demand tends to focus on the existing stock, especially at traditional prime/high value or at key locations. The standard investment has a freehold commercial building let out at its full rental value with a lease guaranteeing rental income regularly reviewed upwards in line with market trends over decades.

Security of this investment is often assisted by the inelasticity of supply as the amount of suitable sites is fixed, mainly already pre-empted by alternative users. Difficulties involving site assembly in older historic central areas, legislative restrictions and the planning and bye-law processes can involve lengthy delays in alternative premises coming on the market. Similarly, the rental income being a prior charge on a company or tenant, irrespective of profits or loss, and the fact that the property can be re-let should that tenant's business fail, can enhance the security of income to the investor.

Other advantages of property investment are the ability to select invest-ments to suit the varying capital requirements of investors and the availability of tax arrangements and incentives associated with property investment in specified sectors or areas. The management of property investments to achieve many or all of the benefits discussed requires identification of current and future market trends and can involve rigorous standards of selection. The many disadvantages associated with incorrect investment decisions lead many potential investors to concentrate their development activity on prime areas only. This results in significant pressures for investment and devel-opment in the existing prime areas, which involve the historic core of the city, and the neglect of other secondary areas, which, despite being ready for and needing development and investment activity, present higher risks than established prime locations. In terms of partnership negotiations, it is these areas that are in need of investment and development that are often in focus. The need to attract investment to areas in need of renewal is often a reason for interventions or for the public sector seeking to attract private partners to invest in such areas.

The chief disadvantages attached to investment in property arise with the large initial sums needed to enter the market. Prices for the smallest commercial investment property available, for example, in the London market would frequently be in excess of £10 000 000, whereas the larger investments can involve sums over £100 000 000. Entry to such markets is beyond the capability of many private investors, and the market was, in the past dominated by larger financial institutions such as pension funds and life assurance companies. These institutions benefit from large-scale long-term contractual inflows of funds with outflows from present income not required in the medium term. This availability of capital ensures that other potential purchasers may not compete with such concerns. The special tax treatment of the return on investments (i.e. rent enjoyed by the institutions) similarly gives a competitive advantage in the market place.

High costs of transfer and liquidity problems with property assets make such investments difficult for many individual investors who might require the capital for alternative uses in the short term. Legal, professional and acquisition taxes make entry into the market prohibitive and while costs of transfers inhibit certain investors, it is the potential losses in forced sale situations that may deter all but the longer term investor. Although a pension fund or assurance company may be able to hold property through a downturn or series of downturns in the property cycle, it is unlikely that many private investors would have sufficient resources to act in this way. Again, the institutional long-term investor can take such risks and look at the time scales required for such investment positions to the exclusion of other market participants.

Subjective valuation monitoring makes the actual performance of major property investment particularly difficult to monitor over time. The open market value of a property is clearly evident in its full sense only on its purchase date and date of sale. However, all estimates of value dur-ing the intervening period are subjective and may be proved incorrect if put to the market for sale or disposal. Issues such as the responsibility for management, maintenance and continual improvements and repairs required on all buildings also make investment in property difficult for the non-specialist investor in property.

The biggest risk any investor in property faces is the obvious impact of changes in demand, creating falling returns. Changes in demand resulting in downward pressure in rental prices and capital prices can occur owing to structural changes in the economy affecting sector demand, real economic decline, obsolescence of the individual building or oversupply. While a decline in the national or local economy cannot be discounted in the decision-making process other than by deferral of investment, choices can be made, which minimise risk if investment is decided on. Changes in demand and obsolescence of building type or function are less likely to affect prime property, often described as modern commercial property at good locations suitable and adaptable for modern needs and for alternative users if required. Risk minimisation therefore leads many investors in property in the United Kingdom to concentrate their efforts on this sector. The combination of resource availability, taxation considerations, complex management expertise requirements and the key knowledge and experience of the workings of an imperfect market therefore give large-scale investors a pivotal role in the shaping of city centre development in particular.

The returns sought from investment in property are normally expressed as a yield, which is the periodic return from an investment expressed as a percentage of the capital sum invested. In turn, capital values are expressed as a multiple of rental income, the multiple being derived from the level of initial yield or return required. Higher perceptions of risk lead to requirements for high initial yields whereas lower yields or return are acceptable on investments that represent low risk of losses and on which growth in rental and capital income is expected. This inter-relationship between the two sectors of the demand present in the property market is of vital importance. Good investments require strong tenant demand. Supply of adequate space for tenants is dependant on adequate returns being available for investors.

Market prices at which investment properties are sold are normally assessed by the following relationship:

$$\text{Price} = \text{full rental income} \times \frac{100}{\text{initial yield\%}}$$

Initial yields at which prime office property is purchased in the current market range from 3 to 5%. This may appear low at times when monetary interest rates are 5 or 6%. However, this ignores the primary importance of rental growth included in calculations; initial yields of 3 or 5% will often be achieving target rates of return of 8–10% on investments. This search for rental growth provided one of the great attractions of property investment, particularly during the past more inflationary periods such as the 1970s and 1980s. A desire to outpace the general rate of inflationary growth has in the past attracted investment funds to property. If the trend in the twenty-first century towards lower inflation levels continues this 'hedge against inflation' attribute of property becomes less important. Indeed, the recognition of the high costs of refurbishment of property and making allowances for depreciation and obsolescence of all property tend to become more recognised during periods of low inflation of downturns in the property market when a strong rental growth is no longer guaranteed.

During such periods, the concentration of investors is often on improving the return from existing investment by increasing the rental return where possible. This can be achieved by refurbishment of buildings to upgrade their function to a higher paying level within their existing use or to a higher value use, for example, residential to office buildings.

The supply of urban built space

Prices, as represented in rentals and capital sale prices, are the prime determinants of construction activity and the provision of new development. However, as most of the urban space has been built for a considerable period, particularly in the centre of older urban areas, the factors that determine its use, refurbishment, redevelopment and obsolescence require examination. The primary relationship between price and supply is illustrated in Figure 2.1.

With quantity of accommodation fixed at A1, demand is indicated by demand line D1, which, through the interaction of supply and demand, has fixed the price of this type of space at P1. Improvement in the general economy leads to an increased level of demand D2 which, in competing for existing supplies, pushes the price level up to P2. At this new price, further accommodation is made available (A2). As the level of accommodation is relatively fixed in the short term, sudden changes in demand can lead to rapid price increases. Within a speculative development market, profit-seeking suppliers respond to the new price level by increasing the levels of accommodation.

The next issue for examination is that of periods over which the property market operates and its impact on development patterns. As a result of the different time frames in which such changes in demand and output occur,

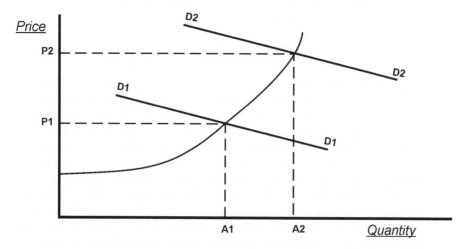

Figure 2.1 Property prices and supply–demand relationships.

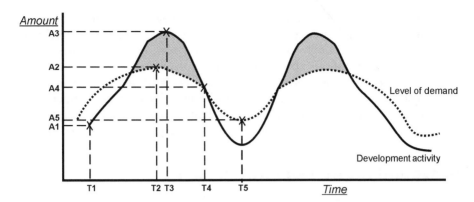

Figure 2.2 Cyclical interaction of demand and supply patterns.

development cycles and booms and slumps happen. Demand for property is capable of changing very quickly owing to improved economic activity, lower interest rates and increased confidence. However, the supply of built space often lags behind such increases in demand and in later stages of the cycle fails to respond to the levelling off or reduction of demand as illustrated in Figure 2.2.

Our example begins during a weak market phase during which development interests have not been active and the economy and property market have been experiencing low growth. With weaker economic and market conditions, levels of development are run down and the risk in market prospects leads to cancellation or postponement of development decisions.

As a recovery or upswing eventually occurs at T1, the amount of development activity A1 lags behind demand as the period for completion of projects will be a minimum of 1 to 2 years from initiation through planning to development. The impact of this time lag with demand levels rising even modestly is to drive rentals up and lower yields on the available stock, making development activity substantially more profitable. As evidence of increases in demand is analysed by development site owners, the expectations of profitability increase and supply of new development is increased. At this point in the market, financiers also become more willing to lend and the supply of property therefore rises to A3. With lead developments attracting sales and rentals at good profit levels this encourages increasing numbers of other developers to enter the market place. All act with imperfect market knowledge as to what the precise level of existing and future demand is.

Early entrants will have made good profits, having acquired sites for low prices during the weak phase of the market. However, later entrants will push up both land prices and levels of supply. The increase in supply, reaching completion at T3, may already have created supply beyond available demand at T2. Nevertheless, the nature of development activity is that once initiated, a construction project cannot be abandoned without incurring substantial losses. The time span over which a project will take to move from inception to completion, 2 years or more, makes judgements of supply/demand relationships difficult, and such occurrences of oversupply are common.

The result of oversupply is falling rentals and reduced investor demand, leading to decreased profitability. At this stage (T4), new development proposals have been suspended and major reductions in development activity occur. With little or no development occurring effectively, a correction or even overcorrection in market activity levels results. Thus, the level of demand, once it stabilises, even at low level will tend to find supplies limited after some time, leading to increasing rentals and the commencement of the next cycle and the tendency to repeat the stages already described at T5.

Finance and the development process

Availability of finance plays a vital role in two of the key stages in property development – project finance and investment finance. First, the short-term costs for the developer in borrowing the necessary capital to initiate and complete the process are crucial for the development of property. Then the onward sale of that building and its retention as an investment by an owner occupier or investor involves the availability of capital for such transfers over a longer term.

Short-term project finance is necessary for the purchase of the site, payment of fees, payments to contractors for construction work and so on. In the case of a property development company, such finance is often sought on an interest-only payment scheme with final repayment on a roll-up basis at completion and sale of the project. At this stage, the project capital plus any remaining compounded interest is repaid in a lump sum. Larger property development companies could fund developments from their own resources of retained earnings or through a stock market issue to raise capital. However, most of the developments would be carried out with borrowed capital.

Although the main clearing banks would often provide short-term working capital, it is the specialist merchant banks that dominate such businesses. Short-term working capital from clearing banks would often only be available at levels that are above variable interest rates and subject to short-term recall. Loans from merchant banks or finance houses can alternatively be negotiated at fixed rates for a term of years. Such loans would be the preferred source for property company finance intended for speculative development activity. Availability of such finance significantly affects the supply of development, as without this input development does not occur. Banking groups as lenders are clearly taking a risk in lending on speculative developments and some arrangements reflect a further extension of this risk with equity sharing arrangements. In such arrangements, the lender takes a stake or equity in the proposed development as part of the funding arrangement.

The criteria on which such loans are granted will often consider the following factors:

1. The borrower's financial strength and record in terms of previous developments completed and repayments. Audited accounts, financial plans and feasibility studies for the proposed development will often be requested.

2. The collateral which is being provided as security, often including the site itself, the development as it proceeds or other property owned by the borrower.
3. The financial viability of the particular project and arrangements for repayment of the loan.

In a weak market, the forward sale of any proposed development can be seen as essential. This effectively pushes the development market to a situation where development is only viable where future occupation is guaranteed or where the developer can utilise funds generated internally. Additionally, in the present situation from 2008 onwards, lending institutions will attempt to reduce their exposure to what is seen as a high-risk sector. Such portfolio considerations and management of risk apply to both lending institutions and borrowers. International experience is that overexposure to the speculative property sector leads to major problems in the banking system such as those that occurred in the early 1970s, 1990s and again in 2007/2008.

The standard mortgage-type loan has diminished in importance as few developers would commit themselves to speculative ventures on this basis even if such loans were still available. The continual, strong rental growth of the 1960s saw sufficient revenue returns guaranteed to cover mortgage capital and interest repayments, which were often based on fixed interest rates. Increasing inflation rates meant that such repayments were increasingly unattractive in terms of return for the lending institutions that increasingly sought a greater share of the returns being generated by the development process. Instead of developers building and selling on, often with large capital gains, investing institutions sought and obtained equity participation in major projects that they were financing. Arrangements for such partnership or equity-sharing arrangements are numerous and often involve ground rent-type agreements involving combinations of land owners, developers, contractors and financial institutions. The share of profits from resulting rental income is normally based on the inputs of the various parties.

The trend since the 1990s was for elements of financing of development projects to merge with the investment process. Major risks undertaken in financing speculative development entail a similar commitment in the event of the project's failing. Some lending institutions therefore extended their role to overlap with that of the investor, with common forms of long-term financing emerging, which combine both roles. A large range of financing models has evolved including the following:

1. *Forward sale.* A typical developer is trading in property rather than investing. As finance is difficult to obtain, a prior agreement with an investor who will purchase or 'take out' a completed development is essential in an uncertain market. Such agreements include precise details of arrangements, including effects of delays, voids in letting out, expected rental pattern, etc. between the funder and the developer. As the investor's main concern is the full rental value on completion whereas the developer balances the potential profit derived from such rental with the risk of uncertain demand on completion, negotiations involve a trade-off between potential profit and risk.

Chapter 2

2. *Sale and Leaseback.* This is a popular term for long-term financing that involves a developer's selling the freehold interest in a completed development to an investor and taking back a long lease on the property at a rent equal to the initial yield as reflected in the selling price. The developer then takes on the management of the completed project and aims to sublet the property at a rent beyond that period to the investor.

3. *Mezzanine Finance.* Major development projects sometimes require borrowing from a number of sources. Often a conventional borrowing arrangement will only provide 75–80% of the amount required, necessitating a 'final slice' or 'top-up' arrangement. This 'top up' can sometimes come from a series of banks or a syndicate and will often be at a higher risk rate than the main loan as the developer's main assets will have been used as collateral to secure the main loan. Often regarded as high risk, these loans will be at high interest rates or involve shares of the eventual profits. Such finance is often regarded as outside conventional banking arrangements, highly speculative and dubious as regards the business ethics of consultants who are often involved in setting up deals.

The general deregulation of investment and financial markets since the 1990s has internationally led to considerable inflows of funds into property development. Free movement of capital combined with complex specialised financial arrangements created major flows of funds available internationally for property development and investment. This climate of ever-increasing property values and strong investment-led development growth created large levels of confidence in property markets throughout Europe into the twenty-first century. Finance was widely available and the market seemed to be on a continual upward movement. It was in this climate that significant levels of private finance were willing to enter the property market. In the United Kingdom and elsewhere, investment in publicly quoted property development companies or unit trusts evolved, which financed the many major developments of the period.

Urban renewal policies, as developed in the United Kingdom and Ireland as examples, attempted to channel the flows of finance towards participation in urban regeneration. This form of finance, tax driven and subsidised, was more easily available for development activity in areas that were treated with caution by traditional sources of finance. Therefore, the lending preferences of traditional lenders to the property market were to some extent bypassed in the finance for development within special incentive-designated areas. Such finance, as would be provided for projects in secondary areas, would normally involve the developer providing a large part of the equity himself/herself, requiring ownership of the land and the provision of both collateral and personal warranties.

Life cycles in buildings and their property development implications

The economic cycle that dictates the utilisation and investment in buildings represents a pattern of replacement or refurbishment, which occurs when the value of the site exceeds the existing building's real value. This increase in site value occurs owing to the nature of the pricing system that reflects hope or potential values in site prices. As the real return declines, continuing growth in an urban area and the potential for new uses or more intensive uses inflate site values over time. Planning regulations, by way of conservation and preservation objectives, prevent the demolition of such buildings. However, refurbishment and intensification of use or changes of use will alternatively occur at this point. This process of obsolescence and redevelopment is illustrated in Figure 2.3.

Nevertheless, buildings in central city areas can be of such poor quality that refurbishment or redevelopment is not an economic option. This can often occur because of the condition of the existing buildings, difficult sites that are unsuitable for development because of site assembly problems or legal difficulties and frequently due to the poor surrounding physical environment. In such cases, decay and neglect of property frequently lead to a deteriorating environment.

While cycles of demand in development activity dictate the overall level of development in urban areas, large areas of dereliction, pockets of vacant land and run-down buildings occur and remain even through the cyclical upswings. Explanations for these seemingly contradictory pockets that defy general trends can be found by examination of the economics of development and redevelopment on an individual site basis. Lack of development at these locations and undesirable pressures for development in established areas often involve the aspirations of the planning process being directly opposite to the intentions of the speculative development interests. The basis for such conflict is the developer's wishes to maximise profit. This often will not take into account costs and effects of new development on the public and differ from the planners' wishes to achieve the objectives of their development plan without their own resources to achieve implementation. The reality of this situation is that development profit is the area in which the essential trade-off between the private market wishes and the planners' objectives occurs. The development cycle of an individual building is indicated in Figure 2.4, with Figure 2.5 demonstrating stagnation of this process.

Chapter 2

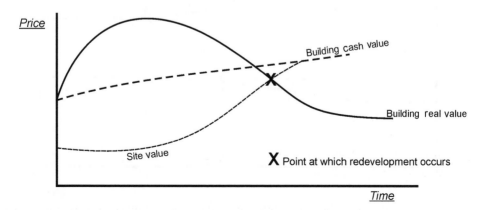

Figure 2.3 Building obsolescence and redevelopment.

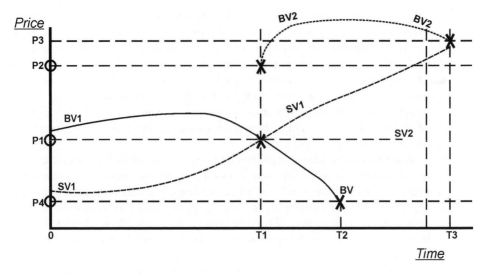

Figure 2.4   Development cycles of individual buildings.

In Figure 2.4 the relationship between site prices, building prices and real demand is demonstrated. The relative relationship between prices and time dictates critical points at which development decisions are made. At Price 1 (P1) the initial relationship at inception of site value situated at one-third of building value has moved to parity.

This represents the decline in building value over the period T1 (20 years plus), at which stage the maintenance and management costs of the building have increased steadily. At this point, the site becomes more valuable than the building and redevelopment occurs. Building value now moves to a new

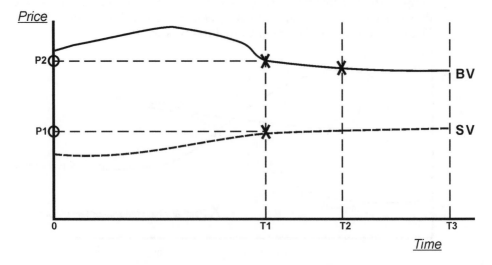

Figure 2.5   Development cycle stagnation.

level BV2, with the life span of the building extended by a further period of 20 years plus to T3, at which point redevelopment occurs again.

Should development/redevelopment not occur, the building's real value will continue to decline until by T2 the building could have a negative value. Here, while the site has a stable value (SV2), the buildings are in poor condition and their demolition may be the most economic option. Typical of such situations is the operation of extended rent control attempted in various countries in the twentieth century. Rents, often frozen by legislation at historic levels, provided owners with neither an adequate return on investment nor adequate sums for basic maintenance of the properties. Decisions were consequently taken to make no investment in the property concerned and the most economic outturn for owners of such property was to allow dereliction to occur to such an extent that demolition became necessary.

Stagnation within the development process also occurred through persistent weak tenant demand, as demonstrated in Figure 2.5. In these circumstances, weak demand over time has ensured that by T1 the relationship between site value and building value has stabilised at a low level, making redevelopment or refurbishment not profitable. Low levels of demand for sites at this location ensure a lack of further investment, whereas a stable and low level of income from the property maintains its value above this level, but without sufficient return to justify even essential repair and maintenance. Low returns keep the building in use but not well maintained, major refurbishment decisions are deferred and a more gradual process of decay occurs. A typical life cycle of a major urban building is represented in Figure 2.6, with one option where refurbishment or redevelopment takes place and the other alternative whose outcome is dereliction.

Public policy choices in the property market

The public sector plays a significant part in all development activity in the role as planning authorities. In the United Kingdom and Ireland, the planning system is often mainly involved in issues of development control. This is often in effect a regulatory and restrictive role. As such, the role of the planning system as it has evolved, combined with the effect of local authority structures, can restrict the role of public intervention in the development process compared to other European jurisdictions. Participants in the development of the urban land market therefore often see planning as having a narrow market-supportive role. Most of the private development interests are often willing to accept this control, in that it can improve the functional interaction between various land users. Such support is also based on intervention being necessary for development to take place in that the provision of physical infrastructure is necessary for further development, and regulating future development militates against haphazard and uneconomic patterns of activity.

Curiously, the more restrictive operations of such control may in the longer term benefit development and investment interests in that such control

Time scale year	Phase/ user	Condition	Costs	Revenue and investment return
−2	Feasibility & site purchase	—	—	Potentially high
−1	Design proposals & Planning	—	—	Potentially high
0	Construction	New	Nil	High
1	New Business or industry single user	New	Nil	High
10+	Established user	Good	Maintenance & modification	High
20+	Old single user	Fair	Substantial maintenance & repair	Moderate
25+	Mixture of older & emerging users	Poor	Substantial refurbishment required	Poor
Option (A) 30+	Refurbishment /development	New	Nil	High
Option (B) 30+	Vacant obsolete	Derelict	Major	Nil

Figure 2.6   Typical property life cycle in central Dublin.

obviously affects the value of developments already made. For owners of existing developments, tight zoning and restrictive permissions for future developments protect the long-term returns and capital values of existing property. Policies that tend to loosen restriction on market supply, although allowing investors to avail of new opportunities in property investment, decrease existing property prices in the longer term. Policies that restrict development therefore can be seen as supporting existing investments. Of course, if such restrictions go against a strong market trend, for example, strong demand for new office space in existing central locations, they can cause displacement of such sector demand to areas where permission is more readily available. This displacement effect is a part explanation of the tendency for office and housing development to move towards suburban locations.

To restrict the role of planning to market-supportive measures in the longer term brings the planning system into a position of bargaining with development and investment interests. Dependent on development and investment interests for implementation of plans, the state and its planning functions are often seen as following market trends, being too weak to affect them. This dependency on capital and development interests for implementation significantly guides planning policy and gives dominant interests in the urban land markets a major role in planning urban areas. Criticism of such dependency sees the state's role reduced to dealing with the socially undesirable consequences of economic growth by changing its institutional or physical settings, with the function and role of the state resulting in major losses in state revenues, while private interests benefit from growth and development without sharing the real costs or gains of new developments. This in turn can lead to poor development management and resultant urban societal problems (Healey 2006).

By its nature, planning control creates limitations on particular developments and conversely monopoly value on sites zoned for high-value developments. It is this large profit or latent value that attracts development and investment interests. The distribution of this development gain obviously involves political choices. The argument that the community should have or share this gain is based on that gain being dependent on public investment in infrastructure and basic services and that gain resulting from community growth and effort rather than private activity. Also prevalent is speculation in property with development potential where buyers purchase or take options on property through identification of development opportunity not already discounted by the market into that property's price.

The inevitable tendency in planning and policy making in urban land markets, such as in the United Kingdom and countries with similar regulatory systems, is a planning system that evolves towards involvement in a facilitative process to smooth the course of development of the built environment, often in a manner that adopts the requirements of development and capital interests (McGuirk and McLaran 2001). Dilution of broader aims of planning is then essential, and development of property by the private sector becomes the basis of development plans. Earlier theories that planning should be a neutral process of public intervention to secure efficient and equitable patterns of development and a good environment have been superceded by the development of an entrepreneurial role for planning, supportive particularly of development interests. In particular, the 1990s saw this new role for planning evolve and consolidate significantly. Planning could, following this mindset, be viewed as an impediment to economic development and its powers were to be limited. With new roles being developed in planning, political processes shifted the emphasis of planning to the need to encourage and stimulate investment and away from control and regulation of development. Jobs and new investment, new business, new industry and a climate for generating developments were adopted as priorities.

Partnerships in property development often link area planning and urban renewal, which are by their nature area specific and long term; property development perspectives are by contrast short term and site specific. Major property investment is concerned both with individual sites and overall areas and is long term. Both the time and spatial requirements of planning, urban renewal and long-term property investment are not served by short-term upsurges in sector supply, distorting markets with often unintended effects. Such periods of development have a great effect on both future development patterns and investments already made. Policies aimed at expanding supply of development space in an unregulated manner often result in short-term benefits of increased activity. However, unless this increased activity is integrated into an effective programme, its impact in the long term can be minimal.

An understanding of the development decision-making process can assist in shaping potential means of integrating such activity into broader policy aims. Development profit at a specific site is normally the single focus of development activity. However, the total of such development decisions represents a major power in directing patterns of urban development. An understanding of the role of the developer in the property market and his or her decision-making process thereby enhances policy initiatives in the property development context whether in terms of planning, urban renewal or public–private partnership arrangements.

References

Albrechts L, Healey P and Kunzmann R (2003) Strategic spatial planning and regional governance in Europe. *Journal of the American Planning Association*, **69**, 113–129.

Barras R (1994) Property and the economic cycle revisited. *Journal of Property Research*, **11**, 183–187.

Baum AE and Crosby N (2007) *Property Investment Appraisal*, Wiley Blackwell, Oxford.

Cheshire PC and Magrini S (2002) *The Distinctive Determinants of European Urban Growth: Does One Size Fit All?* Research Papers in Environmental and Spatial Analysis, No 68, Departments of Geography and Environment, London School of Economics, London.

Evans A (2003) The development of urban economics in the twentieth century. *Regional Studies*, **37**, (5), 521–529.

Gemaca II Project (2002) EU INTERREG II C, *Research on the Economic Competitiveness of the European Metropolitan Areas*, IAURIF, Paris. Publication: Les Cahiers, Economic Performance of the European Regions, Quarter 4, 2002. Sections by Cheshire P, Knapp W and Williams B.

Guy S and Henneberry J (eds) (2002) *Development and Developers*, Blackwell, Oxford.

Healey P (2006) *Collaborative Planning: Shaping Places in Fragmented Societies*, Palgrave Macmillan, Basingstoke.

McGuirk P and MacLaran A (2001) Changing approaches to urban planning in an entrepreneurial city: the case of Dublin. *European Planning Studies*, **9**, (4), 437–457.

O'Sullivan A (2006) *Urban Economics*, McGraw-Hill, New York.

Wyatt P (2007) *Property Valuation in an Economic Context*, Wiley Blackwell, Oxford.

Chapter 3
Partnership Negotiations Using Property Development Appraisal Techniques

The development decision

Partnership negotiations involve decisions in regard to the appraisal of the property development in the future and the property development interests in the area where the property is located.

Development appraisal decisions reflect the analysis by such participants in the development process of future movement in supply and demand, finance and construction capital (Cadman and Topping 1995). Understanding partnerships in urban development incorporates inputs from a wide range of perspectives on the development process including aspects of valuation (Isaac and Steley 1999; Hayward 2008), understanding markets in real estate (Ball 2006) and the priorities of the participants in the development process (Guy and Henneberry 2002). The interplay of these forces can create substantial risk in such decisions involving the physical process of production of buildings within uncertain social, economic and political contexts. A more detailed analysis of the property development decision process and a sequence of evaluations on markets and activities are therefore appropriate to gain an understanding of the high level of risk and return involved (Darlow 1990). It is upon such appraisal decisions that all public–private partnerships (PPPs) and sharing arrangements are ultimately based. In effect the public agency side of such arrangements often trades land at less than open market value for varying levels of required developments or services to be provided by competing/bidding private sector interests. Negotiating a partnership or joint venture with a land development component can be a complex process involving estimates and assessments of future market trends.

Chapter 3

The residual approach or method is normally used in valuation of property where latent development value is the prime determinant of an overall valuation assessment. Categories of land where this approach might be used include sites for development, refurbishment of buildings and other property situations where a future potential use value exceeds the value based on the present use. The concepts involved are that the market is likely to relate the value of the property to the surplus or profit, which can be generated by the potential development. An outline of such an appraisal involves the estimation of development value of alternative projects at the location and a comparison of this value with the costs of achieving development. Recent sales for sites with similar development possibilities can indicate a range of potential prices for the locality, along with evidence of sales and rental levels of completed units for comparison purpose. However, the unique physical location and other attributes of each site necessitate an individual valuation approach to each site. In this way it is possible to carry out analysis on options such as establishing a potential sale value of a development site, determining the feasibility of various development options or establishing the optimum intensity or quality of a proposed development.

The wide range of potential decision makers involved in the decision-making process could include the following:

1. speculative developers
2. residential building contractors
3. local authorities
4. development agencies
5. institutional developers/investors
6. charitable and religious institutional land owners
7. individual site owners

Partnerships between public and private interests

The next issue for consideration is the varying objectives of such partners in the development process. Although profit optimisation and seeking the highest value use and financial return are the obvious starting objectives of the private interest, risk containment and minimisation may also be aimed at in the course of the process. For public sector participants, issues such as providing affordable accommodation and achieving community or public resource goals may dominate depending upon the particular site and policy priority of the time.

In order to understand how both public and private sectors negotiate and determine such arrangements, it is necessary to review and appreciate the essential elements of appraisal and decision-making in the property development process at a specific development site. These can involve the completion of the following processes:

1. The identification and estimation of existing and future demand for new buildings and land uses.
2. The identification and acquisition of sites upon which such uses can be accommodated.

3. The design of accommodation to meet the requirements of such demand on the sites identified.
4. The arrangement of short- and long-term finance to fund site acquisition and construction.
5. The management of design and construction in a cost-effective manner.
6. In the case of private speculative commercial development, the letting out and management of the completed buildings and the onward sale of completed developments to investors.
7. In the case of private speculative residential development, the onward disposal of completed units to potential owner occupiers or investors.
8. The completion of financial obligations with the providers of development funds.

All estimates and evaluations are carried out subject to competition at all levels, which plays a major role in the culture of the property development industry. Specialist companies, evolving often from speculative building concerns, are what would customarily be regarded as property developers. Such interests are involved in regional, national and international markets using experience and imperfect market knowledge to evaluate and test development projects. This involves analysis of uncertain markets, the state of current supply and the proposals of other development interests to supply this market. Each stage of the process is costly, time consuming and involves decisions based upon the analysis of risk. In particular, as the identification and acquisition stage has passed and capital is committed, heavy costs are incurred.

Because of the capital requirements of the development process, a deeper involvement of the financial institutions has evolved over recent decades. Until the 1960s, these institutions were primarily involved as providers of mortgages on development property and as investors. The exposure of such investments and loans to property market corrections highlighted the burden of risk of such investment and loans. As the last resort, property companies were forced into liquidation, contrasting strongly with the disproportionate high returns enjoyed by developers during previous booms, based on low- or fixed-interest loans. More substantial involvement in the development market saw such institutions initially taking stakes in such developments and finally becoming involved as developers in their own right. Such developers will often be acting with an investment interest in view, with the parent company (e.g. a life assurance group) retaining the completed development for rental and capital growth. Otherwise, where developments are for onward sale, the attitude and decision-making of the institutions would be similar to that of the main property development companies.

The remaining property development interests include both occupiers and owners along with public sector agencies. Occupiers, and particularly owner occupiers, are involved in maximising the use and potential of their existing location. Risk taking for development by such participants is normally at a lower level than that for speculative development. The bulk of development activity by occupiers and owners is for their own use and, consequently, the return, by way of their utility of the property, is assessed based on the extra profit that can be derived from such expenditure based on inputs, including known levels of business and costs. When owner occupiers expand the scale

Chapter 3

of their development beyond their own known requirements, they enter the area of speculative development with risks similar to that of conventional development situations.

It is clear that the role of the public sector in providing development is radically different from the other interests whether directly or by means of partnerships. Social and economic considerations are included in the public service analysis of developments. Such analysis would essentially involve the political consideration of social needs allied with evaluation of cost/benefit analysis as to the efficient use of scarce public sector funds. Where public sector agencies combine with private sector interests, the negotiations by the private sector will revolve around conventional development appraisal assessments of profitability conditioned by the requirements of the public agency included as a cost on the development. This cost is, of course, normally balanced by the availability of land at a lower than normal price in exchange. In essence, however, both sides are in need of accurate development appraisal estimates in order to negotiate successfully.

In terms of the general bidding process for development land, competition among property developers, owners and the public sector involves the payment of high prices for suitable development sites. In an active market, potential purchasers compete for the limited suitable development land on the market. Although developers attempt at all stages to minimise the costs and risks involved, land purchase decisions involve upward price movement due to competing bids. Land purchase and financing of development bring the developer into conflict with the other capital interests in the process – land, finance and investment providers – as to shares in the eventual return accruing from the potential property development. Negotiating land purchase price, financing or equity sharing arrangements and onward sale arrangements dictate the level of return to the development company. Although often able to contract out some of the essential elements of the process, the final risk is borne by the developer. A similar process can evolve as development interests compete for valuable sites that are the subject of a bidding process for public–private development projects. Several groups may compete and bid up in terms of the returns for the public agency from the bid. This component effectively becomes the essence of their bid with the risk increasing as these elements of the development must be provided effectively, subsidised by the remaining elements of the development.

Decision-making, which often leads to specialisation in a given sector or market niche, is an obvious route to survival and success in such competitive situations. The capability of such companies to participate in major developments during cyclical upswings, when rents, returns and investor demand are high, has considerable effects on output in such sectors. The tendency of such processes to occasion boom and slump conditions within the commercial office sector particularly is much in evidence. Similarly, specialisation can occur by concentrating on a particular part of the development process. Thus, certain development interests have emerged specialising in land acquisition and assembly, requiring considerable time and management involvement. Other planning specialists will attempt to create added value by achieving planning permission, which rivals could not foresee or achieve in a limited market, requiring high-risk site acquisition and considerable management skills. Finally, in certain enterprise zones or tax concession-designated areas, a taxation specialist has become established who arranges both development and investment processes, and is involved in organising the taxation and incentive system to maximise the total return from any property development to using all allowances including the cost of borrowing. These specialists can also establish strategies in terms of both geographical spread and market sectors in order to minimise the risk of overexposure to a single market or sector.

Investigation of property development companies and their employment of varying strategies to ensure company efficiency indicate some features of good long-term management such as the following:

1. Ensuring that investment on projects is kept to a minimum by favourable funding arrangements.
2. Close monitoring and control of construction phases in developments.
3. Achieving a high degree of pre-lettings or pre-sales prior to commencement by being aware of clients' needs and forging relationships with clients, estate agents and other parties in the sector.

As discussed in Chapter 2, the development industry is basically the facilitator of present and future demand requirements of both investors and consumers of built space. The demand for buildings is a derived demand resulting from the real economy and the structural changes within the economy that continually result in changes in demand for space. The property development industry therefore is attempting to satisfy present and future demand and derive profits from the process.

Profitability and future expectations of profits are therefore the key issues in development trends. A rising market with increased demand produces increasing rents, values and profits. Within a private market, land will tend to have its most profitable use. Therefore, prime sites enjoying maximum accessibility, convenience and suitability to alternative uses will tend to be occupied by the highest bidders. New office development tends to be of the highest value use for locations such as central business districts for a number of reasons:

1. It offers maximum space development efficiency for a developer.
2. It offers a maximum rent-out area of space developed as a percentage of total development.
3. Revenue to space developed is maximised as office rental prices charged are often similar over the period of complete development.
4. It has low management costs compared with either retail or residential developments. It is often let to a single occupier.
5. It is capable of adoption or change to a number of uses.
6. It uses simple construction compared to mixed use or complex retail developments. Often functional designs are based on prefabricated steel or concrete frame.
7. Leasing structures and arrangements allow for maximum benefits to investors and owners.

Major developers have in the past preferred commercial development in central business districts and lower density residential development at green field locations. Efforts to encourage residential development at higher densities through the 1990s saw developers initially reluctant to switch to such residential development where design and density criteria were radically different. Security, servicing and maintenance of common areas were all the more problematic issues within the management of residential development projects. Obviously, the development of a large, high-density residential project with entirely different marketing financing and project management requirements is not the preferred option of some major development companies. However, problems of office cycles and oversupply have increasingly led to a switch in emphasis to residential development in many urban areas. With cheaper building methods and smaller units, it has become possible to develop residential apartments at central locations at profitable prices, and a trend towards development in this sector is evident.

Assessing options

In the following example, an analysis of a development appraisal shows the various options and the resulting profits demonstrating the economic basis of decision-making between options. Here a local authority owns a development site that its valuers advise is worth £8 000 000 with development potential, which they can sell on the open market. Importantly, the owner may wish to retain some control by way of conditions in a joint venture agreement over the future development in addition to normal planning control and building legislation. This would be of particular importance to a public agency whose obligations extend beyond maximising the commercial value of land assets. Alternatively, if they wish, they could assess the development profitability of the site with the aim of sharing that gain with a development partner. In essence, the local authority may negotiate a sale at full market price or amend the asking price in return for community facilities/affordable housing or other priorities, or seek a share in the development profits. All the estimates on the spreadsheet may be altered to give different scenarios or outcomes. In turn, each of the inputs can be assessed to test the sensitivity of development profits to changes in costs or revenues.

In this example, the site that can accommodate a commercial development is assessed as having a potential development profit of over £9 000 000. This gives the participants, including the land owning partner, a clear idea of the possible negotiating positions they hold. Subsequently, both the land owner and the potential partners will be examining the alternative scenarios based on different development projects, costs and revenues. In turn, the spreadsheet can be used to test what effect individual input changes will have on appraisal outcomes independently or combined. Figure 3.1 shows the development appraisal and sensitivity analysis.

Frequently the potential gain is greatest where risk is also greatest and the advantages of such gains can compensate for coping with high levels of uncertainty. The calculations are based on the various participants'

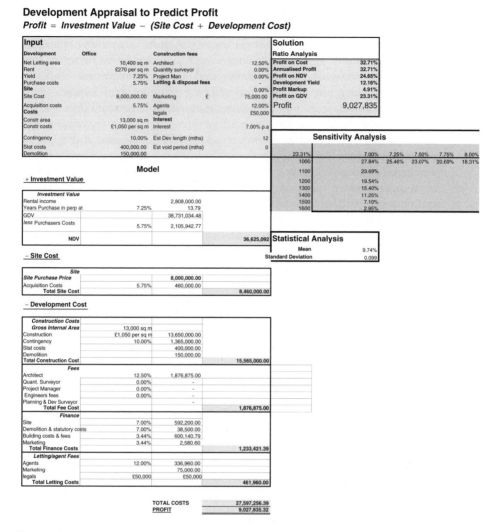

Figure 3.1 Development appraisal and sensitivity analysis.

judgement and analysis of the regional property and development markets, the future trends and actions, and the decisions of other potential developers, investors and purchasers in the same market.

Sensitivity analysis

All initial development valuations and appraisals must be based on a considerable number of estimated inputs. The more complex the scheme, the more likely it is that inaccuracies will occur. This places a premium on experience and up-to-date local market knowledge. With such analysis, the reliability of the outputs and results is not dependent on the method employed as on the quality of information and data used in the analysis. Indicated in the table are the effects of changes in inputs such as rents, yields, building costs and interest rates on profit. Constant reworking of calculations or sensitivity analysis to demonstrate the influence on land values or rental value or other input alterations is relatively easy to assess with the use of spreadsheet packages. Estimates of the effects on the profit of rising or falling rental values can be determined almost instantaneously. In the recent volatile market period, the demand for a more explicitly analytical evidence for property development appraisals has become even more important. While the standard approach remains to estimate whether a proposal or intended scheme is likely to prove viable based on assumptions made, this is usually accompanied by feasibility studies, discounted cash flow (DCF) analysis and scenario testing based on the ranges of probable costs and returns. In particular, PPPs may involve the appraisal of complex development options with cash flows on completed schemes. For such purposes, project-tailored appraisals may be developed in a user friendly manner and options in terms of sensitivity analysis, phasing and financing can be looked at in greater detail by all participants. From such analysis, it can be seen that changes to the various components of rent, yield, cost, finance and time can have dramatic effects upon the profitability of a scheme when tested. The next table from the spreadsheet indicates how such uncertainty can be analysed. Here the best and worst outcomes, which are expected, are inputted and their impact on the outcome assessed. Figure 3.2 shows a scenario summary.

A DCF analysis is considered to produce a more accurate basis for analysis and appraisal of the development situation. Ratcliffe and Williams (2000) found that the principal advantage of using cash flows is that there is considerably more flexibility in assessing the timing of payments and receipts. As the same information (costs and values) is used initially in residuals and cash flows, inaccuracies in these inputs will lead to errors whichever method or approach is adopted. In negotiations with an investment and development appraisal focus, DCF approaches are regularly used. The standard net present value (NPV) approach involves the discounting of all inflows and outflows. The computation of the sum of discounted inflows and outflows produces the NPV of the development profit. Individual developers have their own 'target'

Scenario Summary					
	Current Values:		Worst Case	Best Outcome	
Changing Cells:	50%		30%	20%	
Investment Yield	7.50%		8.50%	7.25%	
Building cost	£1,000 per sq m		£1,200 per sq m	£900 per sq m	
interest	7.50% p.a		8.50% p.a	7.00% p.a	
Result Cells:					Average 18.73%
Profit	23.35%		–3.19%	36.04%	STD 0.20018

Notes: Current Values column represents values of changing cells at time Scenario Summary Report was created. Changing cells for each scenario are highlighted in grey.

Expected risk adjusted profit   17.92%

Figure 3.2 A scenario summary.

discount rates but for initial appraisals it is logical to use the short-term finance rate as this is the real cost of money at that point in time for that interest. A positive NPV indicates that allowing for the time cost of money, the scheme is profitable and a negative NPV indicates on the same basis that a loss is likely. A DCF analysis can be carried out on all elements of the project. A DCF spreadsheet on one of the scenarios for this project is shown in Figure 3.3.

At acquisition and site assembly stage, uncertainty exists often as to the physical suitability of the land for development and its cost implications, along with the legal and planning difficulties that may arise in obtaining permission for the required development. Buying an option on the property, with final payment subject to planning, legal and other issues being resolved, restricts this risk element. The acquisition of development rights on public lands under a joint venture or PPP-type arrangement at a less than market price is, therefore, an attractive option for private market interests, especially during very strong market periods. This makes the prospects of PPPs for land development purposes attractive, especially during periods of upward market price movement.

If a site is purchased or capital committed, the interest payments commence immediately. Risks of unforeseen expenditures increase during the

Discounted Cash Flow

Month	0	1	2	3	4	5	6	7	8	9	10	
Date	Feb-2009	Mar-2009	Apr-2009	May-2009	Jun-2009	July-2009	Aug-2009	Sep-2009	Oct-2009	Nov-2009	Dec-2009	
Site cost	−6,000,000											
Aqu. Costs	−345,000											
Construction			−403200	−672000	−1209600	−1612800	−2822400	−2822400	−1612800	−1209600	−672000	−403200	−13440000
Premlinary & s.278 works			−10,000									−30,000
Fees			−175,720	−175,720	−175,720	−175,720	−175,720	−175,720	−175,720	−175,720	−175,720	−175,720
Agent/letting												−480,620
NDV												28,242,711
NCF		−6,435,000	−588,920	−847,720	−1,385,320	−1,788,520	−2,998,120	−2,998,120	−1,788,520	−1,385,320	−847,720	27,153,170
PV Factor	0.72%	1.0000	0.9928	0.9857	0.9787	0.9717	0.9647	0.9578	0.9510	0.9442	0.9374	0.9307
PV Value		−6,345,000	−584,706	−835,631	−1,355,793	−1,737,874	−2,892,375	−2,871,678	−1,700,833	−1,307,974	−794,662	25,271,545

	NPV	4,845,018
	Check	4,845,018
	Profit:	5,205, 760
	IRR per month	4.08%
	IRR p.a	61.5%

	Period	0	1	2	3	4	5	6	7	8	9	10
Construction costs	13,440,000.00											
start	1											
Build period	10											
Period costs based on S Curve			403200	672000	1209600	1612800	2822400	2822400	1612800	1209600	672000	403200
Cumulative total			403200	1075200	2284800	3897600	6720000	9542400	11155200	12364800	13036800	13440000

S Curve fo construction costs

Period	1	2	3	4	5	6	7	8	9	10	11	12	13	14
6 months	9%	13%	28%	28%	13%	9%								
7 months	7%	10%	17%	32%	17%	10%	7%							
8 months	5%	7%	14%	24%	24%	14%	7%	5%						
9 months	4%	6%	10%	16%	28%	16%	10%	6%	4%					
10 months	3%	5%	9%	12%	21%	21%	12%	9%	5%	3%				
11 months	2%	3%	6%	11%	14%	28%	14%	11%	6%	3%	2%			
12 months	1%	2%	5%	9%	14%	19%	19%	14%	9%	5%	2%	1%		

Figure 3.3   A DCF from a spreadsheet.

construction phase. It is at the later stages following fitting out that major risk is involved. Instead of an option on a site or ownership of a piece of development land with many possible uses, the developer has now a partially finished product. This product is physically fixed at a specific location with its future economic and market context when completed out of the developer's control. Many developments are for sale as investments, on the open market, which can be volatile and unpredictable. In this context, the public sector development element of a PPP must be guaranteed and needs to be covered by the profitability of the remaining components.

In such situations, the developer and other participants are faced with the most difficult uncertainty, that is, the timing, as developments will often take more than 2 years from initiation to completion. The determination of accurate assessments of costs and expenditures throughout the project development period presents major problems and a detailed forecasting is needed for feasibility studies. However accurate these may be, they remain only estimates based on incomplete knowledge. Changes in the property market and other economic cycles present different scenarios and difficult problems for all decision makers. Cyclical development patterns often involve developments being completed during periods of oversupply in the market. Development interests, therefore, at no stage can avoid risks, but different attitudes can be taken to potential risks based on information, analysis and forecasts.

Development decisions therefore rely heavily on the quality of information and analysis. A detailed analysis can highlight those factors representing the highest risk elements of a project and indicate the role of various input factors in deciding on the feasibility of such projects. Such analysis assists in understanding the critical elements in decision-making for property development and highlights those factors most sensitive to change.

Knowing which factors are most sensitive to change and whose movement plays a critical role in decisions to initiate or defer development provides a basis for the evaluation of partnership arrangements in the property development process. In carrying out such analysis, use is made of a conventional spreadsheet to give computer-aided calculations of numerous variations of the inputs involved. With this type of knowledge on the operations of the property development process, it is possible to examine the partnership arrangements in context and assess their ongoing impact on decision makers in the process.

Key inputs in negotiations

With the benefit of this analysis it is possible to isolate those factors that are crucial to the decision-making process. Obviously with variables such as site development costs and professional fees, although their movement improves or disimproves the relative feasibility of the project, their effect is not the most critical. Similarly, items such as agents' fees and advertising costs do not form a significant element of costs or revenues. For large-scale commercial developments small movements in land prices also are not significant and savings in this area, while welcome, would not swing major development decisions. It is when rentals, investors yield, construction costs and finance costs are analysed that the greatest levels of uncertainties and risk are encountered.

Rental income is the developer's forecast of what rent will be achieved when the development is completed. This forecast is shaped by considerations of location and supply and demand in the market at a future point in time. Specialist advice from leading chartered surveyors or estate agents will often be sought regarding expected levels at completion date. Normally, appraisals are based on today's levels of rentals and cost. Expected rentals are difficult to predict as they are dependent on both supply and demand with the intentions of other potential suppliers of development space unknown. Consequently, it is common practice to include a series of rental levels in feasibility studies. This assessment is crucial as it determines the expected capital value of the property from which the developer expects to derive the profits. Investor yields are similarly crucial in their role in determining the expected capital value of the property developed. As a multiple of the rental in assessment of gross development value (GDV) the smallest change in yields significantly influences GDV and development profits. The sensitivity of these two factors combined produces the crucial estimate as to what revenues can be expected from a project.

Construction cost constitutes a major fixed cost on the development. If variation is allowed in this factor due to inflation, wage increases, demand for building services or costs of raw materials, the effect is immediately to reduce development profits. Developers can attempt to ensure that construction costs are contained through maximising the tendering competition between potential building contractors seeking work on the project. Cost savings are also often sought through delaying payment as much as possible to the contractor commonly through phasing arrangements. During periods of low construction activity, this process of cost reductions and competition is at its most intense, involving both initial tender price and phasing arrangements. Boom periods allow contractors to increase their prices and profits in the knowledge that competition is less pressing.

The cost of finance is often the most difficult to predict. The ready availability of finance from 2000 to 2007 contrasts with previous high costs, based on historically high real interest rates in the 1980s and 1990s, which made finance prohibitively expensive on many projects. Movement on finance cost is potentially more complex and more damaging than changes in other cost factors. Changes with major impact can occur either in time or interest rates, which significantly affect profitability.

Timing of the development is crucial to profitability in many respects. With the cyclical movement of the property market, letting or sale of the property may prove more difficult than expected. Rentals and yields, as previously discussed, if underachieved, result in immediate losses. However, delay in the project, even with a successful disposal, has similar results. This occurs because property development is normally carried out with high costs of borrowed money overhanging the development. Delays at relatively high interest rates immediately involve financial costs, which seriously damage viability. Small rises in interest rates alone may be covered by developers in the short term in terms of the project remaining viable or profitable. However, if such rises are combined with delays on completion or disposal of the property, the effect has most serious implications. Reductions in interest rates conversely increase the profitability of projects. It is clear therefore that time and interest rates for the completion and disposal of a development represent a major risk at all stages of the process.

With such a high degree of sensitivity to change present in factors that are at best only reasoned assumptions, the scale of risk involved is often great. Variations of only 10% can potentially double or entirely remove profits. Great care and attention must therefore be taken in arriving at such estimates. While architects or quantity surveyors can with a reasonable degree of confidence predict building costs, the estimates of rentals and yields must be regarded as less certain. The cost of finance, based as it is on time factors pertaining to the development as well as general economic considerations and government policy, is obviously out of the control and expertise of developers and property markets. Best estimates of the input figures included must therefore be based on probability analysis.

No matter how detailed the study of probability, models can never overcome the fundamental dynamic nature of the inputs involved in the development process. It is therefore necessary to treat all major inputs as flexible and revisions on the feasibility of the project would be common as the project proceeds. Even construction cost can be significantly affected by a design change made necessary at the planning stage. To a large degree, however, risks based on costs are within the experience of major develop-ment interests and with the exception of a major redesign, construction costs can be expected to be reasonably accurate. Similarly, funding arrangements secured in advance at fixed rates can help contain the cost of finance. How-ever, unless the building is pre-let or pre-sold, the investment yield and rental and eventual time taken for disposal remain beyond control. It is therefore on these factors that most risk is concentrated. The variation resulting from changes to both these inputs can be calculated over a series of scenarios and the results compared in order to assess results on profitability. Timing of development remains the greatest imponderable since developments will only be coming onto uncertain markets within 2 years. The final decision on development, type of development and timing is therefore based on a series of crucial assessments and estimates. Based on the analysis of these figures, any development interest must use decision-making processes to evaluate what result is most probable and finally decide whether that crucial element timing is correct.

References

Ball M (2006) *Markets and Institutions in Real Estate and Construction*, Wiley Blackwell, Oxford.

Cadman D and Topping O (1995) *Property Development*, E and F Spon Press, London.

Darlow C (1990) *Valuation and Development Appraisal*, Estates Gazette, London.

Guy S and Henneberry J (eds) (2002) *Development and Developers*, Wiley Blackwell, Oxford.

Hayward R (2008) *Valuation: Principles into Practice*, Estates Gazette, London.

Isaac D and Steley T (1999) *Property Valuation Techniques*, 2nd edn. Macmillan, London.

Ratcliffe J and Williams B (2000) *Development Properties in Valuations Principles into Practice*, (eds WH Rees and REH Hayward), Estates Gazette, London.

Chapter 3

Chapter 4
The Private Finance Initiative

History of the private finance initiative

The Private Finance Initiative (PFI) was originally launched in the United Kingdom by the then Chancellor, Norman Lamont, in his autumn statement in 1992 with the main criteria of encouraging private money into public requirements by capital investment, to provide value for money (VFM) and transfer the risks of provision to the private sector wherever possible. PFI is therefore directed towards those areas where capital funding has traditionally been provided directly by government and it is here that supporters of PFI have predicted further benefits. Private sector finance will almost always exceed the cost of government borrowing but it is predicted that recompense will come through 'collateral non-financial benefits', which will provide a better delivery of service as a result of private sector efficiency (Stewart and Butler 1996).

In 1995, the Conservative government clarified its thinking of PFI in evidence to the House of Commons Treasury Select Committee. Originally introduced as a means to supplement public capital spending (PCS), Kenneth Clarke as Chancellor gave evidence to the select committee and stated that the purpose of PFI was to 'replace public capital spending'.

PFI deals proved difficult for those involved with them, particularly private sector bidders. Kenneth Clarke's laconic statement in his 1995 budget speech that 'the Government chooses the quality services the public require and then goes out and acquires those services from private companies with the finance and expertise to deliver' implied that the process was a simple business transaction, but in practice, PFI has proved complex. The problems were summarised, and solutions proposed, in the government-initiated review of PFI by Malcolm Bates, which was announced by the Paymaster General on 23 June 1997. This resulted in the creation of the Treasury Taskforce to help build PFI expertise in government. The most common form of PFI is where the private sector is responsible for design, building, financing and operating the proposed facility (known as *DBFO*) (Allen 2003). It is this model that is assumed to be used in the discussion in this chapter.

The taskforce gave momentum to the sentiments expressed by Tony Blair nearly a year before his party won the 1997 General Election when he stressed his support for PFI but proposed certain reforms. He proposed that the terms of the partnerships would be brokered by specialists, that there would be a better definition of risk between private and public sectors and that civil servants would be better trained to deal with PFI schemes (Blitz 1996). A continuing problem has been the interface between the civil servants and the private contractors responsible for building and managing PFI facilities and there has been a succession of initiatives intended to make the process more efficient. The latest of these is the employment of Partnerships UK as part of the Treasury Taskforce. This initiative has received a mixed reception. Speaking in July 1999, Alan Milburn, Secretary of State for Health, said 'Partnerships UK will provide the public sector with the expertise of the private sector. It is the final piece of the jigsaw in the modernisation of PFI that we promised in our manifesto' (Milburn 1999). Others take a more phlegmatic view. 'It has an uncomfortably complicated sort of feel. It could also be a centralising device' (Kemp 1999, p. 28). PFI can also be seen as part of the Labour government's agenda to modernise the public sector. In a revealing speech to the British Venture Capitalist Association in July 1999, Prime Minister Blair said 'You try getting change in the public sector or public services...I bear the scars on my back after two years in government. Heaven knows what it will be like after a bit longer'.

There has been no fundamental change of government policy in respect of PFI since the Labour party's election victory in 1997, but a number of administrative reforms show the commitment of government to PFI. Partnerships UK has become a public–private partnership with 49% of the company remaining in public sector hands. In addition, the Office of Government Commerce (OGC) has been created to replace the policy arm of the Treasury Taskforce with the primary intention of addressing the procurement problems associated with PFI deals.

The Labour government's stubborn refusal to change its stance on PFI is illustrated by the result of a motion to the Labour Conference of 2002, calling for a moratorium on any future PFI projects pending an independent review. The motion was carried in the hall by a 2 to 1 majority but this was ignored by the Labour party executive. In part, this appears to be caused by a new pragmatism on the part of those driving the new Labour project. Tony Blair stated at the conference, 'Are we going to force local communities to put up with crumbling Victorian buildings just because we have some ideological objection to a private company building their new hospital?'

The role of Partnerships UK is supplemented by the OGC, which advises on procurement and is chaired by the Chief Secretary to the Treasury with a Board of Permanent Secretaries. The Private Finance Unit, part of OGC, develops and promotes PFI policy for public bodies (Allen 2003).

Chapter 4

The PFI process

A PFI project commences with the preparation of an outline business case (OBC) by the department, Quasi Autonomous Non-Governmental Organisation (QUANGO) or local authority promoting the scheme. The OBC is the basis for justifying the project to the relevant government department and the process for a typical, local authority-promoted scheme is summarised below:

1. appraisal of project options;
2. statement of need;
3. financial appraisal and cost estimate;
4. identification of preferred service delivery option;
5. draft output specification and payment mechanism;
6. approach to development of information pack, pre-qualification questionnaire and model contract;
7. proposals for monitoring the contract;
8. risk register;
9. procurement timetable;
10. establishment of reference project or public sector comparator (4Ps 2004).

When the OBC has been approved by the relevant government department a project owner, director and a team are appointed. The first of these chairs the Project Board, the second is responsible for the detailed negotiation with the PFI contractors and the third provides technical support as required. Outside consultants may also be appointed where there is a skills gap. A Project Board to take responsibility for strategic matters and also a Stakeholder Board, where the project involves a number of outside bodies not directly connected with the procurement process, may also be required. Government has tried to reform the PFI process by introducing a new procedure intended to reduce the number of changes required to a project after the preferred bidder has been selected. This 'competitive dialogue' should make the process more competitive and reduce the time and costs involved with the preferred bidder stage. It is acknowledged that there may be a need for negotiation with more bodies before a preferred bidder is selected and this may weaken the bidder interest. The old and new procedures are summarised in Figure 4.1.

The sponsoring authority is obliged to publicise the opportunity by advertising in the official European Economic Community (EEC) journal (Official Journal of the European Union (OJEU)) and through a prior information notice published in relevant publications. The remaining process is a series of investigations and negotiations. Some potential bidders will be excluded following shortlisting for financial reasons or because expertise in the type of project proposed cannot be proved. Up to four bidders will be invited to negotiate and, following receipt of final offers, one or two preferred bidders may be selected. The sponsoring authority will have prepared an output specification that will describe the performance required from the proposed building but not how that performance is to be achieved. Design and specification solutions are part of the final negotiation that leads to the award of

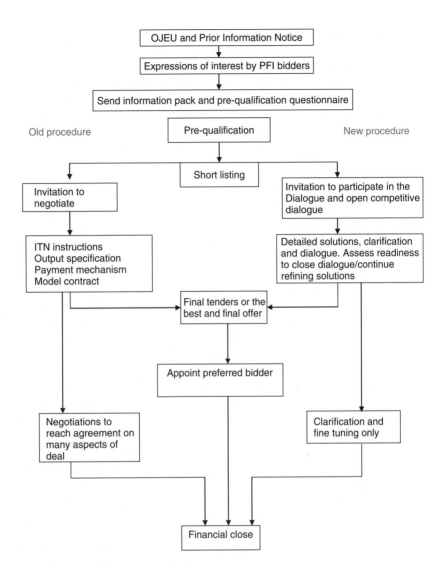

Figure 4.1   PFI process. Adapted from 4Ps (2004).

the contract. A National Health Service (NHS) scheme has a further stage of completing a definitive investment appraisal and Full Business Case for government approval before the contract is finalised and awarded. This is seen as a more refined process for arriving at one preferred bidder and there is then a final negotiation with this company only (NHS Executive 2008).

Justification for PFI

The unwavering support of government for the PFI has attracted interest as various commentators have sought to analyse government's true incentives.

Derek Kerr (1998) identifies the necessity to control the public sector borrowing requirement (PSBR) as the primary reason for government promotion of PFI. The state in the 1980s suffered from a crisis of overaccumulation with the policy of easy credit resulting in inflationary growth in the money supply rather than capital growth. Kerr believes that PFI is a direct result of this problem. 'This has forced national states to introduce policies designed to improve their position in the global price hierarchy, to depoliticise their domestic policy, further to reduce state expenditure and to reshape the relationship between state and civil society' (Kerr 1998). The argument here is that in the absence of global financial regulation (such as was provided under the Bretton Woods agreement in the aftermath of World War II), states that accumulate increasing amounts of debt will be rewarded with an outflow of capital and a run on the currency. The consequent high interest rates, which would of necessity be imposed by government to support the currency, would lead to falling investment and aggregate demand and increased unemployment. Government unpopularity and rejection at the polls would be the likely result.

As the UK economy demonstrated in the mid-1970s and the Argentinean economy more recently, governments are well advised to avoid levels of debt which effectively put domestic policy in the hands of a body such as the International Monetary Fund (IMF).

Grahame Allen (2001, p. 23) acknowledges that 'the PFI helps government overcome a perceived fiscal dilemma: it enables the government to increase public investment through higher capital spending while maintaining a tight fiscal stance'. He quotes statements by HM Treasury (2001) concerning 'the golden rule' and 'the sustainable investment rule'. The former states that over the economic cycle the government will borrow only to invest and not to fund current spending. The latter states that net debt will be maintained below 40% of gross domestic product (GDP) over the economic cycle. Strict control of government debt is therefore seen to be a major policy incentive but in the economic circumstances that prevailed until recently, it is doubtful that the adoption of PFI was necessary to achieve that end. As Allen points out (2001, p. 24), since 1997, the PSBR has been negative in three of the four financial years by a total of £35bn with public sector debt as a percentage of GDP falling from 42% in March 1997 to 31% in January 2000 (National Statistics 2001).

Allen concludes that the two treasury rules would not have been broken even if all the PFI projects currently signed had been funded directly by the public sector. It should be remembered, however, that PFI projects and projections of public need have long-term influences and government will not always benefit from favourable economic circumstances. Adoption of PFI as an overarching policy means that capital expenditure is replaced by long-term revenue expenditure and the present government appears to believe that the risk of capital overspending in the future is therefore reduced.

One major incentive for government in using PFI is that it is possible to regard state expenditure as 'off balance sheet'. Thus, in comparison with a conventionally procured project, the cost of provision is not accounted for as it is a future stream of payments rather than a one-off expenditure; moreover, the project is financed by private money. Government is therefore protected from the risk of breaking two of its most well-known fiscal rules. Too much emphasis should not be placed on the off balance sheet incentive compared with others; however, as Allen points out, if the project was conventionally procured, the finance would be defined as capital investment, not current spending, and therefore would not break the two rules.

The government's case to support its use of PFI is put strongly in the long report *Meeting the Investment Challenge* (HM Treasury 2003a). The 'small but important role' that PFI plays in public investment is explained in persuasive detail. Increased public expenditure since the election of the Labour government in 1997 is emphasised and it is clear to see that only a very small percentage of the £50bn investment in 2006 was a result of PFI (Figure 4.2). The 'on or off balance sheet' argument is given a short shrift in this document; 'the decision to use PFI is taken on value for money grounds alone, and whether or not it is on or off balance sheet is not relevant'. At the heart of government's support of PFI is the transfer of risk to the public sector and VFM. This is defined as 'the optimum combination of whole-life cost and quality (or fitness for purpose) to meet the user requirement' (ibid. 3.12). To put this statement another way, the function of PFI is to provide public services at a specification which represents the best trade-off between cost and value in use. Reference is made to 'optimum whole-of-life cost and quality' (ibid.), which will be determined by using 'the best professional judgment based on the best available evidence' (ibid.).

Overspend from past public procurement is used as evidence that a new method is required. The list of late and overspent projects includes Guy's

Chapter 4

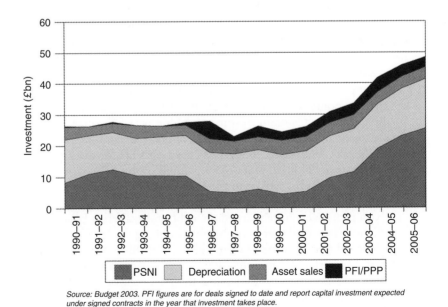

Source: Budget 2003. PFI figures are for deals signed to date and report capital investment expected under signed contracts in the year that investment takes place.

Figure 4.2 Total investment in public services. *Source: Meeting the Investment Challenge* (2003a). Crown Copyright.

and St. Thomas' Hospitals where costs rose by 29% with the completion date slipping by 3 years and the Trident submarine base at Faslane where the cost rose from estimate to final cost by 214% with completion drifting by 30 months. The reasons cited for past overspend and lateness of delivery are as follows:

1. the full cost of projects not counted accurately beforehand;
2. risk management procedures not implemented;
3. insufficient incentives for either management or organisation to ensure that the projects are driven forward successfully (*Meeting the Investment Challenge* 2003a).

These factors will be more fully considered in the case study that follows. In particular, it is interesting to speculate why projects are not costed accurately from the start. The report concludes that a National Audit Office (NAO) (unreferenced) survey found that only '30% of non PFI major construction projects were delivered on time and only 27% were within budget whereas . . . over 70% of the PFI projects were delivered on time and no construction cost overruns were borne by the public sector' (ibid.). The lesson drawn from this statement is that 'construction risk transfer has been effective, as cost overruns were not borne by the taxpayer' (ibid.). Other commentators have drawn different conclusions from these statistics. If the specification has not been changed or updated, this would have kept cost within original limits. Similarly, if the procurement timetable only allows the full cost to emerge after final negotiations with the preferred bidder, this would tend to massage the figures. Figure 4.2 shows a chart that tabulates total investment in public services.

Financing of PFI projects

Apologists for PFI stress the private sector efficiencies that may result from the input of private finance in terms of both capital and revenue costs. From the viewpoint of the private sector funders and contractors, however, a viable PFI project is a sound investment with returns guaranteed by an undoubted covenant and with risks restricted to familiar areas. With falling interest rates in the past (but not recently) it has been possible for private sector consortia to refinance PFI loans and achieve capital profits. This came to the attention of Alan Williams, MP, a member of the Public Accounts Committee, and it was reported that Carillion and Group 4 (PFI contractors) made £13m extra profit when it refinanced the debt on Fazakerley Prison in Liverpool. It might be expected that government would require some claw-back provision (financial reimbursement) from PFI deals of this nature but Williams reports that Fazakerley is one of many where this was unavailable (Glackin 2000). It should also be borne in mind that it is conventional business practice for private companies to examine their debt profile at regular intervals. Refinancing by private companies involved with PFI has raised a storm of protest in certain sections of the media (e.g. *The Observer* 7/7/01) and it is implied that PFI contractors are making additional profits in an underhand manner. Yet, this is no more than normal business practice and once again neatly illustrates the dichotomy at the heart of PFI. Government is constrained from imposing 'unduly onerous conditions' as to do so 'may result in these (bidders) being unwilling to participate in future procurements, thereby weakening competition, and thus value for money, in the long term' (NAO 1999). 'Unduly onerous conditions' may reasonably be taken to mean anything that does not accord with normal business practice and this may explain why, initially, government was relaxed about the additional gains that accrued to private companies when refinancing as project risk declined.

PFI projects require an all-embracing service from the private sector, which may last 30 or 35 years. The initial contract phase is regarded by the financial markets as high risk, whereas once the building is completed, the facilities management (FM) phase is far less risky. This is mirrored by a private sector development project where the short-term finance to buy the site and build the building is usually more expensive than the long-term finance that replaces it. Normal business practice is for companies to keep their funding arrangements under constant review as cheaper funding may become available. Directors of companies have a fiduciary duty towards the company and it is possible that a failure to take advantage of a favourable funding package could be regarded as negligent. However, normal business practice does not necessarily fit with the PFI procurement route and in the early days of the initiative, criticisms were made of PFI contractors refunding at the completion of construction and making a windfall gain of many millions. As a result of this, new rules have been introduced for PFI projects. Contracts signed from July 2002 onwards provide for public authorities to receive 50% of any gains arising from debt refinancing and there is also a voluntary code where authorities would expect to receive 30% of refinancing gains where the provision is not included in the PFI contract (NAO 2006b).

The NAO reports that government has secured gains of £137m up to February 2006 through the operation of the voluntary arrangement. The sale of equity shares in PFI schemes is not covered by the new rules and PFI contractors can take advantage of the growing market for PFI schemes as investment vehicles without any payment to the government except taxation. These arrangements once again illustrate the dichotomy at the heart of any public–private partnership. Where public money is involved, the government is obliged to depart from normal business practice even though the initiative has been set up to revolutionise the way in which public buildings are procured.

The windfall gains experienced by PFI contractors from refunding led to questions in the House of Commons and the government had to respond. In a normal business climate, however, the code and the sharing requirements put the PFI project at a disadvantage with others where normal financing can occur. At present, there is little sign that PFI deals have become less attractive for this reason and this may be as a result of the size of the returns from successful PFI schemes compared with (until recently) the low funding costs.

In 2008, it was revealed in the newspaper *The Guardian* (Hencke, *Guardian*, 4 March 2008) that PFI vehicles were being moved into offshore funds where most capital gains tax could be avoided. The example quoted is the Home Office headquarters in Marsham Street, Westminster, a £311m PFI project, which required the PFI contractor to build, finance and operate a new headquarters building for a 29-year concession. Some commentators have criticised this arrangement because taxpayers are paying rent on a building where the tax base is declining but once again it is normal business practice to avoid paying tax where this is legally possible.

Rates of return for PFI projects are often shrouded in commercial confidentiality. Highly geared projects will offer the best return to equity so long as the cost of borrowing is exceeded by the rate of return. Pricewaterhouse-Coopers (PWC) in Appendix C of Meeting the Investment Challenge (2003) state that the normal equity return bid declined for PFI projects from over 15% in 1995 to 13.5% with an average from 1995 to 2002 of 14.5% per annum. PWC were unable to comment on the returns expected form PFI projects in total as 'insufficient data is available' (PWC, para C12).

Value for money and procurement in PFI projects

From the above it will be appreciated that a PFI project is a complex process. Originally, the use of private finance to satisfy public requirements was governed by the rules proposed by a committee chaired by Sir William Ryrie. Privately funded solutions were tested against publicly funded alternatives and had to be shown to be cost effective. Secondly, public expenditure had to be reduced by the amount of private funding obtained. Current PFI policy has dispensed with the second of these rules and, indeed, from 1994, the Treasury has not approved any capital projects unless private finance options had been explored. It is still necessary, however, for 'Value For Money' to be demonstrated in all PFI projects where public money is used in addition to private.

The VFM test is set out in the 'Green Book' (*Economic Appraisal in Central Government –A Technical Guide for Government Departments 1993*). The costs of the private option (payments by users or the public sector) are estimated and discounted at 6% (recently revised to 3.5%). The Green Book identifies this as a 'pre-tax cost of public financing to compare with the pre-tax cost of public funding'. Intangible costs and benefits are evaluated using a method of points scoring against an appropriate scale.

The Treasury has sought to justify PFI by citing the overruns on publicly funded capital construction projects but it has not been explained how projects to provide long-term services can be better controlled in comparison with a conventional route. It has also been suggested that the pattern of public investment may well be skewed towards those projects that are attractive to the private sector. Some commentators have used the example of the Jubilee Line Extension to the London Underground network as an indication of the way in which government allocates priorities. 'We build the Jubilee Line Extension not because it is for passengers ... than many other improvements to the London Underground network, but because it has a small element of private finance' (*Financial Times* 31/1/97).

Scepticism has also been expressed about the handling of PFI procurement by government departments. An early study of 200 companies and financial institutions carried out by James R Knowles (*Financial Times* 27/6/96) found that many companies experienced difficulties in the handling of PFI contracts by civil servants. Inconsistency of approach by government departments and the lack of a clear framework for PFI projects resulted in time and money being wasted on schemes that were unlikely to go ahead.

The IMF, in a study of the UK economy (IMF 1996 reported in the *Financial Times* 25/11/96), rejected the prospect of allocation of public need being determined by the possibility of attracting private funds. Claims that PFI would result in additional investment were said to be 'illusory' and the assumption that PFI would result in greater efficiency over publicly funded alternatives 'must be taken largely on faith'. The IMF had similar criticisms to the James R Knowles study in citing administrative problems in the procurement process as a cause of frustration and delay.

Risk and value for money

David Heald (2003) notes that certain financing routes are not available for public authorities wishing to replace or upgrade facilities. The choice is restricted to three options: a conventional project, a PFI project or the 'do nothing' option, which Heald terms as unacceptable and therefore can be discounted. The conventional exchequer financed scheme is the fall back position as it provides the only option if the PFI scheme is rejected. VFM is defined as net present value (NPV), which is the discounted value of benefits and costs discounted over the life of the project. Heald sees a number of problems with the VFM procedure adopted by the government, which compares the NPV of a public sector comparator (PSC) with a PFI project:

1. The standard of comparison may be inconsistent if it is known that the PSC would not be adopted even if it showed superior VFM.
2. The calculation of NPV uses the rate of discount required by government which is 6% per annum. Demand risk and residual value risk always remain with the public sector and the impact of present value cost will be lower at 6% than with a lower real discount rate. (The article pre-dates the 3.5% revision.)
3. VFM analysis is done from the viewpoint of the purchasing body without taking into account any impact on other public sector bodies. These negative externalities may be significant.
4. The risk estimate inherent in the VFM test quantifies a comparative situation of public versus private provision but there is no estimate of the total risk in the project or whether risk is created elsewhere.
5. Satisfaction with the project may vary over the life of the project as benefits and costs vary. Over time, the incentives of the construction arm of the PFI consortium and the finance arm may diverge. It may be that this is one incentive for PFI consortia to refinance projects upon building completion.

Broadbent *et al.* (2003) attempt to evaluate the PFI in the NHS and, in doing so, come to conclusions about the PSC and VFM. Their definition of VFM is the one used by the Institute for Public Policy Research (IPPR 2001): 'giving equal weight to quality considerations: it is the optimum combination of cost and quality in meeting the needs of service users'. It should be noted that there is no mention of risk in this definition, whereas in all government publications risk is a central feature in VFM calculations. However, in discussing the use of the PSC the authors note that the VFM calculation compares the PSC with the PFI option by a discounted cash flow cost analysis, which is discounted at 6% (recently revised to 3.5%). The cost figures are adjusted for inflation rises and also for downside risks. This means that the PSC cost is inflated for risks that are not explicit in the bald figures for procurement. Therefore, the risk of construction overruns and other contractual problems, which are assumed to be factored in for the PFI scheme, are explicitly added on to the PSC. The risks of construction cost overruns are estimated by using data from previous experience with directly procured projects. Broadbent *et al.* note that 'design and construction risk accounts for 50% of the total risk adjustment that leads to PFI being the best' (ibid.).

A different view from Gaffney and Pollock is taken about the widely held belief that in order to afford PFI, bed numbers in NHS hospitals must be reduced. Alyson Pollock cites the reduction in bed numbers as a result of the cost of PFI schemes. 'Therefore the new buildings have to be smaller so that bed numbers and staff can be reduced. These reductions are driven by financial necessity, not by any analysis of health care needs' (Pollock 2004). Broadbent *et al.* see the proven reduction in bed space mainly due to changing clinical practices, but the point remains that if fewer facilities are being provided, is this point given sufficient weight in the PFI/PSC decision-making process?

A Public Accounts Committee paper (Committee of Public Accounts 2007) has reviewed the PFI bidding and tendering process. Problems are perceived in the way the process deals with the need for competition and market testing. The report concluded with the following points:

1. Since 2004, the proportion of deals attracting only two bidders has more than doubled with the average tender time between 2004 and 2006 being 34 months. These two factors are seen to be linked with firms being reluctant to commit to a lengthy, expensive and uncertain process.
2. Changes to projects after the selection of a preferred bidder were made by one-third of project teams.
3. The application of benchmarking and market testing have had the effect of increasing prices by (up to) 14%.
4. It is difficult for project teams to find appropriate benchmarking data.
5. In order to keep contracts affordable, services in hospitals have had to be reduced.
6. Public procurement teams do not possess the necessary PFI skills and experience (NAO 2007).

The conclusions of the Committee summarised above can be compared with the critical success factors for PFI schemes that emerged from research by Dixon *et al.* (2005, para 4.1). These are paraphrased as follows:

1. A robust business case demonstrating need and long-term financial viability.
2. An output specification that firmly establishes quality and quantity of infrastructure and services over the contract period.
3. Input from users into the specification.
4. Balancing of performance measurement and risk transfer to ensure that incentives are in place and the project meets the needs of the end user.
5. Commitment and resourcing by awarding authorities.
6. Avoidance of abortive financial negotiations by involving financiers at an early stage.

Policy responses

Government rhetoric in promoting PFI does not emphasise macro economic incentives. Much is made of the transfer of risk, previous overspending on public projects in the past and the involvement of private sector expertise and efficiency. The concept of risk is indicative of the way in which government policy has been tailored to meet private sector funding requirements. Initially, PFI was promoted on the understanding that the private sector would take responsibility for all the risks associated with building and running the facility within agreed performance criteria. This was discussed in a paper written in 1997 (Gallimore *et al.* 1997); 'The government's view has been that it is reasonable to expect a project consortium to take on systematic risk, such as a future change in Civil Service accommodation policy . . . the interviews suggested that contractors appear comfortable with risks with which they are familiar (e.g. construction), this is less so for longer-term risks such as usage'. Problems were experienced in funding PFI schemes where private sector consortia were expected to carry systematic, or demand, risk. The result is that in PFI schemes this risk is retained by the public sector. This is reflected in a survey by Akintoye *et al.* (1998), where demand risk was ranked second in importance from a list of 26 risk factors in PFI projects. In many types of PFI projects, the carrying by the private sector of demand risk is not considered as a viable option by the government. 'Volume is difficult to forecast and in the case of prison provision this risk has been retained by the client'. Further research by Bing *et al.* (2004) divides risk into three factors: macro, meso and micro. The first of these are risks that are external to the project such as economic conditions, the second are internal to the project such as design and the third are risks derived from the different nature of the private and public sectors and their incentives. A survey of organisations concerned with PFI carried out by the authors (Bing *et al.* 2004) found that the risks that should be retained by the public sector include the political decision-making process, political opposition, government stability and site availability. Apart from the latter, all these are seen to be macro risks. Risks that respondents thought should remain with the private sector are a combination of macro, meso and micro risks such as industrial regulatory change (although some thought this should be shared), interest rates, weather, environment, ground conditions, financial market and all risks associated with design, construction and operation. Many risk factors are thought better to be shared between the parties or allocated on a case-by-case basis.

Graham Leach (2000) sees risk transfer as 'the main benefit expected from PFI' and he points out that if a private sector supplier is asked to carry high levels of risk, VFM will decline. Premium payments will be required by the private sector if it is required 'to take on risk better managed by the public sector'. Demand can be considered to be the type of risk that a private supplier would find unattractive, but this raises the question of whether the private sector is being asked only to carry those risks that it would normally carry in a conventional project. The NAO takes a similar view to Leach in its examination of deals under the PFI (NAO 1999). Risks should be allocated 'to those parties best able to manage them' and this is seen as a crucial factor in obtaining the best possible deal for the taxpayer. A report by the Kings Fund (reported in *The Guardian* 9/5/02) emphasises the level of demand risk that will be carried by the public sector as requirements change and technology develops. John Appleby, Director of Health Systems, is quoted as saying 'continuing change in medical and information technology suggests that hospitals as we know them may not be needed in 10 or 20 years, yet the PFI is locking the government in for 30 years or more'.

Justification of PFI on the grounds of cost and VFM has been challenged by research carried out by Gaffney and Pollock (1999) into PFI hospital schemes. In order to show VFM, PFI projects are tested against a PSC. Gaffney and Pollock first of all consider the existing capital charging regime in the NHS. NHS trusts are obliged to make an operating surplus of 6% of relevant assets after inflation and, in addition, a straight line depreciation charge is levied against the lifetime of the assets. The prices charged by the trusts are passed to purchasers who are in turn funded to reflect a component equal to average capital charges. The authors point out that, firstly, the 6% charge for the cost of capital does not reflect the cost of capital to the public sector but has been imposed 'to ensure that there is no inefficient bias against the private sector supply' (HM Treasury 1997 quoted in Gaffney and Pollock 1999). Two problems are seen with this system. As the circulating funding must also provide for payments to PFI contractors a leak is created from a formerly closed system and any shortfall must be made up from other budgets available to the public sector procurer.

Gaffney and Pollock also analyse increases in capital costs for the first wave of PFI hospital schemes from the statement of the OBC to the current cost. It was found that cost increases for a total of 14 hospitals averaged 69% and the authors conclude that the reason for this 'is largely accounted for by the incorporation of financing costs to the private sector, which amount to

25% and 15% of the overall cost respectively' (ibid.); the authors considered the two hospitals where full data were available.

Evidence is also available that the government is at pains to offer PFI schemes that are tailored to be attractive to private sector consortia. For example, the Princess Margaret Hospital scheme in Swindon was originally envisaged as a town centre project and was costed at £48m at OBC stage. The project has now been relocated to an out-of-town site, thereby releasing valuable town centre land for development by the PFI consortium. The current cost is reported to be £148m 'which was uniquely determined by the interests of private investors' (Gaffney and Pollock 1999, p. 59).

Since these relatively early examples of PFI procurement, government has changed the procedure for analysing the risks in comparing a proposed PFI project with a PSC. It is stated that PFI is not suitable for projects of under £20m capital expenditure and VFM is tested at three different times in the life of the project; at programme level assessment (commencement), at OBC and at procurement level just before financial close (The Treasury 2006). The latest edition of the Green Book confirms that the preferred discount rate is 3.5% (Green Book 5.49) but a range of discount rates are recommended for projects where the concession will last over 30 years.

One early example where PFI was claimed to be an unequivocal success in terms of VFM was in respect of prison contracts. Former Paymaster General, Geoffrey Robinson, sought to justify PFI by citing the '20% savings on the most recent prisons constructed and run under PFI contracts' (Robinson 1999). A former career civil servant at the Home Office, David Wright, confirms this by referring to 'significant savings on operating costs, in the order of 13–22%' (Wright 1996, para 22) but the obvious point to make is that these savings may serve merely to increase the profits of the PFI contractor. In terms of capital cost a major problem appears to be that the Treasury, in seeking to control spending, requires accurate costings to be produced at an early stage. If the facility is to be produced using private finance this problem is avoided. This situation can be better understood by considering the way in which publicly funded projects were procured before the adoption of PFI and this is dealt with later in the comparative case study.

In spite of the many early criticisms of PFI, the government continues to argue strongly for its efficacy. In *PFI: Strengthening Long-Term Partnerships* (HM Treasury 2006) (The Report) the Treasury states the government case for PFI in detail and it is therefore an important milestone document. Partly written in defensive tone, it reports on the success of PFI to date, recommends further improvements to the process and accepts that not all projects are suitable for this type of procurement. The transfer of risk and the importance of 'value for money' are both major items in The Report. As a result of 'the most extensive survey of operational projects to date' the success of PFI to date is asserted. The argument rests on four main planks:

1. Seventy-nine per cent of the projects report that service standards are delivered always or almost always.

2. Public authorities report that the overall performance of 96% of projects is at least satisfactory, and that in 89% of projects services are being provided in line with the contract or better.
3. With 83% of projects the contracts always or almost always accurately specify the services required with recent contracts showing more improvement.
4. PFI incentives are working with payment deductions being low and when applied the response from the contractor has resulted in good or very good levels of service (The Treasury 2006).

The operational performance of PFI projects is one area where the Report sees the need for further improvement in the following areas:

1. operational performance, flexibility and better long-term VFM;
2. ensuring that contractual incentives align more closely with service provision;
3. handover from procurement to operation;
4. the length of the contract in relation to the nature of the services and assets being provided;
5. the cost of contract termination by the government 'changing its approach to certain aspects of the financial structure and the calculation of the payment made if the public sector wishes to terminate the contract' (para 1.21);
6. flexibility in the provision of soft services;
7. length of time from OJEU advertising to financial close. This is stated to be 2 years on average;
8. PFI procurement and monitoring expertise in government;
9. improved competition for senior debt.

It is therefore recognised that in spite of reported satisfaction with the PFI process, there are many areas where improvements are required. Attention is also given to the procurement process itself. 'The key goal in managing a procurement process is to maintain competitive tension while achieving the requirements laid out in the project preparation stage' (ibid., para 3.10). Government here is setting out its belief that VFM is achieved through competition but it tacitly recognises the difficulties of doing this when complex services are being negotiated with a preferred bidder. The VFM drivers are listed as follows:

1. appropriate allocation of risks;
2. optimisation of whole-life costs throughout the life of the project;
3. an output-based specification that allows innovation and solutions that deliver VFM;
4. flexibility to allow changes in service requirements but allowing certainty for the private sector to innovate;
5. private sector incentive structures;
6. risk management expertise (para 3.11).

When these drivers are considered as a package it is difficult to escape the conclusion that government is attempting to reconcile fundamentally opposing incentives and requirements. How can 'flexibility' and 'certainty' be achieved at the same time? Who decides on the 'optimum' cost (which means costs in relation to performance) throughout the project?

Certain projects are not considered suitable for the PFI route based on past experience. These include front-line service delivery where the terms of employment offered by PFI contractors would be unacceptable. This is called 'pre-conditions of equity and accountability' in The Report. Also for projects with fast changing service requirements and for projects of less than £20m, PFI is thought unsuitable, as the PFI contract cannot cope with the flexibility required, for example, in an information technology (IT) project. It is also accepted that PFI procurement is too expensive for small projects to be financially viable for contractors.

As stated earlier, certain risks were assumed to be borne by the private sector in the initial stages of PFI promotion by government. Demand risk, for example, is one area that was unacceptable to the private sector and is therefore borne by the public sector. This is rationalised by government as the view that risk should be carried by the party best able to manage it; although, as seen earlier, certain changes to PFI procurement will improve the public sector risk level. The Report sets out those risks 'typically' transferred to the private sector, which can be summarised as follows (para 3.39):

1. standards of delivery;
2. cost overrun during construction;
3. timely completion of the facility;
4. underlying and future costs associated with the project;
5. industrial action and physical damage;
6. certain market risks which would be scheme specific.

Figure 4.3 illustrates the risk profile of a typical PFI project.

The risks to be transferred to the private sector come within the all-embracing 'value for money' requirement but it is noticeable that there

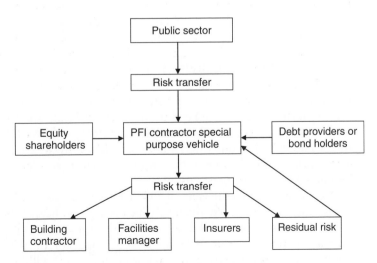

Figure 4.3   Risk structure for PFI project.

is an acceptance that projects that require a high level of flexibility are not thought suitable for PFI. Government also recognises the importance of the 'people' factor in projects and procurement. This is defined as 'partnership working' (paras 5.48 and 5.49) and will be given advisory weight only by being documented in a 'shared vision' document that, although not contractual, 'sits alongside' the PFI contract.

Government also believes that the structure of a typical PFI contract inherently protects the public sector by the incentives of the various parties involved in the project. These are listed as follows (para 5.75):

1. Senior lenders will require construction bonds and parent company guarantees and will scrutinise the PFI company closely.
2. As the PFI company will not receive service payments until the facility is running there is a strong incentive to make the facility available, in accordance with the service contract as soon as possible.
3. Investor equity is at risk if the PFI company defaults and will therefore have a strong incentive to manage the PFI company effectively.
4. The ability of lenders to 'step in' will be exercised in the case of difficulty and there is a strong incentive for lenders to do that as their debt repayment is at stake.
5. The right of the public sector client company to terminate the PFI contract gives a strong incentive to both equity and debt providers as both will be at risk in the case of default and termination.

Although government appears happy that the PFI structure contains an inherent risk protection, as the penalties for default are great, it is not satisfied with the time taken to procure and complete projects. More emphasis will be placed on defining the project before bidders are involved and schemes will be more closely examined before a preferred bidder is selected. A final approval prior to financial close will be introduced to ensure that the scheme is within the previously approved parameters. These measures are designed to minimise cost increases and time delays when projects come to the market but it is worth recording the financial risk that the public sector accepts with all PFI projects. The risk of inflation is retained by the public sector as a proportion of the unitary charge made by the PFI contractor is indexed to the Retail Price Index (RPI). How much of the contractor's costs are to be indexed is confirmed in the bid for the project. The retention of this risk is seen as a benefit to the public sector because, if it was not there, the contractor would be obliged to factor the risk into the bid. The risk of interest rate rises is borne by the PFI contractor but government continues to consider whether this offers the best VFM as, in the case of contractor default, the cost of breaking the contractor's short-term loan commitments becomes a government responsibility.

One of the major criticisms of PFI has been the cost of private finance in comparison with public finance, which is always cheaper. Government is aware that raising public finance through gilt issues tends to push up interest rates as a competitive rate of return must be offered on the gilt issue. Also, if government is in the market as a major debtor, funds will be attracted to a relatively low-risk debtor and this will tend to 'crowd out' the private sector from the debt markets or make the available debt unnecessarily expensive. The Report (para 8.2) acknowledges that the cost of government borrowing is lower than that enjoyed by private sector institutions and proposes credit guarantee finance (CGF) to reduce the private sector risk premium. The CGF works very much like the securitised debt described in Chapter 7 when Chase Manhattan Bank was able to lend at a small fraction over London interbank offered rate (LIBOR) as a result of a promissory note provided by the developer. With CGF the government lends to the PFI contractor at the prevailing rate of interest as if the contractor was borrowing in the market. The government's loan is guaranteed by one or more financial institutions of undoubted covenant and for this guarantee they are paid a fee. Even after paying the fee, the government is able to show a positive cash flow, which is a net surplus of funds. The Report states that pilot studies of this method have shown cost savings at Leeds Hospital at 8% of financing costs and at Portsmouth Hospital at 16% of total financing costs.

Design of PFI facilities

Broadbent *et al.* (2003) see two results flowing from the public sector performance specification provided to PFI bidders. Firstly, it is assumed that this will lead to innovation in service delivery and secondly that as the private sector will own, run and maintain the buildings, it will be concerned with the quality of the design and the building. Evidence for design and build quality is, however, scanty, although government publications such as *Meeting the Investment Challenge* (HM Treasury 2003a) assert that users are mainly satisfied with the design and use of the buildings provided under PFI. Sir Stuart Lipton is quoted as saying that the design of PFI hospitals is 'not uplifting and won't do anything for society' (Broadbent *et al.* 2003) and in the *Observer* newspaper (20/8/2000) it is reported that the emphasis in PFI is on speed and cost to the detriment of good design. In *The Guardian* (29/8/05) Larry Elliott mocks government claims of the satisfaction expressed by users of PFI schemes. 'The quality of design and the likely longevity of a building come way down the list of priorities if you've been working in a draughty 100-year-old hospital where the roof leaks'.

The Commission for Architecture and the Built Environment (CABE 2005) has investigated the design of PFI buildings. It sees a number of factors acting as barriers to good design and these can be summarised as follows:

1. inexperienced public sector clients;
2. discussions dominated by contractors whose main incentive is time reduction;
3. unrealistic budgets combined with unrealistic VFM exercises;
4. little or no incentive for the private sector to innovate or take risks for service delivery;
5. little account taken of changes in service delivery over time;
6. high-quality design outweighed by 'best value' issues;
7. the step-like nature of the PFI process that leads to lack of design continuity;

Chapter 4

8. protracted initial stages in PFI leading to barriers to entry, thus reducing the pool of talent available;
9. overall quality compromised by pressure to produce detailed designs for a start on site to reduce costs.

In the words of Larry Elliott, 'Originality means risk, and risk can be expensive' (*The Guardian* 29/8/05). In terms of design, the picture that emerges is that the main drivers for PFI contractors are time and cost and this cannot be regarded as surprising. When dealing with an inexperienced user client, the emphasis will probably be placed on producing a facility that satisfies need rather than spend expensive consultant hours, seeking innovative design solutions or elevations and floor plates that will win architectural awards.

The NAO (2003) reported on PFI construction performance. The Report repeats the data for publicly procured projects before and after PFI and concludes that 73% of pre-PFI projects exceeded the price agreed at contract stage and 70% were delivered late. Post PFI, the figures are 22% and 24%, respectively, and it is noted that the cost increases arose from the client, not PFI consortium changes. Most public sector managers are reported as satisfied with the quality of design and construction and 'mostly satisfied' with the performance of the building. Feedback from users was patchier but it is reported to be 'generally favourable' (2003, para 11). An analysis of price increases after contract award shows that the public sector procurer was responsible for most changes and the reasons were, in order of frequency, new facilities, and extensions or enhancement to facilities. A minor amount of extra cost was expended on work to buildings that were not originally expected to be retained – refurbishment work and design changes. The advantage of PFI in transferring the risk of extra construction cost caused by weather conditions, unforeseen ground conditions, labour problems and changing building regulations to the private sector is noted.

The Report states that the public sector would have been responsible for these costs in traditional procurement but it fails to compare like with like. PFI is essentially procurement based on an output specification, very much like a lump sum contract with contractor's design (design and build). If a design and build contract had been used for a conventional project, the situation would have been the same as for the PFI project and the contractor would have been responsible for the extra cost of the items stated. Client changes after contract would have led to additional cost just as they do with a PFI contract.

Graham Leach (2000) in a paper produced for the Institute of Directors (IOD) does not believe that PFI should be seen as a mechanism that results in minimum risk for the public sector. If the private sector is required to accept risks over which it has no control, the bids received for the PFI project may well be unacceptably high as the extra uncontrollable risk will be factored in. This can be illustrated in Figure 4.4.

The PFI procurement route therefore elicits controversy in the way it deals with VFM. Government analysis tends to regard each PFI project as discrete but, as Heald points out, public expenditure should be seen in terms of

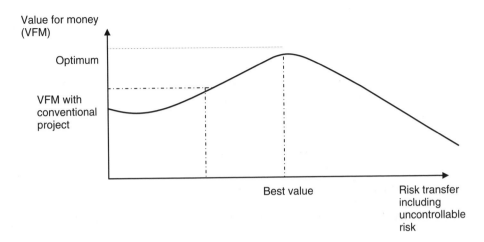

Figure 4.4   Risk transfer. Adapted from Leach (2000).

the total risk profile not just the project. In bidding for a scheme, a PFI consortium will take a view of the risk involved with the project should it be won. High bidding cost is cited by Dixon *et al.* (2005) as a factor in reducing market competitiveness and this must be regarded as a further risk factor that firms have to quantify. Also, semi-structured interviews suggest that success criteria varied depending on the party involved. These are recorded as follows (Dixon *et al.* 2005, p. 417):

1. *Special purpose vehicle (SPV)*. Efficient and cost-effective procurement process.
2. *Lawyers/financiers*. Reaching a financial close.
3. *Investors*. A good quality covenant and certainty of income.
4. *Awarding authority*. Project on time, cost and to the required specification.
5. *Project sponsor*. Feedback from end users.

It is not surprising that what can be regarded as the client body, the awarding authority, should measure success as satisfying the accepted project criteria of time, cost and performance. Not every client, however, will attach the same weighting to each factor although each will be important to some extent. Client objectives may be weighted in a multiplicity of ways and a typical example of incentive weighting is provided in Figure 4.5.

The project in Figure 4.5 seeks to quantify client incentives in a more sophisticated way than time, cost and quality. This client has a bias towards quality and aesthetic qualities are important. Price and time are seen to be of equal weighting with a distinct importance given to capital expenditure. The client here has a short-term commitment to the project but surprisingly wishes it to have a pleasing design. The client here might be the developer of a major civic facility where the building will be passed on to the public sector when complete. The eventual owner will, of course, have different incentives. It is unlikely that a PFI scheme would display such a profile

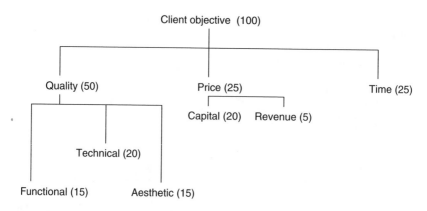

Figure 4.5   Client incentive weighting. Adapted from Walker (1996).

from the project sponsor's viewpoint as it would be likely that the relative importance of capital and revenue would be much closer and aesthetic qualities, which receive scant regard in government advice on PFI, would be relatively unimportant.

Project changes

PFI procurement as described in government publications such as *Meeting the Investment Challenge* (2003a) is analogous to a lump sum contract with contractor's design, in other words, a design and build contract. Changes to this type of contract are always fraught with danger as, without a Bill of Quantities, the contractor has an opportunity to load the cost of any variations demanded by the employer client. For this reason, the 'design and build' contract is not recommended for complex projects that may require changes during the construction contract at the instigation of the employer. PFI contracts operate as a tender based on a performance specification followed by a negotiation to finalise the details of the project. There should not be a need to change the project after financial close but circumstances may arise where this is necessary.

Where a change is necessary to a PFI project, government emphasises the preference for the work to be competitively tendered. It is reported in the NAO report *Making Changes in Operational PFI Projects* (2008) that in 2006, 70 changes with a cost of £100 000 or above were made in 43 PFI projects. Only 29% of these were competitively tendered. The main reason for this was 'complex interface issues with the ongoing risks and obligations borne by the incumbent private sector contractor' (NAO, para 2.6). The NAO cites evidence that changes to PFI projects are more expensive than equivalent changes in conventionally procured projects in the opinion of 59% of PFI contract managers (NAO, para 2.9). Part of this expense is caused by the inclusion of high fees to cover overheads and profit and NAO reports that these fees are typically 12.5% with a range from 5 to 28%. The NAO also reports that the mark ups for FM contractors are in line with a range of 10–20% as recommended by the Royal Institute (sic) of Chartered Surveyors (NAO, para 2.11). The NAO identifies change management as a problem in PFI schemes and recommends the following guidelines to keep costs down and avoid delays.

1. Control the flow of changes to avoid overstretching resources.
2. Ensure that the 'change' is not already specified in the contract.
3. Keep good records of changes.
4. Brief the private sector partners clearly.
5. Employ effective methods to check costs.
6. Maintain open lines of communication among all stakeholders.
7. Approach the need for changes strategically to minimise cost (NAO 2008, para 3.5).

Most of the recommendations listed here are sensible project management policies but the NAO also noted the importance of soft management issues in this area. Relationships between the public and private sectors are described as 'good' or 'excellent' in 75% of projects surveyed and the value of good relationships is clear. Some PFI contractors will not charge for minor changes, for example, and some innovation to the benefit of the public sector is noted (NAO, para 3.14).

Public sector ethos

Some commentators perceive a loss of public sector ethos resulting from the growth of PFI. Hebson *et al.* (2003) identify five main principles associated with the public sector ethos. These are paraphrased as follows:

1. *Accountability.* Acceptance of the legitimacy of the political structure without allowing personal views to influence behaviour.
2. *Bureaucratic behaviour.* Show honesty, integrity, impartiality and objectivity.
3. *Public interest.* Serve the public good.
4. *Motivation.* Altruistic motivation rather than personal gain.
5. *Loyalty.* Loyalty to public sector organisations.

The authors conclude that, based on case study research, 'transparency of decision making that is the hallmark of accountability and bureaucratic behaviour, albeit often at the price of time consuming structures, has been replaced with contract-led decision structures that are negotiated and fought over' (Hebson *et al.* 2003). Conflicting priorities are recorded between public and private sector managers and the authors believe that this causes manipulation, strategic behaviour and an erosion of other features of the public sector ethos. Before he assumed office Prime Minister Tony Blair envisaged the delivery of public services based on trust. Cooperation was emphasised more than VFM and competition. Later government statements have moved away from this initial stance and government publications that seek to explain and justify PFI place greater emphasis on the maintenance of competitive tension as a means of securing VFM.

Chapter 4

Comparative case study

It is instructive to compare a project procured by the traditional route with a typical PFI route. The comparative study compares a project procured by conventional means with another similar project. The first is the National Physical Laboratory PFI project (the PFI project), which was terminated in 2004 and is the subject of an NAO report (NAO 2006a). As both the case study and the PFI project are similar in the type of facilities provided, this comparison seems particularly appropriate.

The PFI project

The PFI project consisted of 16 linked modules providing over 400 laboratories to replace existing buildings. The planned cost of the new buildings was approximately £96m, financed, as in most PFI projects, mainly by bank loans. The PFI contractor was Laser, an SPV owned jointly by Serco Group and John Laing. It was agreed that the responsible department, The Department of Trade and Industry, would pay Laser a yearly sum of £11.5m when the project was complete and this was subject to annual indexation to RPI.

Ownership of the buildings would revert to the department at the end of the 25-year contract. Laser contracted with a wholly owned subsidiary of Laing plc, John Laing Construction Ltd (JLC) to design and build the new buildings and a subsidiary of Serco contracted to manage the scheme when complete.

Progress with PFI project

Following the signing of the PFI contract in 1998, construction commenced but 1 year into the project, JLC encountered problems in completing the mechanical and electrical systems in the first-phase modules. The consequent delays knocked on to other phases so that some were delayed by up to 45 months (NAO 2006b). Two technical problems proved particularly intractable. The design of the environmental control systems in 29 laboratories was problematic and it became clear that design would take a long time. As a result, the public sector agreed to withdraw these requirements from the contract but, nevertheless, delays amounted to between 38 and 46 months. Secondly, subaudible noise requirements clashed with requirements for temperature control and it was concluded by the contractor that the conflict could not be resolved. The independent certifier concluded that the fact that the noise requirements could not be met did not result in a loss of beneficial use of the modules and these areas were regarded as complete.

As the project progressed further problems emerged. Among those listed in the NAO report are unsafe gas extraction systems, ineffective fume hoods, ineffective water dilution tanks, incorrect humidifiers and a multiplicity of other technical defects. In spite of the defects identified, the independent certifier was able to issue completion certificates for the laboratories that presented defects but the department called for adjudication and the adjudicator found for the department as non-compliance prevented beneficial use of the buildings. The design and build contract meant that JLC could not pass on cost increases to Laser and Laser was running short of funds. Laser, the PFI consortium, had access to £100m of funds to pay its predicted capital expenditure of £96m. It intended to use revenue from the completed facilities to fund part of its payments to JLC. The financing structure of the project was as follows:

Laser's source of funds	£	Use of funds	£
Prepayment from governments Sale of land pre project	8.8m	Fixed price contract	82.0m
Senior debt Mainly Abbey National	81.8m	Fees, preparation of FM contract, debt interest, working capital	17.6m
Junior debt Abbey National Treasury Services	4.6m		
Shareholder's equity Serco and John Laing plc	4.4m		
Total	99.6m		99.6m

Adapted from NAO Report diagram 7.

As a result of losses on this project and the Millennium Stadium, Cardiff, John Laing plc sold its construction business including JLC. Although Laser had parent company guarantees for the construction contract, the delays meant that the income it should have received for the completed buildings was not available. It became clear that the design as envisaged was not going to meet the specification required by the department and John Laing plc estimated that the cost to complete the new buildings would be £45m. The company had already been paid £76m of the agreed fixed price of £82m. The predictable result was that the Laings considered walking away from the project and the department's interests would not be best served if this was allowed to happen. A supplemental deed was therefore agreed between Laser and JLC, whereby the stringent performance requirements would be relaxed and the buildings would be completed based on specified inputs rather than performance outputs. Any outstanding work that was required post contract would be project managed by Serco.

Although the supplemental deed was not accepted by the department, the work went ahead but further difficulties led to serious cash flow problems for Laser and it was eventually sold to Serco by John Laing plc. Laser's bankers kept its debt facilities open but it became clear that the company would not be able to complete the buildings to the specification required. Finally, an agreed termination of the contract resulted in serious monetary losses for the private companies involved in the deal, summarised as follows.

Private sector investment	£	Outcomes	£
Equity investors Serco + John Laing plc	4m	Lost	
Bank of America Abbey National Treasury Services plc	85m	Recovered	67m
Subcontractors		Not known	79m loss
Total private sector investment	89m	Total private sector loss	101m

Adapted from NAO, para 13.

In dealing with the problems listed here, the Department of Trade and Industry was advised by a number of legal and technical consultants. Eight major companies were paid a total of £8.53m in fees between 1998 and 2004 when the contract was terminated. Prominent among these payments were over £1m to Herbert Smith for legal advice, £3.3m to HDR for engineering advice and £2.1m to Turner & Townsend for quantity surveying advice. In summing up the causes of the problems experienced with the project, the NAO cites the following:

1. A complex specification where the client, as required by PFI, provided an output specification. The solutions were 'very demanding'.
2. Of the two bids received for the project neither bidder demonstrated satisfactorily how the demanding specification was going to be met.
3. There is evidence that the PFI contractor, after Laser had been appointed the preferred bidder, tried to make design drive the outputs rather than the required output drive the design.
4. There was little competitive tension in the project. There were few expressions of interest and only two bidders, one of which 'hardly merited being considered a reserve bidder' (para 2.14).
5. None of the parties realised that meeting the stringent requirements of the specification would prove so difficult but the department, in accordance with PFI procedures, kept design risk with the contractor.
6. By maintaining the design risk with Laser, the department hoped that the incentive imposed on the contractor would result in a solution to the design problems. As the NAO laconically put it 'the Department was mistaken in this expectation' (para 2.20).
7. Construction of the facility commenced before detailed designs of the mechanical and electrical systems were available. The shell and the footprint of the building were therefore fixed before the contents were understood or fully designed.
8. Contractual arrangements with the various private sector companies concerned with the project were too loose to allow a sufficient measure of control when problems were encountered.

9. The department refrained from relaxing the output specification in case this was regarded by the contractor as a variation that would have passed some of the design risk to the department.

10. Upon termination of the contract, the department was obliged to meet the value of the contract and did so, after considerable negotiation and advice, with the sum of £75m.

11. The department was left with buildings that are largely complete and its £122m investment exceeds the £85m valuation carried out by King Sturge in 2004–2005 (para 4.3).

12. An £18m completion package was agreed and specified although the original subaudible noise requirements will still not be met and at the time of writing this requirement, which proved so damaging and problematical for the original PFI contractor, had not been resolved.

The case study project

The project that is the subject of this case study is the development of a series of buildings providing $4500\,m^2$ of laboratories and ancillary uses on a site of 4 Ha. The facility opened in 1987 following the completion of a capital building project, funded by the Department of Health and Social Security (DHSS) (as it was then) at an approximate build cost of £25m but with a further £25m in equipment. With a highly serviced project of this nature, the equipment is classified under four heads. Group 1 equipment is supplied and fixed by the contractor as part of the building contract; Group 2 equipment is supplied by the employer and fixed by the contractor; Group 3 equipment is supplied and fixed by the employer and Group 4 equipment covers minor and loose equipment, such as tables and chairs, supplied and fixed by the employer. Although basic information regarding the scheme is in the public domain, the details of procurement and the problems experienced in the management of the project are not. For these reasons the scheme cannot be identified in this chapter.

The project was designed in the conventional way by a design team led by the architect, a practice well experienced in public sector work. The new facilities were required to replace existing partially dilapidated buildings on a cramped and unsuitable site. The project was overseen by a team of engineers from the DHSS and was managed by a private sector project management consultant acting as project coordinator. Responsibility for the completion of the project rested with a client board and the facility itself was managed by a director heading up a team of 12 department heads. A senior civil servant was seconded to advise the director in his dealings with government departments and the project team.

The project was procured by the traditional route of well-established procedures. These were published in CAPRICODE (HMSO 1987), a government publication designed to provide a system of procedures and approvals to ensure that projects were delivered to the required time, cost and performance targets. A summary of the stages of CAPRICODE up to the time a contract was awarded to build the scheme appears at the end of this chapter.

Comparison with PFI procedures

CAPRICODE provides a good example of the way in which the government sought to control capital projects before PFI. The project followed the established procedures, which in many ways appear very different from a PFI route. However, there are distinct similarities.

Each milestone of government approval resulted in further funds being committed to the project, but only up to the next stage of approval. These stages were Approval in Principle (1e) and Budget Cost Approval (2h). Unless these submissions were approved, the project would not proceed. Under PFI, government departments are still obliged to proceed through most of the stages leading up to Approval in Principle, although the emphasis is placed on VFM. Although under CAPRICODE all options were to be evaluated, these did not include the option of agreeing a contract with a private company or consortium as a complete solution to the public need.

PFI procedures still retain evaluation of options by cost/benefit analysis within the investment appraisal and Treasury approval is still necessary before a scheme proceeds. There are also similarities with financial commitments from government. Under the CAPRICODE procedures it was possible for the Treasury to refuse to commit funds to the scheme immediately prior to tender. The same problems were acknowledged with early PFI in the Paymaster General's response to the Bates Report (HM Treasury 23/6/97), where it was reported that the practice of the Treasury becoming involved too late in the process led to frustration and increased costs.

After CAPRICODE Stage 1e has been reached, there is a major change in procedure. Under conventional procedures the government department takes on the role of employer and arranges for the facility to be designed and specified by a project team. A project team is still necessary under PFI, but its role is to define the output specification rather than produce a design team brief.

In the case study project, the design team brief consisted essentially of four separate elements. These were the architect's sketch layout drawings at 1:50 scale, the client's operational policies, the client's equipment schedules and the sum of money allocated to the project by the Approval in Principle and Budget Cost. Although a PFI project will seek tenders on the basis of an output specification, there will still be operational and design constraints, which will require considerable input from the user body, its consultant team and those firms wishing to tender. Further work will be necessary by the preferred tenderer when final negotiations take place. In the opinion of an early PFI tenderer, 'the costs of bidding for a PFI project can be up to five times higher than for conventional public contracts' (John Laing quoted in Madden 1997). With a complex facility this comment is not surprising, as the contracting consortium will be bidding to agree a performance specification for a complete facility, rather than merely a construction contract.

A perusal of the contract for a PFI facility shows that the contractor is placed with obligations concerning the specification and operation of the building, which would normally form part of the briefing documents in a conventional public sector contract (Wright 1996). Under the terms of the contract, the contractor must supply an exhaustive list of drawings and specifications to the public sector user and, once approved, further approval is necessary for any changes. The case study project was managed in a more flexible manner, with the design team brief providing a framework for future design development and approvals from the user client.

Cost time and performance

Although a study of DHSS procured buildings at the time suggested that a management contract might be suitable, it was decided to follow precedent and adopt the fully designed, fully billed option of a lump sum contract under Joint Contracts Tribunal (JCT) 1980. This route requires a full design to be prepared by the team and the decision was made that the services engineer should be instructed to perform full duties. This consultant would be responsible therefore for designing the whole of the services installation sufficient for the services subcontractor to construct the services. For a building that was to be air-conditioned with differential air pressures and full of complex equipment, the challenge for this consultant was great. The services engineer was also appointed to produce coordinated drawings for the whole of the building at the time of the pre-tender estimate and these would provide evidence that all parts of the design worked and no conduits, for example, were designed to penetrate parts of the structure.

The case study project was complex in terms of design solutions to scientific requirements. Effluent discharges required a lengthy simulation study and the requirement for differential air pressures within the building increased the time required to complete the design. Problems were also experienced with design team coordination, which did not become finally apparent until coordinated drawings were produced by the services engineer. During the whole of this process, consultation continued with the client, particularly in terms of the equipment to be supplied and fixed by the contractor (Group 1 equipment). User awareness of technical developments in scientific equipment led to changes being requested, which in some cases had unfortunate consequences in terms of time and cost. As the design progressed, it was increasingly apparent that the refinement of the brief in terms of the equipment specification was problematic. Heads of Department needed considerable time to decide on the specification of new equipment and for major pieces of equipment, this led to design changes in the building envelope. These changes were not welcomed by the architect or project manager in view of the programme and cost implications.

Some equipment presented a real procurement challenge to the team. The user decided, for example, that a machine was needed to cool a large number of eggs (used to grow pathogen cultures) in a very short time. The power plant needed for what was in effect a giant refrigerator was unacceptably large and this necessitated further meetings, and associated delays, with the user client. There was also a requirement to construct a separate building, where dangerous category A pathogens could be exposed on an operative's bench. Category A includes very dangerous viruses such as the rabies virus. Sensibly, the design team recommended that this facility should be built by a specialist contractor and it was therefore made the subject of a prime cost sum in the Bill of Quantities and the contractor became nominated. This nomination did mean that the client was accepting an increased risk should the nominated subcontractor fail. The effluent from exhaust-protective cabinets also required design resolution as the effluent would, after filtering, be discharged to the atmosphere through flues on the roofs of the laboratories. A decision on the height of these flues only emerged after extensive simulation tests.

The design consultants in the case study were appointed under the normal terms and conditions, which meant that the client would not be expected to meet the cost of redesign unless this had resulted from a change of instruction. The process of design development inevitably resulted in the picture becoming blurred as the user client and the design team arrived at solutions to technical problems and changes to scientific procedures. This, together with the coordination problems referred to earlier, led to increased costs and a pre-tender cost estimate that is 12% over the budget cost. A simultaneous study by DHSS officers illuminated coordination and technical mistakes in the design, which necessitated a redesign of the project and a further submission to DHSS for additional funds. The requirement for additional funds did not sit well with established Treasury procedures for controlling government expenditure through Public Expenditure Sub Committee (PESC) forecasts, which voted money to projects on a yearly basis and this type of cost increase is that which now provides justification for the use of PFI in public procurement.

Solving the problems mentioned earlier had predictable consequences in terms of time and cost. Design team fees increased substantially and solutions to technical problems required additional funds for construction. The threat of cancellation by withdrawal of Treasury funds also pressurised the redesign programme, and in some areas, the user client was obliged to accept specifications that were less than ideal. A change of project architect, services engineer and client project manager, together with commitment to a redesign programme by all parties resulted in the project proceeding to tender. However, the redesign took a considerable amount of time as the new services engineer accepted no responsibility for the designs produced by the original firm. Also, as time had passed since some of the design had been specified, there were enhancements proposed, such as a building management system, which would reduce revenue cost when the building was operational. Updates to the design were also required as a result of a change in the building regulations or best practice. Galvanised wall ties were replaced by stainless steel wall ties, for example.

The user client who had to approve all the design changes proposed was understandably nervous in view of the problems experienced with the project and this tended to delay the programme while instructions were confirmed. Eventually, the project proceeded to tender. Tenders were received within the (new) approved budget cost and a construction contract awarded. Difficulties were experienced on site with unexpected ground conditions and the design of the air-conditioning system that resulted in claims by the contractor for additional time and cost. The project was eventually completed in 1987, although residual problems with the air conditioning required further work after completion.

Comparison with PFI project

It is always dangerous to compare two types of procurement when the subject cases involve complex facilities but the following conclusions can be drawn. The nature of the PFI route requires an exhaustive study of requirements to take place before contracts are agreed and the user is pressurised to consider all aspects of the facility in terms of its performance output. When the PFI project is agreed, there is little scope for the public sector to seek changes to the specification and this should result in additional cost being contained. With the case study project, design development continued until late in the briefing process, and this resulted in an unclear brief and extra cost.

In the PFI project the public sector was concerned that design risk should remain with the private sector contractor. A real transfer of risk will only take place if this process produces the required performance. If this is not the case, cost reductions will result not from greater efficiency but an inferior specification, and the risk can never be transferred absolutely in the case of contractor failure. The failed contractor in the PFI project was compensated to the amount of £75m but this did not save any equity investment in view of the large outstanding bank loans. In the case study project, design problems came to light some time before a start on site and before the pre-tender estimate. In both the cases, considerable sums were expended in solving or attempting to solve the design problems but with the PFI project the public sector client did not become involved with the solution of the problems to ensure that risk and design responsibility remained with the contractor. When the contractor failed, the risk immediately rebounded to the public sector client as the PFI contract contained compensation clauses if the contract was terminated. With the case study, there was considerable expenditure of design team fees and a new services consultant had to start the design from first principles, which resulted in further delay. In theory, the earlier a design mistake is discovered in a project, the lesser the cost will be. If the case study project had proceeded to contract and contractor mobilisation, the cost would have been greater than it was. The PFI project used a procurement route that placed all of the design risk on the contractor so long as there was no change of instruction, and this type of procurement attempts to provide the client with a detailed input by way of a performance specification with the added cost certainty of design and build. That the route chosen failed in this instance was in part due to the stringent requirements of the performance brief that proved impossible to satisfy completely.

In the case study project, the user client found that financial and time pressures resulted in some areas of specification being changed for non-operational reasons, although this, perhaps, would not have been necessary

Chapter 4

if the briefing process had been more thorough early in the project. With conventional projects, and the case study is a good example, the user is not motivated to think in detail about commissioning until late in the programme and this adds to the risk of increased costs and time. Conversely, there is a loss of flexibility in the project if the scheme is effectively frozen when contracts are agreed with a PFI contractor.

PFI contractors are used to taking on responsibility for design and construction risk and have a direct incentive to proceed quickly and smoothly. At the time of incurring expenditure on design development, the PFI contractor will have achieved preferred bidder status and there will be a strong incentive for all parties to complete the scheme. There may be some risk that design solutions may not provide the same performance that would have been achieved by a conventional route, but the risk of major cost overruns should be reduced. In essence, what is assumed to be achieved with a PFI scheme is project management by a private contractor rather than by civil servants. When the public sector has agreed upon the performance specification, the development of the design becomes the responsibility of the PFI contractor. Theoretically, the risk of cost increases over and above the budget should be reduced as cost control of building projects is a risk well understood by contractors. Government should be provided with increased cost and time certainty but as Gaffney and Pollock seek to show, other factors such as funding requirements tend to cloud the picture. With the PFI project the design problems associated with the stringent technical requirements of the laboratory modules were insurmountable and eventually the public sector relaxed the specification. This was too late, however, for the contractor to stay financially viable.

It should be remembered that a consultant project manager from the private sector managed the case study project, and this was a feature of most DHSS-funded projects at the time. Those commentators who write about PFI sometimes assume that civil servants commonly took on the project management role and this was and is not the case. The NAO states, 'Traditionally many departments have themselves been managers or providers of services and directly responsible for the construction of capital assets' (1999, p. 6). The problems associated with the case study project stemmed from an indistinct development of the brief with considerable delays from the original programme resulting from technical work involved with satisfying the user client. Yet, the NAO acknowledges that 'value for money will be compromised if the public sector's requirements take second place to providing an attractive opportunity for the private sector' (1999, p. 3). There is little doubt that with the case study, progress would have been quicker and budgets more robust if the user client had been restricted to performance criteria only. In this situation, however, the PFI contractor would have a direct incentive to provide the cheapest possible solution to meet the public sector requirement and this may have led to a design that fell below the optimum. The comparison between the case study project and the PFI project is summarised as follows.

Comparison between conventional (case study) project and PFI project.

Item	Conventional project	PFI project
Brief	Detailed brief extracted from user client by design team and equipment officer	Performance brief
Design	Full design by architect engineers and others	By contractor to above brief
Structure	All consultants and contractor contract with client board	Contractor SPV. Complex web of contracts and guarantees between closely associated companies
Client contract	As above	PFI contract with SPV
Payment	Monthly stage payments based on architect/quality surveyor (QS) certificates. Time-based design fee for early work and change of client instruction. Other fees on normal percentage	Unitary charge of £11.5m per annum linked to RPI for 25 years
Funding	DHSS/Treasury	Small percentage equity, primarily bank debt. Over 94% geared
Design complexity	Fairly complex structure bespoke requirements for equipment complex a/c brief	Demanding performance requirements
Management	Private sector project manager and assistant reporting to client director and board	Initially by contractor. Department used large project team and advisers as project ran into problems
Risk	Design team for design. Contractor for normal contracting risk. Client for all other risk	Contractor and guarantors for design, performance and funding; underlying risk with client including demand risk. Contractor compensated if contract terminated on default
Problems	Protracted equipment brief. Full engineering design faulty. A/c performance, ground conditions	Irresolvable engineering requirements
Solutions	Redesign with partly new team	Contract termination. Redesign with additional management. Design performance not fully resolved

Chapter 4

Conclusion

In terms of procurement, cost savings on PFI schemes over the conventional route have been reported. Peter Coates (2000, p. 18) reports that before PFI 'expensive cost and time overruns were the norm' and he quotes the example of the Kensington and Chelsea hospital project, which had an estimated cost of £134m and eventually cost £236m. 'Meeting the Investment Challenge' makes similar points. Conversely, Gaffney and Pollock (1999, p. 59) provide figures to show that the differences between outturn and original approved tender sums on NHS capital construction projects over £1m show average cost increases of between 8.8 and 6.2% in the period 1990–1997. In conclusions to the PFI laboratory case study described earlier, the NAO compared the cost of the procurement to the department with the value of the facilities produced. It is noticeable that in 'Meeting the Investment Challenge', the emphasis is on cost benefits of PFI in comparison with earlier pre-PFI public sector projects. If the concept of value is introduced, as it is in the NAO report on the failed National Physical Laboratory, a different picture may emerge.

The value of PFI projects as a percentage of Public Capital Spending (PCS) shows a distinctive upward trend. Yet, PFI in 2001 still accounted for less than 20% of PCS in 2001 (IPPR quoted in *The Economist* 30/6/01). The size of the overall PFI market is now in excess of £6000m and the projects are tending to become larger (PFI State of the Market 2006, p. 6). The average capital value of projects was £148.57m in 2006–2007 with the main sponsoring department being the Department of Health followed by the Ministry of Defence (ibid.). Supporters of PFI stress the efficiencies of private sector consortia and the advantages of risk transference, yet there is evidence that risk for PFI contractors is limited to those areas where it is most easily managed. Indeed, apologists for PFI see this as a logical step because risk should remain with the party best able to manage it. The case study provides the example of a publicly funded scheme before PFI and it may be inferred that some of the problems associated with its procurement may have been managed better had it been a PFI project. Fundamental questions remain, however. The case study project was managed, designed and built by private sector companies and this was not unusual before PFI. A PFI scheme would not allow the user client to influence the detailed design late in the project and therefore cost and time certainty should be improved. Whether or not the specification produced provides the optimum remains open to debate and there may be collateral benefits for the private sector with the release of development land. Refinancing as project risk declines may yield further benefits but if government seeks to claw these back, it runs the risk of making PFI less attractive to the private sector.

There is little doubt that an attractively structured PFI project is regarded as a sound investment for private sector funds. 'Annual 30 year PFI payments from the Government to the private sector prove a lucrative and secure return on investment. This is a form of hypothecated tax that the public sector can only dream of' (Pollock, Business *The Observer* 8/7/01, p. 5). The IOD confirms the popularity of PFI schemes to the private sector. In a survey, 70% of a sample of IOD members who had been involved with PFI deals considered that PFI 'provided the private sector with an investment opportunity with a reasonable return without unmanageable risk' (Leach 2000). A PFI scheme is usually highly geared with bank finance providing over 90% of the development funding for schemes of a value of up to £250m (Partnerships UK 2007). Although it may be considered a strange statement in the current climate, banks are risk averse and a well-managed PFI scheme provides an excellent low-risk investment. Returns are guaranteed by the State and the State is funded by many millions of taxpayers. With such a diverse source of funds the risk of State default is minimal and the investment becomes safer than all others with the bonus of growth guaranteed by linking returns to the RPI. If, during the construction phase, the contractor runs into insurmountable difficulties and the public sector terminates the contract, as in the case of the National Physical Laboratory, the PFI contractor is compensated and all this compensation will go some way towards repaying outstanding bank debt.

The government remains committed to PFI and it appears that predictability of public capital expenditure and the timing of delivery are seen as major incentives. There is an implication in government policy that whatever the circumstances, private sector management will always be preferable to a more active public sector role. Although there are strong economic and practical arguments against PFI, it appears likely that government will maintain its policy stance in the future.

CAPRICODE summary

1a

Review strategy and development plans

Formulate service development proposal

Obtain authorisation for option appraisal and appoint appraisal team

Prepare programme for option appraisal

1b

Define objectives for service development

Identify constraints

Investigate present activity

Research future demand for services

Assess potential for better use of resources

Decide on criteria for option selection

Prepare brief for option appraisal and state preliminary functional content

1c

Conduct local consultations

Identify all options

Identify/evaluate alternatives for support services

Evaluate options by cost/benefit

1d

Select the preferred option

Prepare option appraisal report

Confirm that report meets objectives more efficiently than other options

Finalise Approval in Principle submission

1e

Approval in Principle

2a

Appoint project team

Prepare scheme brief for design team including statement
    planning and operational policies

2b

Sign certificate of readiness to proceed to design

2c

Sketch design

2d

Prepare programme

2e

Estimate capital and revenue costs

Update development control plan

2f

Select procurement method and contract strategy

2g

Confirm that building solution offers the prospect of a cost-effective scheme
    providing efficient accommodation of identified service and functions

Finalise budget cost submission

2h

Budget cost approval

3a

Design brief –whole scheme

Confirm design brief

Design brief not to be changed after this point without clear justification and DHSS approval

3b

Certificate of readiness to proceed with design

3c

Design development

Consider contract method and programme

Confirm site access and contractor's areas

Assess commissioning requirements in building contract

Equipment schedules

3d

Detail design

3e

Tender documentation

3f

Pre-tender checks

3g

Certificate of readiness to proceed to tender

Confirm that resources will be available to build and operate scheme

Proceed to tender

4a

Select tenderers

4b

Tender period

4c, d, e

Evaluate tenders

Award contract

References

4Ps (2004) *A Map of the PFI Process*, 4Ps, London.

Akintoye A, Taylor C and Fitzgerald E (1998) Risk analysis and management of PFI. *Engineering Construction and Architectural Management*, 5, (1), 9–21.

Allen G (2001) *The Private Finance Initiative (PFI)*, Economic Policy and Statistics Section, House of Commons LibraryResearch Paper 01/117, London.

Allen G (2003) *The Private Finance Initiative*. House of Commons Research Paper 03/79.

Bing L, Akintoye A, Edwards PJ and Harcastle C (2004) *Risk Allocation Preferences in PPP/PFI Construction Projects in the UK*. COBRA Conference, Leeds 2004, RICS, London.

Blitz J (1996) Labour Plans Reform of PFI. *Financial Times* 16/9/96.

Broadbent J, Gill J and Laughlin R (2003) Evaluating the private finance initiative in the National Health Service in the UK. *Accounting, Auditing and Accountability Journal*, **16**, (3), 342–371.

CABE (2005) *Design Quality and the Private Finance Initiative*, CABE, London.

Coates P (2000) Don't shoot the messenger. *Public Finance*, August 25, 16–19.

Committee of Public Accounts (2007) *HM Treasury: Tendering and Benchmarking in PFI*, The Stationery Office, London.

Dixon T, Pottinger G and Jordan A (2005) Lessons from the private finance initiative in the UK. *Journal of Property Investment and Finance*, **23**, (5), 412–423.

Gaffney D and Pollock AM (1999) *Pump-Priming the PFI. Why Are Privately Financed Hospital Schemes Being Subsidised?* Public Policy and Management January–March 1999, 55–62.

Gallimore P, Williams W and Woodward D (1997) Perceptions of risk in the private finance initiative. *MCB Journal of Property Finance*, **8**, (2), 164–176.

Glackin M (2000) *MP Threatens to Shame PFI Profiteers, Barbour Expert Archive*, http://wwwbarbourexpert.com.

Heald D (2003) Value for money tests and accounting treatment in PFI schemes. *Accounting, Auditing and Accountability Journal*, **16**, (3), 342–371.

Hebson G, Grimshaw D and Marchington M (2003) PPPs and the changing public sector ethos. *Work Employment and Society*, **17**, (3), 481–501.

HM Treasury (1993) *Economic Appraisal in Central Government–A Technical Guide for Government Departments* (The Green Book), HM Treasury, London.

HM Treasury (1997) *Public Sector Comparators and Value for Money*, HM Treasury, London.

HM Treasury (2001) *Financial Statement and Budget Report 2001*, HG 279, 2000/01.

HM Treasury (2003a) *PFI: Meeting the Investment Challenge*, HMSO, London.

HM Treasury (2003b) *The Green Book: Appraisal and Evaluation in Central Government*, HMSO, London.

HM Treasury (2006) *PFI: Strengthening Long-term Partnerships*, HMSO, London.

HMSO (1987) *Capricode*, HMSO, London.

Institute for Public Policy Research (2001) *Building Better Partnerships*, Commission on Public Private Partnerships, Central Books, London.

Kemp P (1999) Stop fiddling the books. *New Statesman* 18/10/99.

Kerr D (1998) The private finance initiative and the changing governance of the built environment. *Urban Studies*, **35**, (12), 2277–2301.

Leach G (2000) *The Private Finance Initiative*, IOD Policy Paper, Institute of Directors, London.

Madden R (1997) *A Study of Private Sector Risk Perceptions within the Private Finance Initiative*, Unpublished Dissertation, Kingston University, London.

Milburn A (1999) *A Speech on PFI*, http://www.hmtreasury.gov.uk, 27/3/08.

National Audit Office (1999) *Examining the Value for Money of Deals Under the Private Finance Initiative*. HC 739, Session 1998–9, 13 August 1999.

Chapter 4

National Audit Office (2003) *PFI: Construction Performance*, The Stationery Office, London.

National Audit Office (2006a) *Central Government's Use of Consultants*, The Stationery Office, London.

National Audit Office (2006b) *The Termination of the PFI Contract for the National Physical Laboratory*, The Stationery Office, London.

National Audit Office (2007) *Improving the PFI Tendering Process*, The Stationery Office, London.

National Audit Office (2008) *Making Changes in Operational PFI Projects*, The Stationery Office, London.

National Statistics (2001) *Public Sector Finances October 2001. First Release, 20 November 2001.*

NHS Executive (2008) *Public Private Partnerships in the National Health Service: The Private Finance Initiative*, Treasury Taskforce, London, accessed on 17/6/08.

Partnerships UK (2007) *PFI: The State of the Market*, Partnerships UK, London.

Pollock A (2004) *NHS plc, the Privatization of Our Health Service*, Verso, London.

Robinson G (1999) Long neglect is at an end, *New Statesman* 18/10/99.

Stewart A and Butler E (1996) *Seize the Initiative*, Adam Smith Institute, London.

The Treasury (2006) *Value for Money Assessment Guidance*, HMSO, Licensing Division, Norwich.

Walker A (1996) *Project Management in Construction*, Blackwell Science, Oxford.

Wright D (1996) *The United Kingdom Experience*. Conference Paper, PFI in Practice, Kingston University, London.

Chapter 4

Chapter 5
Public–Private Partnerships in the Urban Development Experience of Dublin

Background

The process of linking public and private partners in urban development projects is a feature of recent urban development experience in Ireland. In the modern development period, since the 1960s, an evolution has occurred through three types of partnerships. The early attempts at urban regeneration saw individually negotiated joint venture schemes for key projects. This was succeeded by area-wide urban regeneration incentive schemes and by 2008 a prioritisation of public–private partnership (PPPP) arrangement in key sectors with arrangements similar to standard international models is in place.

The concept of public–private partnerships (PPPs) has a long historical background in Ireland. Arrangements bringing together the state's powers of compulsory land acquisition and private business were at the forefront of the development of key historic urban and regional infrastructure, including the canal and railway system. In addition, major city development including the existing central city pattern of Dublin was shaped by the Wide Streets Commission of the eighteenth century, which used public powers to acquire land to enable development incorporating private interests to proceed. In the modern era, the planning legislation introduced in 1964 to manage planning and development in Ireland intended local authorities to have a major role in engaging in the development process for the regeneration and development in city areas.

The housing programmes and slum clearance measures of the post-war period were by the 1960s leaving in their wake large areas of the inner city vacant and derelict. The continuing priority of the government in Ireland as across western Europe was housing, closely followed by infrastructure development, especially road building programmes. However, due to lack of resources, the local authorities took a more passive role in development than envisaged and largely concentrated on development control responsibilities. The extent of public confidence in public planning systems and the ability of statutory authorities involved in tackling city development problems decreased significantly in the late twentieth century. Their inability to implement development plans often coupled with the negative effects of previous developments undertaken, especially, in the housing area led to much criticism. This criticism was often directed strongly at the local authorities who had statutory responsibility for planning and development within their areas. The result of such criticism was that central government and interested parties internationally commenced looking at alternative forms and structures to deal with existing and emerging urban development problems, including the combining of public and private development interests.

Criticism of central government is often less strong although, often equally if not more, justified. In Ireland, the thrust of central government initiatives over many decades has been to reduce the financial resources and sources of funding for local authorities with Irish local government systems lacking independent taxation powers such as property taxes which, in Ireland, only relate to commercial property users since the removal of rates from the residential sector in the 1970s. Present local government structures are heavily dependent on central sources for most of their funding and frequently have been criticised as incapable of providing adequate local government comparable to other European urban governance models. This centralisation of power and resources reduces the impact of the local state authorities to deal effectively with development problems. The combined results were that in the face of the mounting urban problems of the 1980s, programme policies and initiatives had to be entirely reviewed. Often the existing agencies dealing with planning and urban development problems were found unsuitable and new specialist agencies combining public and private sector interests were required. The reasons for such major initiatives are found in the complex and difficult pattern of decline, which evolved especially in central urban areas in recent decades.

By the 1970s, the major problems identified were the movement of population to the suburbs, pollution and congestion making central areas unattractive for central city users and the damaging effect of the continued expansion of office space in central areas and infrastructural development on the urban fabric to cope with increases in motorised traffic. Additionally, the involvement of non-building and speculative interests in property development was acting to reduce the proper functioning of the development process as were planning systems, and the granting of building permissions which did not take due regard in ensuring the implementation of development.

Compulsory purchase legislation was used by local authorities to carry out such matters as road developments or improvements and the clearance of obsolete and slum areas. Lack of finance and legal complications were the obvious principal restraint over the use of such powers. The role of the public sector in providing development was radically different from private sector interests. Social and economic considerations were mixed in the public service analysis of developments. As the public sector financial constraints mounted in recent decades, and the capital available to local authorities in particular reduced, so also did the role of the state in the general development process. Consequently, the bulk of development activity in central Dublin since 1960 (excepting infrastructure developments carried out by the public sector) has been the result of the activities of the private sector. The dependency of this sector on profits, allied with the high rates of return and risk, has attracted a high level of public mistrust. High levels of profits, losses and risks quite obviously make decision-making in the development industry of necessity to concentrate on short-term trends rather than long-term development needs.

Competition between property developers, owners and the public sector involves the payment of high prices for suitable development sites. In an active market, potential purchasers compete for the limited suitable development land on the market. While developers will attempt at all stages to minimise costs and risks involved, land purchase decisions often involve upward price movement due to competing bids. Negotiating land purchase price, financing or equity sharing arrangements and onward sale arrangements dictate the level of return to the development company. Although often able to contract out some of the essential elements of the process, the final risk is borne by the development interest.

The combining of public and private partnerships in a variety of forms has shaped the development of modern Dublin and this chapter will deal with the evolution of such arrangements. First to be noted are early and largely unsuccessful attempts at joint ventures for major urban regeneration initiatives. These were succeeded by the modern urban renewal schemes, a largely market incentive-driven facilitation of private capital investment in urban regeneration, often involving partnership arrangements with public land holders and finally, the evolution of the modern PPP process.

The modern development of Dublin has experienced a variety of forms of PPP relationships with varying levels of failure and success. A transition in the engagement of private capital in urban development projects can be clearly identified. This involves a movement from area-based urban development programmes involving the use of taxation incentives to encourage investment and development to a more standardised PPP-type approach in line with similar related programmes in the United Kingdom and other jurisdictions. In reflecting on such initiatives, past and present, we can hope to learn what approaches will succeed for present and future initiatives. Evidence of development experiences in Dublin is supplemented by the results of interviews with policy making, planning and development interests on the operation and effectiveness of the various schemes.

Engaging in public–private partnerships: from urban regeneration to PPP

The recent major impetus for the PPP policy approach evolving in Ireland can be viewed as the requirement to achieve a major input to exchequer funding to invest in current major public sector investment programmes. This is particularly so in relation to transport infrastructure, which is seen as essential to future economic competitiveness and increasingly for social infrastructure needs. Ireland joined the euro monetary zone on 1/01/02 and under the criteria of the Stability and Growth Pact for participating member states, budget deficits were to be kept below 3% of GDP which imposed strict budget discipline. While these criteria were relaxed for member states, in recent years, the intention to keep public sector finances within this range remains a government priority.

Ireland is considered as coming relatively late to the international standard PPP approach to delivery of a wide range of infrastructure and service requirements. Equally, it is widely regarded as a major example of the innovative engagement of private capital and interests in major urban development and regeneration projects pre-dating such standard PPPs. Previous policies involved the extensive and successful use of taxation incentives to encourage investment and physical development in designated areas of inner cities and urban areas which are being terminated in relation to urban renewal by July 2008. PPP is now developing an important role in hard infrastructure such as road and rail projects, education, housing, health care and prison projects with the retention of a limited range of taxation incentives supporting investors in specific sectors. Planned PPPs include the proposed Dublin Metro North rail proposal with estimated cost ranging from €3bn–€6bn, Thornton Hall prison in north Dublin and a variety of social housing regeneration projects. Strong support from central government for moves towards PPPs is now clear, including the creation of the National Finance and Development Agency (NFDA), a central advisory and procurement agency for PPPs in Ireland.

In particular, the recent economic downturn makes the exchequer look where possible for the involvement of the private sector to fund the major spending requirements envisioned in recent national development plans (NDPs) in 2000 and 2007 with 80bn in capital spending planned in the period from 2007 until 2013 with 15bn of this spending planned to be provided through PPP initiatives.

Expectations of the role private capital and interests could play are shaped by the major property development boom recently experienced in Ireland. A period of sustained low interest rates followed the adoption of the euro as a single currency. Low interest rates applicable to the broader European economy have significant consequences in regions such as Ireland which had sustained rapid economic growth. Access to easy credit fuelled a long period of sustained upward movement in property prices and, as a result, general development activity boomed. Although this period has now ended, the expectations of such trends continue to contribute to a major expansion of positive interest in all forms of urban development involvement including PPPs.

Earlier less successful examples of PPP in Dublin include the development of the Dublin Corporation and Irish Life shopping centre and mixed-use development known as the ILAC centre in Henry Street, Dublin's main central retail area. In the 1960s and 1970s, Henry Street was identified as a key urban regeneration site in the city centre. With the involvement of the city council as land owner and Irish Life, the city's major life assurance company as financier, the project had ambitious aspirations in terms of its own success and its intended impact on the adjacent area. However, relationships between the various parties and the overall success of the project were significantly less successful than initially expected. With a guaranteed level of estimated rental value (ERV) to the developer and shares for other partners only above this threshold, the public agency did not get the return expected. In addition, the drafting of the agreement provisions did not deal with refurbishment issues satisfactorily. This resulted in a combination of rent and cost sharing arrangements, which gave the parties involved no incentive to refurbish, and management problems also occurred. At a more basic level, difficulties were also encountered in terms of final agreement as to what was built and, in many important respects, the partnership failed. Negotiations ensued over a period of time and the consortium eventually broke up with the parties agreeing to subdivide the development. The centre has recently been redeveloped successfully under new ownership arrangements. This experience meant that both the concept of PPPs and the urban regeneration plan-led agenda were set back to some extent by the problems evident in this experience.

A second public private-type partnership arrangement in the 1990s, which attracted significant negative attention was the agreement by the state transport company construction industry and expansion (CIE) to allow a telecommunications group rights to use its rail network as a basis for developing a telecommunications network. The company's own need at a later date to upgrade its signal network was significantly compromised by these arrangements and costs were greatly affected. This resulted in a Parliamentary enquiry or Oireachtas sub-committee report into why signalling originally costing €17.8m later rose by an extra €45.7m and resulted in 26 public sittings of 235 hours, including 102 other private meetings. Several conflicts of interest were found notably with consultants working for both principal parties to the arrangement simultaneously. The process was eventually curtailed due to complex legal issues, but the outcome negatively influenced attitudes on the issue of joint ventures involving state assets (Irish times, 2002).

Another much publicised early PPP-type project that attracted much criticism was the development of the Beaumont Hospital car park in Dublin. The contract agreed was found to be extremely generous in financial terms to the contractor, with very poor terms made in respect of the hospital interests. The public controversy surrounding this development centred on complaints that the direct provision of this facility by the public sector would have cost €9m–13m less than the cost of a public–private partnership arrangement aided by additional benefit of taxation incentives for the investors in the project (Department of Finance 2008).

Evolving public–private inputs in urban renewal in Dublin

From 1986 to 2008, fiscal incentives for private investors in urban regeneration formed a major component of urban development policies. The extent to which such initiatives influence the property market can be gauged from the numbers of completed and ongoing developments, which have benefited from the scheme. The evolving role of fiscal incentives for private investment in urban regeneration, their impact on investment and development and implications for the market of their termination are now examined.

The experience of the Dublin property market over the period 1986–2008 was greatly influenced by the evolving role of fiscal incentives in urban regeneration initiatives in central Dublin. With a rapidly changing economic development context, policies evolved from blanket subsidisation of development in designated areas towards a more selective approach. The rationale for policy shifts will be examined over various phases, 1986–1994, 1994–1998 and 1998–2008 and finally an examination of future prospects. Quantitative analysis of the costs and benefits of a selected number of property developments is developed and results can be compared with evaluations of similar schemes internationally. Particular attention is paid to the direct and indirect impact of such incentives on the feasibility of development projects, private investment trends and real estate values including rental and site values. It is also necessary to consider the effects of the termination of regeneration incentive programmes on urban regeneration activities and the general property market in 2008.

The ideal conditions for implementation of urban renewal strategies in any region would include a strong economy, adequate public resources and a determined commitment to solve urban dereliction problems while achieving social and economic benefits. In such circumstances, planned improvements to infrastructure, transportation and environment should coincide with renewal and new development that has the support of all social partners. The challenges facing many European cities of globalisation and economic restructuring resulting in urban blight, social exclusion or segregation and property market failures are evident. Many commentators identified the attraction of property-led development to public sector interests as being centred on the proactive nature of the approach (Williams 2006). These agencies often have few powers in terms of local economic development but they do have a range of powers relating to property development. These include planning, infrastructure and compulsory purchase powers together with the availability of public land assets. If used proactively, it is possible to influence local economic development, stimulate employment and boost activity at least in the short term. Problems however exist with increasing demand on urban management structures to produce a more sustainable urban environment on diminished public finances and are well recognised.

The origins of inner-city decline in cities including Dublin are variously attributed to economic restructuring, suburbanisation of land uses and inappropriate policy structures. Urban analysts identified weak planning and

Chapter 5

development policies as a common problem in European cities post World War II and as a significant factor in later urban and social problems. Economic social and electoral pressures promoted immediate solutions to housing and development problems often at newly developed suburban locations. Solution to housing shortages was achieved through the creation of large-scale state-subsidised housing schemes, often under resourced and without any corresponding supporting area development. Decline and dereliction in older central areas now vacated along with declining demand for commercial space due to economic restructuring, suburbanisation and inappropriate policies combined to create the classic inner-city decline. The necessity for intervention and initiatives to deal with such problems does not mean however that any consensus as to ideal approaches exists. Commentators have noted that much research on the effectiveness of regeneration policies in the United Kingdom and internationally tends to be critical with a persistent sentiment that urban policy has failed cities. The European model of sustainable cities with aspirations to building sustainable communities and cities has proved an attractive, if difficult, policy option (Department of the Environment and Local Government 2002; ODPM 2003). Subsidisation of development activity as has occurred in Dublin and internationally offers an area-based renewal approach particularly where a weak property market exists. In addition, if the public authority has land assets that it wishes to see develop in areas viewed negatively by the current market, the availability of incentives may act as a catalyst for development activity.

In Ireland, a long period of subsidised property development-led urban renewal commenced in 1985–1986. The core objectives of such schemes has been the promotion of investment by the private sector in construction and reconstruction of buildings in what became known as *designated areas* of towns and cities. The priming of the schemes through fiscal incentives has seen major successes in terms of physical developments created as the Irish economy grew. The trend towards a more entrepreneurial approach with the advent of special purpose renewal agencies has been interpreted as a diminution of the traditional planning authority's role (McGuirk and MacLaran 2001). Senior State Revenue officials, from the early stages of the scheme, outlined recognition of the political difficulties of addressing the reviews and termination of such measures. Mullen (1991) noted that the tendency was for such fiscal supports to become capitalised in land values in designated areas. Thus the officials found interventions acceptable up to a point in a weak property market. However, when a self-sustaining level of development was reached and the designated areas' property market recovered, the benefits would simply accrue to the owners of property and business without social benefit.

From a liberal economics perspective, such interventions are considered not justified in that they cause general taxation rates to remain higher than they should and this excess burden hampers general economic activity. As the results and the costs are not clearly demonstrated, the optimum subsidy is difficult to establish and market distortions can occur. From another political/economic perspective, the development gains accrued by individual investors and developers without defined community gains give cause for concern. It is also clear that requests for the continuation of such schemes, *albeit* on a more selective and conditional basis, will be a feature of the current debate even though termination has already been decided upon.

From its inception, the decision-making on selection of areas for incentives has been a major issue in that the areas selected differed from the areas for rejuvenation proposed under previously existing development plans. The localised nature of political decision-making processes and the ability of coalitions of vested interests to sway political selection procedures undoubtedly limit the overall effectiveness of such initiatives. While such concerns are well founded, it is evident that urban renewal initiatives are often responding to problem situations rather than developed in optimum conditions as previously described. As such, they often reflect a political response to an urban economic issue with the problem continuously changing over the duration of policy initiatives.

Urban regeneration policy in Ireland can be described as resulting from an ongoing experiential learning curve, which has moved from a simplistic approach based largely on stimulating any form of new development activity, to a broader, integrated, area-planning approach encompassing social and economic objectives. By examination of the changing policies and their impacts, it is possible to evaluate past initiatives and examine likely improvements and future directions. What is clear is that urban renewal and development policies have both contributed to and been reshaped by the major improvement in the region's economic and business confidence which commenced in the 1990s.

Understanding that the demand for urban development is a derived demand with complex relationships between construction activity, property demand and the general economy provides an essential background to assessing policy initiatives. Policies, which improve the functioning of these various activities, can form an important part of urban renewal strategies. Given the cyclical movement in such economic trends, it is evident that urban development and renewal strategies must be flexible and capable of adaptation to changing circumstances, while at the same time, maintaining confidence in the renewal and development processes.

Phase 1: 1986–1994

The 1980s economic context, within which the urban renewal policy for Dublin was developed, provides a statistical picture of a local and national economy in severe recession (NESC 1985; OECD 1987). National unemployment was over 18% with the construction industry sector figure estimated at 48% and gross fixed investment including building and construction development activity had declined by 20% from 1982 to 1986 (CSO 1986–2008). High levels of emigration and population decline and severe dereliction problems in older urban areas provided a strong pressure on national government to intervene directly to undertake urban economic development and revitalisation measures. The aims of such measures would be primarily to generate development and employment.

Chapter 5

Following recognition of the seriousness of the problems, political events in the 1980s ensured that the inner-city issue became a political priority. During negotiations on the formation of a new government in 1982, the intending governing majority was dependent on the support of an independent community candidate representing Dublin North Central. Highlighted during such negotiations were local development issues in economically deprived areas of central Dublin. Some progress in terms of attempted physical regeneration of system-built local authority estates had commenced in the 1980s with the Remedial Works Scheme. The limited success, if any, of such schemes pointed to the deeper social and economic issues causing such problems, which in turn led to the recognition of the broader long-term issues related to urban decline in Ireland. Subsequent initiatives, working parties and proposals consolidated policy maker's interest on the urban development and renewal area. The poor state of public finances limited the ability of public sector intervention to act, as illustrated in Figure 5.1.

Following an Urban Renewal Bill in 1982 (not enacted), the 1986 Urban Renewal Act was introduced and included the following aims:

1. designation of areas for special incentives with the aim of revitalisation of those parts of the city which, in the absence of such intervention, were likely to remain derelict or undeveloped;
2. the stimulation of investment in the CIE of employment.

While the original aims of the programme were extremely wide, envisaging integrated economic development programmes, job creation and other initiatives, the serious state of public finances in the late 1980s and early 1990s

	Grants	vs.	Tax allowances
Financial constraint	Immediate cost		Deferred cost
Recipients	Targeted at individuals and companies		Generally available
Cost	Quantifiable		Estimates based on take up rate and taxation rate % (foregone)
Future benefit	Builds up future revenue base and increases economic activity in short term		Same
Tax equity consideration	Can be allocated to specific groups		Higher tax payers avail of tax expenditures

Figure 5.1 Exchequer options and comparisons.

militated against this broadly based approach. Instead, tax-related incentives for development and occupation of property dominated the early policy approach as represented in Figure 5.1. The original package of incentives was adapted to suit different areas and included the following:

1. taxation allowances in respect of expenditures of a capital nature for the construction or reconstruction of commercial buildings to be set off against income or corporation tax;
2. a double rent allowance, which occupiers could set off against trading income for a period of 10 years for new leases on commercial buildings;
3. remission of rates for a 10-year period;
4. income tax relief for owner occupiers of residential units newly built or refurbished;
5. taxation relief for investors in rented residential property within specified size limits;
6. a reduced corporation tax rate of 10% applied to licensed companies involved in international financial services located in the International Financial Services Centre (IFSC) (Williams 1997).

The adoption of an area-based approach placed the emphasis on physical renewal in the original schemes. Alternative approaches involving a more integrated approach were considered, but not pursued, due to limitations on resources and public finances and the administrative complexities that they might involve. The initial designated areas within Dublin comprised 101.1 ha with an additional 10.9 ha at Custom House Docks. Special schemes were operated for the Temple Bar area –18.2 ha and the extended Custom House Docks/IFSC site now expanded to 20.2 ha. The addition of extended designated areas in 1990 brought the total amount of general designated area land to 302.4 ha. Other related programmes included the introduction of enterprise areas with incentives specifically for industrial/commercial development at locations close to the docks in 1994 and the introduction of designated streets, where particular incentives were made available for the refurbishment of underused upper floors of commercial buildings (MacLaran and Williams 1995).

Direct sales of city council-/corporation-owned land with development agreements in place were a feature of early urban renewal initiatives in Dublin. Here land sales occurred often at less than open market value in a weak land market with the local authority primarily interested in achieving project delivery rather than optimum prices. In such conditions, developers were brought in to the city centre to consider the viability of such locations. This was a simpler process dealing primarily with smaller infill sites with conceptual drawings of mixed-use development indicated often including a standard mix of ground floor retail and upper floor apartments. Title was withheld by the city council until required developments were substantially completed and then freehold was transferred. In comparison to later PPP processes, this means of engagement with private interests to achieve development was extremely flexible and direct.

The Custom House Docks was the major flagship scheme of urban renewal in Dublin in the 1980s. A previously derelict docklands site was the object

Chapter 5

of a major integrated development comprising business, residential and recreational functions. The creation of a new IFSC was added to this objective and a single-purpose development agency established, with effective planning functions for the area under its administration. The financial services sector in Dublin was dominated by the flagship IFSC, located in the Dublin docklands area.

The IFSC was established in 1987 as policy makers recognised the growth potential of the international financial services sector and added this major development to the existing proposals for the development of the Custom House Docks Development area in central Dublin. The Finance Act of 1986 had introduced financial incentives encouraging urban renewal investment by the private sector in designated areas of Dublin and other urban centres. A generous package of incentives included capital allowances for investment in the construction of the new centre, double the standard rent allowances which occupiers could use to reduce their tax liabilities, and remissions from city property taxes or rates were made available. In addition to the general taxation incentives for urban renewal, the Finance Act 1987 established a 10% corporation tax for certified companies trading in international financial services locating in the IFSC. This special rate of corporation tax was amended from 2006 when the special IFSC rate was replaced by the national 12.5% rate which is still low by international standards.

Construction commenced in 1988 and the first buildings were occupied in 1990. The first phase of development at the IFSC by 1992 involved the completion of the IFSC and ancillary office space totalling 40 000 m² then costing of £120m (€152m). The state has a role as a participant in the development process and resulting profits. Under the confidential master agreement, the development is funded by the developers who are guaranteed a specified minimum economic return. Surplus final development profits are then shared between the developer and the state on a reported 60/40 basis in favour of the state, with the developers also paying a lump-sum premium to the state (Williams 2006).

After a period of little new development, a second, more rapid and sustained phase of development took place at the IFSC after 1994 and by 2000 over 8000 persons were directly employed in over 485 international financial companies and a further 8500 employed in related firms, with mutual funds under management valued at €387bn. By 2003, the IFSC had consolidated its position, with over 370 international financial companies operating in the centre, see Table 5.1. Funds under management at the IFSC expanded to over €435bn in 2003. Estimates of numbers directly employed in the centre range from 10 000 to 12 000 with the official IFSC estimate of 10 700 in 2007 with a growth of 1000 expected in the coming year. In addition, the importance of the IFSC in economic terms is illustrated by its contribution to central government revenues with an estimated €700m in corporation tax paid in 2002 (IFSC 2007).

In May 1997, the Custom House Docks Development Authority was dissolved and the Dublin Docklands Development Authority was established. This authority took responsibility for the original 11 400 m² of

Table 5.1 Analysis of company activities at IFSC

Origin	Banking	Insurance	Fund management	Securities trading, investment management and others	Total
Germany	9	3	2	5	19
USA	5	3	2	4	14
Italy	6	1	1	3	11
Ireland	5	–	–	2	7
Netherlands	3	3	–	1	7
France	3	1	1	1	6
UK	1	3	1	–	5
Other European countries	6	–	2	1	9
Rest of the world	4	3	1	2	10
Total	**42**	**17**	**10**	**19**	**88**

Source (Williams 2008).

office accommodation, 333 apartments, hotel and other facilities comprising IFSC Phase 1 and facilitated the further development of the IFSC Phase 2. For this phase an additional 4.8 ha of land was redeveloped. This has created an overall area of 15.8 ha with the financial services office development complemented by two hotels, retail, residential and educational facilities.

The IFSC in Dublin can be regarded as an exercise in integrated urban renewal and economic development. The development of this sector is regarded as a flagship project in the general urban renewal in the Dublin Region. With a total of over 10 700 persons directly employed in this economic cluster and similar numbers in support services, its importance to the city in terms of both the levels of employment generated and increased tax revenues is critical. The Dublin IFSC experience is of particular interest as it represents an induced development process, which is now maturing and shows signs of having attained a strong critical mass needed to sustain the long-term future of the sector/cluster. The future development of the IFSC remains a primary component of the Integrated Master Plan of the redevelopment of the Dublin Docklands.

Figures 5.2a and 5.2b show two photographs of the International Financial Services Centre in Dublin.

The 1990s witnessed the renewal of Temple Bar as the second historic area development of the city as a newly rejuvenated cultural, artistic and entertainment quarter. In addition to IR£40m funding under the cultural development programme, enhanced incentives existed in this area for refurbishment and considerable amounts of public finances were committed to developments under the Urban Pilot Programme. This area also possessed a single purpose development agency, Temple Bar Renewal Ltd that controlled spending of public funds and had the responsibility of maintaining

Chapter 5

(a)

(b)

Figure 5.2   The International Financial Services Centre in Dublin.

a functional mix and promotion of desired activities in accordance with the prepared plan for the area. For the general designated areas, the local planning authority retained planning control over all renewal schemes and often provided land for development purposes. In these areas, development by normally private interests was required to comply with controls as established in the existing development plan. Reliance on private investment capital was augmented in a limited manner by small-scale urban improvement grants to local authorities.

Results of the schemes

In order to assess any policy intervention, it is useful to consider the original stated policy parameters:

1. to designate areas in need of development without damaging surrounding areas;
2. identify land uses to be promoted in such areas;
3. quantify amounts of development, which could take place;
4. identify appropriate incentives;
5. minimise cost to national exchequer (adapted from DOE 1986).

With the wide range of schemes operating, isolating individual effects is complicated; however, trends can be identified. From 1986 to 1992, development in Dublin's designated areas was slower to gain momentum than in other urban centres in Ireland due to the relatively large sized commercial developments that dominated this phase of activity. New office development, provided mainly on a speculative basis, comprised 70% of the total 136 846 m² space developed in designated areas (Williams 1997). Incentives to occupiers and investor's subsidised rental and investment returns ensured a profitability of developments in secondary areas previously regarded as uneconomic. A major surge in development activity resulted in the displacement of existing demand to incentive-aided locations. Overdevelopment in the office sector resulted by 1991 with a vacancy rate of 45% of new office buildings in the designated areas, followed by a major slowdown in the entire sector. This was followed by a virtual cessation of development activity caused by this miscalculation of real demand and the urban renewal scheme was subsequently modified to exclude speculative office development from the schemes for general designated areas.

Within general designated areas, levels of development activity remained high throughout the period. The switch from office development to mixed use and residential developments since 1992 resulted in substantial areas of the city being rebuilt with new developments, attracted by strong profit levels and low risk. The apartment market remained particularly strong throughout this period with some evidence of oversupply in retail and leisure developments at secondary locations. Strong tourism growth ensured rapid expansion of development in the hotel and ancillary services sector. It is perhaps appropriate, however, to single out the residential sector for particular attention. At all stages of the urban renewal process, a significant emphasis has been placed on the need to revive and sustain the concept of a living city. If one sector was to be described as the litmus test for the success of Dublin's urban renewal policy, it is the residential sector that should be so selected.

Returning residential population to central Dublin

This period saw a major reversal of the continued drift residential development trends and population and from the inner city, which had been continuing in central Dublin since 1961. Positive views as to the success or failure of the designated areas programme are often partly based on its role in reversing this trend. In the early stages of the scheme, its inherent commercial bias ensured that progress was not achieved in this area. Within the designated area wards of central Dublin, a continuing loss of population occurred throughout the 1980s. A change in the emphasis of the scheme towards favouring residential development occurred in the 1990s. This change was both market and policy driven; a downturn in the office market occasioned partly by oversupply of offices in designated areas was accompanied by a focus on residential development incentives on designated areas. This coincided with a major increase in residential demand in the Dublin area. Within 4 years, over 5000 residential units had been completed and over 3000 units were in construction or at planning stage. These trends are clearly reflected in an analysis of census population figures for the 36 Central Dublin Wards affected by designation policies which shows a population increase of 80 630 or 23.7% over the period 1991–1996 when urban renewal programmes were introduced. This trend has continued with high levels of residential development activity through to 2007/2008 (CSO Data, 1991–2006).

In particular, large increases were evident in wards such as North City and the general quay areas where substantial development has occurred. This compares with the period 1986–1991 in which even with the initiation of urban renewal schemes, declines had occurred. Analysis of the residential development in the 1990s situated in urban renewal areas reveals a significantly different profile of occupier for such housing to the traditional residential market as previously experienced in Dublin. Most developments comprise medium- or small-sized apartments for a young population of mainly professional income individuals or groups. A major promotional campaign was undertaken by the city authority to promote living in the city. The demand for small apartment units to cater for young mobile professionals attracted to the city by strong economic growth was welcome, although concerns have been expressed as to the potentially transient nature of such a population. Refinements to the guidelines for such schemes were followed with the aim of improving the standard of development and widening the mix of apartment types being built.

Phase 2: 1994–1998

Changing economic context

The altered economic circumstances of the late 1990s provide a significant statistical contrast to those observed at the initiation of the urban renewal scheme in 1986. From 1994 to 1999 real growth in gross national product (GNP) averaged 7.5%. Building and construction output rose rapidly and unemployment fell to below 6%, the lowest level seen since the 1960s with labour shortages in evidence (ESRI reports 1994–1998). Emigration had ceased to be a problem and immigration into Ireland, particularly in the Dublin region, was growing. Public finances were returned to a surplus situation and inflation and interest rates were low. Ireland's entry to the Economic and Monetary Union (EMU) necessitated a stability in public finances to comply with the Maastricht Treaty criteria. The reduction in interest rates to EMU levels and the prospective stability of low long-term rates had a significant impact on construction and property markets. Lower interest rates stimulated economic growth and investment with significant rise in demand for property. With a common currency in the EMU area, uncertainty was reduced on investment decisions and the exchange rate risks were reduced. Identification of the impact of various factors causing growth in construction output other than the obvious link to economic growth is difficult. Nevertheless, the growth in construction output exceeded the general growth rate. Over the period 1994 to 1998, the volume of construction output rose by 81% (DOE 1998).

By 1994, urban renewal aided by a resurgent economy was proceeding successfully and the need for reform was evident. At this stage, residential development incentives, which had been more widely available, were restricted to designated areas only and measures to attract greater use to vacant or underutilised portions of buildings were introduced. A major official study of the urban regeneration schemes nationally was carried out in 1996 (DOE 1996). At this stage over IR£1.7bn of development schemes had been generated with approximately IR£1bn of this development occurring in Dublin. This study and other independent research highlighted the success of the schemes in physical redevelopment of derelict areas along with the identification of problem areas in policy implementation. The stimulation of property-based urban renewal in areas that would otherwise have remained undeveloped did occur. The absence of sufficient improvement in terms of employment, public amenities education and training was noted along with the following specific issues:

1. deadweight/levels of projects, which would have proceeded anyway;
2. displacement and relocations of commercial users;
3. shadow effect of new developments on old;
4. conservation and refurbishment proved problematic as structure of scheme favoured new development;
5. the favouring of single-use commercial developments over mixed-use development.

In addition, the general pattern of development was sometimes viewed as piecemeal with the absence of urban design/planning criteria leading to poor-quality architecture and urban design. The longer-term sustainability and coordination of development were regarded as having been more appropriately dealt with in the selected areas of Custom House Docks (CHD) and Temple Bar than general designated areas and this model was preferred for future developments (DOE 1996). The official estimate of exchequer cost in tax allowances was IR£367–461m assuming a dead weight of 25–50% and balancing such losses against additional tax revenues generated. This set of estimates would appear to underestimate the direct cost of the scheme due to the following factors:

1. the exclusion of infrastructure and administrative costs directly funded by public sources;
2. the treatment of valuation of public land assets;
3. exclusion of the cost to local authorities of rates remissions.

In turn, it is also likely that the indirect benefits of the scheme in terms of overall taxation returns generated may be underestimated in that employment patterns were not clearly established in 1996 and numbers estimated working in the IFSC and so on were likely to be lower than later realised. Separating such employment gains attributable to urban regeneration from general economic growth, which accelerated throughout the 1990s, is extremely unreliable. The Positive Aspects of Growth for Dublin included the high levels of economic confidence engendered by employment increases with significant inward investment and a major growth in tourism. These development successes are balanced by the negative aspects of growth patterns and urban management issues arising such as the emergence of housing affordability problems and major transportation and infrastructure deficiencies. At this stage, serious questioning arose as to whether the incentives were in fact inflating an already overheating housing market. A variety of related tax incentives for investors in private rented property were amended to deflect investors and favour first-time buyers. The government's concern over lobbying was that this was producing a housing supply downturn that led to a reversal of these measures.

Phase 3: 1998–2007/2008

The demand for development activity in Ireland in this period was driven by several main factors including strong growth in the general economy, high levels of inward investment, particularly in the information technology (IT) sector, expansion of the services sector and growth in tourism. Over the period 1990–2004, Ireland's economic profile changed from one of the weaker economics of North West Europe to one of the strongest in terms of economic and employment growth. Irish GNP growing by 8% per annum by 2001 resulted in unemployment reducing from 12% in 1996 to a low of 4% in 2000. From 2000 to 2004 continued economic and employment growth resulted in unemployment remaining below 5% in 2004 (ESRI Quarterly Economic Commentaries 2000–2004). Recent economic growth in GDP terms continued at 5% in 2005 with sustained employment growth and unemployment remaining low, estimated at 4.3% in mid-2006 (CSO 2005, 2006).

Approximately 49% of all employment growth in Ireland in the 1990s occurred in the Dublin region and similarly 47.5% of all immigration into the state comes to this region (Williams and Shiels 2000). The most recent regional population projection (CSO 2005) indicates that the population of the Greater Dublin area (GDA) is due to increase by a further 500 000 in the period 2006–2021. This projection will be heavily driven by inward migration of an estimated 232 000 into the Dublin region according to CSO estimates.

The pace and form of change in the urban economy of Dublin had yet to be fully appreciated in terms of their impact on urban development trends. This failure to provide for the region's expanding infrastructure requirements may place constraints on the future economic potential of the region. The continued consolidation of the urban core was being complemented by the rapidly expanding edge city growth. Despite the absorption of the concepts of sustainable development, the current housing crisis demonstrates tensions between such policy goals and the means of implementing changes required for their achievement. Record growth in house completions has failed to match demand for housing, particularly in the Dublin area, and resulted in an expanded commuter belt up to 100 km around the Dublin area. The emphasis of policy evolved towards measures that would stabilise house prices and demand and medium-density apartment development has become the norm. The speed at which infrastructure development proceeds is slow despite the opening of new city trams and is significantly behind requirements in the central city and metropolitan area. Policy deliberations followed by planning delays are the principal causes cited for such delays. The resulting urban policy shifts reflect a diminishing emphasis on urban regeneration as a political priority issue. In turn, the level of infrastructure investment required has undoubtedly pushed the government towards PPP as a means of addressing in an urgent manner the transport issues arising in particular.

The publication of a major strategic report on Strategic Planning Guidelines for the Dublin Region occurred in 1999. The introduction of an NDP for the period 2000–2006 at a cost of IR£38bn underwritten and committed towards the necessary catch up infrastructure development required included an emphasis on public transport development in Dublin. This also included a shift towards the incorporation of PPPs in the delivery of infrastructure. With relation to the construction industry, stated policy priorities now include mechanisms to stabilise demand rather than boosting such demand and to determine how the construction industry can optimise its contribution to a sustainable development strategy.

These policy shifts have had major implications for the thrust of urban renewal policies. The necessity to boost demand and development is obviously no longer a priority. Issues that now dominate are the management of ongoing development in a sustainable manner. Alternative priorities now become critical to sustain improvements achieved through economic growth, urban renewal programmes and other policy initiatives. These include the development of proper and effective urban governance and management structures, the development of integrated planning with effective implementation methods and optimising the benefits of recent and continuing development activity.

This policy shift was represented in the altered approach to urban renewal outlined in the programme Urban Renewal 2000 – New Approaches. The introduction of a major new approach to urban renewal in Dublin commenced with the 1998 Urban Renewal Guidelines. The intention to create a more coherent and holistic approach was represented in the introduction of a structured programme based on Integrated Area Plans (IAP) prepared

Chapter 5

for selected areas. These reports are prepared by local authorities for areas based on criteria established by an expert advisory panel to the Minister of the Environment. These plans are intended to be detailed area-focused plans identifying the strengths and weaknesses of the districts involved, target those districts with the greatest need or potential for rejuvenation and select sub-areas or key projects for special incentives. The creation and implementation of such plans were intended to include consultation with representative groups in the area concerned. Fiscal incentives from this point on were part of the overall renewal strategy and were intended to be available only where proven barriers to development exist. Such incentives would apply only to key sites or catalyst projects as defined in the guidelines. The criteria by which areas were selected for IAPs are that such areas contained significant amounts of urban decay or obsolescence. Other indicators include vacant sites/buildings, underutilised infrastructure and a general lack of investment over a prolonged period. It was intended that priority be given to areas, which experience a high level of social disadvantage indicated by the prevalence of relatively high unemployment or low income and education levels.

Contents of IAPs include broad issues such as urban design, sustainable land uses, education training and local economic development, environmental improvement and traffic management. A major feature of the IAP scheme is the requirement for a specific monitoring and implementation strategy for each plan. Progress is required to be monitored on a periodic basis by local authorities and authorised companies. Public monitoring committees with cross-sectional community membership are required to examine physical, economic and social benefits in an annual report. Following a selection procedure a total of 49 IAPs were given ministerial approval in 1999 including a number in the Dublin area. The largest area proposed for urban renewal includes the Docklands area of Dublin for which a master plan was prepared and published following public consultation and a new development authority established. Clarification on the availability of incentive packages has caused delays in the implementation of these plans. European Union (EU) opposition to double rent allowances and rates relief, which were regarded as operational state aids distorting competition, have resulted in alterations to the intended package (Williams 2006). The new package, which commenced in its present form on 1/07/99, and expired in July 2008, consists of the following incentives for private investors:

Commercial/Industrial development

- taxation allowance on eligible construction costs of project of 50% in year 1 and 4% per annum to total 100%;

Residential development – owner occupiers

- new building – taxation allowance of 50% of eligible construction costs allowed at 5% per annum over 10 years;
- refurbishment – taxation allowance of 100% of eligible construction costs allowed at 10% per annum over 10 years;
- residential development – investors;

- taxation allowance of 100% of eligible construction or refurbishment cost may be set off against Irish rental income.

In general, it is intended that these incentives will complement local, national, EU and other funding proposals for each area. The transparency of the new scheme is assisted by Freedom of Information procedures. Relevant extracts of the minutes of advisory panels involved in all decisions are intended to be available on the Internet and give details on individual plan decisions and their reasons. Refusals of IAPs have been explained, deletions or inclusions of individual sites discussed and the need for granting of various incentives debated for individual projects. For the Dublin area a major feature of the discussion of the various IAPs was the interrelationship of the IAPs throughout the city centre.

Phase 4: 2008 onwards

Economic prospects for this period were initially expected to be positive with continued growth, albeit at a lower and perhaps more sustainable level than the late 1990s (ESRI 2005). Consumer confidence and improved retail spending provided an optimistic short-term outlook (CSO 2005). With the continuation of growth to 2007 the policy review of area-based renewal incentives recommended the termination of the use of fiscal incentives for urban regeneration (Department of Finance 2006). Announcing the commencement orders on 26/06/06 giving legal effect to the phasing out of tax incentives as announced in the Budget Statement of 2006 the Minister cited improved economic conditions and public finances as major factors in the decision. However by 2008, these forecasts were being moved downwards with property markets fragmenting and prices falling, expected growth levels cut and credit problems mounting within the financial sector. Prospects for future development by this period carried a substantial additional risk element compared with any time in the past decade.

Future policy trends relating to urban development, the National Spatial Strategy (NSS), in 2002 provided the spatial framework to guide future investment priorities by policy interests and to encourage sustainable development. The Spatial Strategy can be linked with the NDP, which deals with the planned provision of infrastructure, in providing guidance for government policies, regional and local plans at the national spatial and strategic level. The role of major urban areas, particularly Dublin, in promoting economic development is recognised in the NSS in line with international policy experience identifying the significant role of agglomeration and clustering in economic activity.

In particular, the NSS ruled out completely new towns or cities as not being required for the expanding population and expressed the preference that population increases be accommodated at or within existing settlements. This involves a focus on the reuse of vacant or underutilised existing urban spaces rather than Greenfield development. In essence, urban regeneration and suburban renewal should be more actively pursued. The strategy envisages the consolidation of the existing Dublin metropolitan area for a more efficient

Chapter 5

and competitive regional future. Some essential improvements identified in the NSS for Dublin include improved land access to the airport and broadband capacity throughout the region. A central feature of general urban development policy debates has been the sustainability of dispersed housing settlement patterns, particularly in the Dublin area. The review of Regional Planning Guidelines for the Dublin region highlights the importance of quality of life and accessibility issues.

Issues emerging from urban development policy experiences

The difficulty in maintaining the selectivity- or restrictive criteria originally intended for use in property market-based interventions is clear. Incentive-based programmers were introduced in 1986 to deal with problem areas of Ireland's five largest urban areas and the schemes were subsequently extended in 1999 to include areas in another 38 of Ireland's towns and villages. A further 100 towns were included in 2001 for related packages of measures under the Town Renewal Scheme. The inclusion of 13 000 linear metres of streets nationally for Living Over The Shop allowances completes the extensive use of the package to areas and schemes not originally included. While many of these centres have experienced renewal, it seems that the pressure for replication and duplication of the scheme is a continual process unless structures for termination of the scheme are in place. Expectations that PPP-based urban development schemes would continue the progress achieved in urban renewal were viable so long as property markets remained strong but are a major doubt with the weakened states of the markets at present. In addition, the selectivity and prioritisation of key achievable projects may be compromised by overextending and expanding the PPP process.

Development interests argue that weak inner-city locations will continue to need some form of incentives for investors to reduce the risks of developing at such locations compared to other parts of the city located in a generally strong market. Community development interest's principal concerns revolve around their perception of the absence of meaningful consultation and planning gain in urban renewal projects including those involving PPP-type approaches.

Major urban regeneration programmes with a property component are likely to continue with the project at Ballymun (an EU-assisted urban renewal scheme replacing a high rise social housing project of the 1960s) underway. Smaller initiatives such as at Ballyfermot, an inner suburban housing district chosen from the 10 most disadvantaged urban areas in Ireland, are the subject of an environmental regeneration programme supported by EU and national funding in an €11m project and are an example of likely future trends. Many recent projects aiming at social regeneration of deprived areas are now dependent on PPP schemes to replace or refurbish obsolete social housing estates. These projects are critically dependent on favourable market conditions providing revenue streams from proposed developments funding regeneration costs.

A major issue for urban development markets in the coming years is the expiry of urban renewal and area-/property-based taxation schemes given legal effect in 2006 with a phased termination for expenditures until July 2008. While beneficiaries of capital allowances will continue drawing down reliefs over the following 14 years to 2022, no new projects can avail of such allowances after July 2008. This creates a situation in which those areas where weak property demand exists will have no available subsidy effect for the first time in over 20 years.

A major rationale for the exchequer to move towards the reduction or termination of fiscal incentive regeneration schemes includes both cost and concern at the extent of tax sheltering permitted. Extensive use of such tax shelters resulting in some top income earners having no legal taxation liabilities at all has caused public and political disquiet. Pressures for change appear likely to consolidate a switch from general area-based supports towards targeted and sector-based supports perhaps with linkages to broader-based urban regeneration initiatives. These could include fiscal incentives for specific programmes dealing with social and affordable housing for renting with investor agreements. By 2008, economic conditions were deteriorating with property markets in particular experiencing a major downturn. Sliding property prices provided a pessimistic background with, in particular, the development prospects for the housing sector becoming very difficult.

Analysis of individual property development incentives

The debate as to the specific impacts of incentive programmes requires some quantitative analysis of the costs and taxation foregone through the operation of the scheme. While data exist as to the direct costs associated with the scheme, there is no systematic tracking of the precise impact of the various incentive schemes. Estimates have been made in response to parliamentary questions qualified by the difficulties associated with such assessments. These include the fact that while costs of qualifying developments are known, the rate at which allowances are drawn down depends upon the individual or company's year-by-year tax position over periods of more than 10 years. This means that developments completed in the first stages of the scheme from 1986 to 1994 would still potentially be the subject of drawing down of allowances in 2007/2008. For this reason, it is necessary for research purposes to examine retrospectively the impact of the schemes. The method devised for this purpose as part of ongoing research was to make a detailed analysis of the first 100 developments completed between 1986 and 1992 in Dublin and to determine in the case of individual development types the maximum direct cost of tax allowances relative to the cost of each development. For this purpose, it is necessary to compile detailed data on construction costs, rentals, investment yields and interest rates over the period to present. This allows valuation appraisal-type assessments to be carried out incorporating discounted cash flow techniques to arrive at net present value (NPV)-type appraisals concerning the value of incentives.

Table 5.2 Comparative potential tax and rates savings

Total tax and rates savings as % of total development costs	
Refurbishment of existing commercial building	17.6%
New office development	87.9%
Custom House Docks (CHD) new office development	99.4%
Section 27 investments residential	25.8%
New owner-occupier residential in Temple Bar	15.93%
Refurbished owner-occupier residential in Temple Bar	32%
New owner-occupier residential in designated areas	12.8%
Refurbished owner-occupier residential in designated areas	10.7%

Table 5.3 Comparative present values of total potential tax and rates savings (Based on new residential in designated areas = 100%)

New owner-occupier residential in designated areas	100%
Refurbishment of existing commercial building	137%
New office development	686%
CHD	777%
New section 27 investment residential	202%
New owner-occupier residential in Temple Bar	125%
Refurbished in Temple Bar	250%
Refurbished owner-occupier in designated areas	83%

(Williams 2006).

Initial results as illustrated in Figures 5.2 and 5.3 showed ratios in terms of private development funding attracting the residential scheme as the most effective with leverage ratios of 6:1 while some commercial developments showed significantly lower leverage ratios at less than 1:1. Initial conclusions based on such analysis are that only continued selective use of smaller designated areas with controlled use of incentives, perhaps biased towards residential and refurbishment activities, is justified. The question of reallocation of benefits has become a major issue for affected communities with the perception that wider community benefits are being ignored.

The qualified success of urban renewal initiatives in Dublin demonstrates that such programmes can make an effective contribution to urban and regional development. The movement towards a more complex urban renewal programme with broader policy aims is appropriate, although achieving its objectives will present obvious difficulties. In the Irish policy context, such interventions were largely based on tax breaks that have become a feature of the urban development process. Moves towards comprehensive and integrated area-based approaches incorporating PPP-type arrangements will continue to place demands on public finances for the foreseeable future. In this context, examination of international models of current and alternative fiscal policies to guide land uses and optimise community benefits may be required. Examples of such models include Economic Impact Fees, Business Improvement Districts and Tax Increment Financing.

The rapid economic growth of the Irish economy in recent years has seen a major expansion of development activity in all sectors of the Dublin property market with significant beneficial impacts on the physical renewal of designated urban renewal areas in Dublin. Urban renewal and development policies are undergoing major changes from a position of encouraging new development in a recession-hit market to ensuring that the current level of development and investment are maintained in a manner consistent with the NSS, which aims for sustainable development patterns. The economic context for urban regeneration policies has altered greatly from 1986 to 2008. The critical lack of public finance in the 1980s militated against direct government spending on regeneration projects and led to the extensive use of fiscal incentives to generate private investment in designated areas. By comparison, the relatively healthy state of public finances in 2005/2006 allowed for a wider range of policies, including direct intervention and major infrastructure investment to be considered. A corresponding shift in urban land policy has involved a movement from designated area development incentive schemes to integrated area development plans and prioritising catch up infrastructure investments. By 2008, the falling property market and weaker economic conditions presented a more challenging environment for continuation of the successful physical redevelopment of Dublin involving public and private sector inputs.

Future public–private regeneration projects

The major example of what is the next phase of urban regeneration involving public and private partnerships is the Spencer Dock Development adjacent to the IFSC area in Dublin Docklands. This is the largest urban development site in Ireland comprising a total site area of 88188 m² (21.79 acres). The master plan for its development includes c.278 000 m² of new residential development and 232 000 m² of office development and 46 500 m² of service leisure retail and other amenities. The development incorporates a new National Conference Centre, which is being developed under a PPP arrangement with a capacity for 8000 people in total with related hotel developments (Source: Interviews with Development Participants).

The development evolved with proposals from the state transport company CIE, which held a large underutilised piece of land adjacent to dockland with the company wishing to maximise the benefit of land holdings for its own group company. With the company reducing rail freight operations, it was keen to realise the value of this site. The option of a direct sale on the open sale, if taken, would potentially see the price realised partly to central exchequer and the loss of control of a long-term strategic land asset. A more attractive option for the company was to enter negotiations with interested parties for a joint venture development first agreed in 1998. Under this agreement, CIE retains ownership of the lands until required for development. The developer Treasury Holdings is obliged to secure planning permission, find tenants or purchasers, arrange funding and procure construction. This process has involved a long and controversial path to fruition in the creation of a consortium for the development of the entire area.

It is believed that the confidential joint venture agreement for the project guaranteed a return of under 20% of the gross development value (GDV) of all sales/lettings for the land owner with certain other uplift arrangements written into the confidential master plan agreement with the consortium involved in the project. Some commentators argued that this should potentially have been higher given the central location of the site; however, such profit sharing arrangements can prove complex and difficult to manage. Often in such situations, renegotiations occur as difficulties arise. Examples of difficulties that can arise include substantiating actual costs and revenues, which are a potential problem with all such arrangements. In such cases parties may resort to constant evaluations and monitoring by individual stakeholders and, of course, arbitration as an option where agreement cannot be reached. Difficulties, of course, occur in covering all eventualities and the major problem remains as to cut-off points for partners who fail to complete their commitments.

The development is now ongoing and has, following a lengthy and difficult planning process, commenced implementation. Such negotiations have included the use of a community planning approach to the development of the northern phase of the project, incorporating community forums and a consultative approach. This perhaps reflects the earlier and protracted planning appeal and experiences with the differing agendas of both development agencies and development perspectives. Following are the important milestones in the development of the scheme from inception in 1998 to 2008:

1. a significant pre-letting agreement with PricewaterhouseCoopers who are in occupation of a major office building in 2008;
2. residential launch in 2001 with a first phase of 500 apartment units largely sold off plans;
3. apartment construction commenced in 2004 with first completions in 2007;
4. the commencement of the National Conference Centre in 2007;
5. the creation of a new rail station servicing the site.

The transition of this development site is underway with takers of commercial space who are often international concerns and have no traditional bias in terms of city locations and used to new waterfront/docklands developments. The obvious strength of the development going forward is the proximity of the site to central Dublin being walking distance. The clearest threat to its future prospects is the downturn in property market demand and the associated credit/finance problems going forward to the next decade. The development of the National Conference Centre commenced in 2007 following the selection of the consortium involved in Spencer Dock as the preferred bidder with the PPP for its delivery. This creates a unique and complex situation for the state interest in terms of double involvement in both the public/private consortium involved in the overall development and a second engagement by the state through the Office of Public Works with this consortium in the development of the National Conference Centre through

Figure 5.3   Ongoing development in Dublin Docklands.

a PPP process. This development can be viewed as part of the continuing property development-led regeneration of Dublin Docklands as illustrated in Figure 5.3.

The aim of continuing urban regeneration and extensive development on brown-field sites is unlikely to be supported by fiscal incentives to the extent it has been in the recent period. There may remain a role for incentive-based supports to broader urban renewal initiatives, particularly in the residential sector, where, or if, shortages of housing are evident. A shift towards a greater reliance on PPP processes is therefore likely in the attempt to achieve required major urban development and sector development aims. The influence of changing policy on all aspects of the region's property market area is significant in both long and short terms. The Dublin experience combines elements from many public and private inputs that can be seen in the continued evolution of the schemes. While there remains a continuing public policy commitment to urban renewal and solving development problems, it is this commitment that gives the best opportunities of success rather than any combination of formula-based solutions.

The emerging role of public–private partnerships in 2008/2009

The central PPP unit in the Irish government's Department of Finance plays a critical coordinating role in the evolution of the PPP process in Ireland. The department makes available publicly full details on the evolution of the concept as used in Ireland, guidance notes on their implementation, briefing notes and advice to the parliamentary committee responsible for public accounts that provide an overview of the development and progress

Chapter 5

of PPP to 2008 (Department of Finance 2008). In this section a comparison will be drawn between the intentions of the PPP process, which is comparable to similar schemes internationally, and the actual progress achieved in light of evidence from project experience to date in Ireland with specific reference to ongoing PPP projects in the Dublin area in particular. For purposes of clarity, a PPP in Ireland is generally defined in official policy documents as a contractual arrangement between public sector organisations and private interests, with clear agreement on specific shared objectives, for the delivery of an asset or service that would otherwise have been provided through traditional public sector procurement processes and mechanisms.

The essential elements of a PPP in such guidelines are that the private sector will carry out at least one or more of the following:

1. provide private finance or capital to a specified project;
2. should enter into a long-term (defined as more than 5 years) service contract;
3. agree to and undertake the design and construction of an asset on the basis of a stated output specification prepared by a public sector unit or agency and designed to meet performance targets that are agreed in advance;
4. enter into a joint venture-type arrangement with the public sector to provide a specific service or asset.

The basic criteria by which such projects are deemed suitable for PPP are that such project proposals must provide long-term 'value for money' for the exchequer; ensure that environment and public health and safety standards are maintained and that the public interest is fully protected. PPP projects are intended to provide an opportunity to participate fully on major infrastructure development and to contribute new ideas to the design and construction of works. PPP guidance documents also state their aspiration to allow for the best use of public and private sector management skills in providing infrastructure and service delivery.

In an Irish context, PPPs are seen as an important element in delivering the capital investment programmes such as set out in the NDP 2000–2006 and its successors. The approach has been endorsed in social partnership agreements including the Programme for Prosperity and Fairness. Social partnership agreements between the Irish government and social partners have been a major element of successive Irish economic growth strategies since 1987. These agreements with representation from government, employers, trade unions, the voluntary sector and other social partners negotiate an agreed framework for economic growth and development over a period of several years. Priority issues agreed include a framework for general national pay agreements, infrastructure development and priority social programmes for government over the term of each agreement. A framework for the introduction of PPPs was agreed between the government and social partners with a view to overcoming resource constraints and a need to increase the capacity of the Irish economy to provide the major infrastructure catch up required following recent strong economic growth.

Co-operation between the public, voluntary and private sectors in Ireland to deliver services or to build infrastructure has occurred on an extensive basis in the past. In particular, the voluntary sector with a major input from various religious orders played a pivotal role in development of Ireland's health and education systems. Linkages with voluntary groups would, of course, primarily have been based on shared social objectives rather than motivated by private profit, making the emerging PPP process a steep learning curve for all concerned.

The PPP process has evolved in Ireland over the period from 1998 to present. Many of the dominant political parties and social partner groups are committed to the principle of engaging the private sector in the delivery of what were predominantly state activities. Equally there is ideological opposition by some groups to the principle of private/for profit involvement in the delivery of infrastructure and particularly health care and social services. The PPP was raised by the social partners in the context of discussions on potential resource constraints in achieving national infrastructure development objectives. In 1998, the government commissioned a consultancy study to explore the potential for the PPP in Ireland. Following the production of the report indicating that PPP should make a contribution to provision in infrastructure and that this could increase the level of funding available for investment, dedicated PPP units were set up in key government departments to oversee the process.

The pace at which policy direction changed to prioritise PPP approaches accelerated over the following years with strong political support and direction. Pilot projects were announced in June 1999 with a total expenditure of €760m. This included road, water supply, waste, light rail and education projects. The intention to proceed with an accelerated PPP process by learning and doing without necessarily pausing for evaluating and making judgement on the pilot projects was immediately evident. A second policy study in May 2000 contained sector guidance on implementing PPP in Ireland. The Central PPP Unit in the Department of Finance was to be engaged in bringing forward generic guidance on PPP in Ireland during the later half of 2002 and early 2003, using experience gained in the pilot projects. In early 2001, PricewaterhouseCoopers were asked by the Department of Finance to carry out a review of PPP structures in Ireland and this report was published in July 2001. The recommendations contained within this report were mostly accepted by the government and these recommendations are reflected in the support structures for the PPP that have developed in Ireland since that date.

On 1/11/01 the then Minister for Finance, Mr Charlie McCreevy, officially launched the Framework for PPP in Ireland. The Framework sets out scope, principles and goals of the programme, the definition of key project implementation issues including the requirement for central coordination of the programme by the Central PPP Unit. The Framework was negotiated over a 2-year period in the Informal Advisory Group on PPPs which is chaired by the head of the Central PPP Unit and includes representatives of the Irish Congress of Trade Union, the Irish Business and Employers Confederation and the Construction Industry Federation,

Chapter 5

alongside representatives of the sector PPP units. In December 2001, the first in a series of Regional Information Seminars was held on implementing the PPP programme. On 28/12/01, the Department of Public Enterprise (now Transport) enacted the Transport (Railway Infrastructure) Act 2001, which set up the Railway Procurement Agency. Within 1 year, the basic framework for commencing the PPP process had been established.

The next important step was in March 2002 when the State Authorities (Public–Private Partnership Arrangement) Act 2002 was enacted. This is an enabling legislation that provides certainty as to the power of various organisations to enter into joint ventures. Also in early spring of 2002, the programme for government stated an intention to set up a National Development Finance Agency (NDFA) to finance major public projects and to evaluate financing options for potential PPP projects. The NDFA's task is to enable the government to apply commercial standards in evaluating financial risks, costs and options associated with projects thereby attempting to ensure that the optimum financial package is availed of in each PPP process.

The NDFA has been set up under the aegis of the National Treasury Management Agency (NTMA) with the stated objective of maximising value for money for the taxpayer. PPP projects and major infrastructure projects are often extremely complex arrangements, requiring expert technical, legal and financial advices. A centrally resourced expert advisory service to all state authorities was intended to be more economical than employing experts in each of these areas in every procuring authority, including the local authorities. The role will be filled by NDFA in respect primarily of financial advice, project evaluation and risk analysis. It was hoped that significant cost savings could be achieved by this approach over time. The NDFA is able to assist in identifying optimal financing arrangements for major infrastructure projects and if necessary, can raise finance for PPP projects. NDFA itself may advance money to a special purpose company or consortium, such as is often set up for the purposes of a PPP project. State authorities also have powers to convey, assign or transfer land or other property (not including equity holdings) to a special purpose company formed by NDFA for the purpose of a PPP project.

In order to assess the optimal means of financing projects, NDFA has a core of expertise to assess the relative advantages or disadvantages of different project structures. Project prospectus and invitations to tender indicate that NDFA will be involved in assessing and advising on proposals and where appropriate will reserve the right of the relevant state authority to accept or reject any particular package or perhaps instead to utilise funds provided by NDFA. The objective will be to ensure overall value for money and to encourage the maximum private sector involvement in financing projects. State authorities will now be obliged to seek NDFA advice for projects above the €30m thresholds. The NDFA Act 2002 also provides that the Minister for Finance will issue guidance on the circumstances in which NDFA advice should be sought which can be amended by regulation as required.

Experience in PPPs to date

In their 2004 review of PPPs for the Dail/Parliamentary Public Accounts Committee (PAC), the Department of Finance, Central PPP Unit stated that PPPs were a viable procurement option in infrastructure development. Merits of such approaches were stated to include the following:

1. allocation of risk to the private sector that is assumed to be capable of managing it best;
2. inclusion of performance-based payment systems;
3. capturing the benefits of evolving private sector innovation, commercial and management expertise by involving the private sector more centrally in the provision of assets and services;
4. use of long-term contracts often up to 25 years whereby bidders should be encouraged to focus on the whole life-cycle cost of it, hoping that this can lead to more innovative designs with lower life-cycle costs and higher maintenance and operational standards;
5. faster project delivery of essential infrastructure projects.

Rather than reporting any in-depth review of the pilot projects, this review stated that valuable experience had been gained through the projects and that issues such as the establishment of the NDFA and the shaping of its role resulted from early project experiences. The road infrastructure PPPs experience was cited in this review as demonstrating the potential for real risk transfer and value for money outcomes for the exchequer with one contract in the outer Dublin region being awarded Project Finance International (PFI) Infrastructure Deal of the Year 2003; in making the award PFI commented on the level of risk transfer achieved, combined with a cost of finance comparable to less risky roads infrastructure projects.

Based on success in such projects, consultations between the Department of Finance and each department were undertaken with a view to signing a multi-annual investment framework agreement to give practical effect to the capital spending envelopes planned. Such agreements will, among other things, set out key objectives of the investment, the extent of delegated sanction and related conditions. A deliberate upscaling of the PPP programme was envisaged with a target that PPPs would increase their total share of investment in NDP from 3% of total in 2004 to 15% of total in 2008.

In terms of administration, PPPs as a method of public procurement are intended to be subject to an open and transparent tendering process in accordance with national and EU procurement rules. The reporting and accountability arrangements for PPPs are dealt with under the general financial procedures for capital investment and spending on projects and are liable to scrutiny by the Comptroller and Auditor General. In turn, the responsibility for advising on financing arrangements in place and ensuring optimum value for money for larger projects particularly rests with the NDFA. State authorities must refer all major projects or grouped projects over €30m to the NDFA for advice, who carry out a full financial appraisal on the project and test the financial robustness of the potential bidder. In practice this can prove to be more expensive on parties involved and involves full financial appraisals on aspects of the project and the bidder. The requirement that delivery will be guaranteed is very difficult to achieve. To formally comply could involve the bidder in taking out insurance or performance bonds, bank or parent company guarantee, all of which increase costs (Public Accounts Committee 2006–2008).

The inclusion of a Value for Money Comparison stage in the PPP process is stated in the review to be designed to evaluate the total cost of the private sector bid, which includes the costs associated with private finance, with the costs of traditional procurement as set in the Public Sector Benchmark (PSB). For a PPP tender to demonstrate better value for money in this quantitative assessment, the additional costs associated with private finance must:

1. either be justified by risks transferred to the private sector;
2. or be otherwise offset through innovative proposals to address the sponsoring agency's output specification.

Any disproportionate rewards for limited risk transfer are intended to be identified by a rigorous application of these systems.

It is intended that the PPP assessment stage should cover the wide spectrum of options from traditional procurement through to PPPs on a Design, Build, Operate and Finance and on a Concession basis.

In practice, a variety of procurement options have been utilised in Ireland in the early years of this approach, including the following:

1. Design, Build and Operate for Waste Water Projects;
2. Design, Build, Finance and Operate for Bundle of Schools Project;
3. Concession Type Arrangement for Toll Roads;
4. Long-Term Operate Contract for Luas a Dublin Light Rail development.

The assessment and procurement process has evolved to include the following stages:

Preliminary appraisal

Prior to any determination regarding a PPP route or otherwise a preliminary appraisal is carried out for all capital investment projects including defining objectives, options, costs and benefits of each option.

Public sector benchmark (PSB)

This is a detailed budget of the cost of securing the project by conventional procurement routes discounted to NPV.

Affordability cap

Basically the PSB cost is used to set an absolute limit on the outturn cost usually slightly above the PSB on the project elements to be provided by the private interests.

Value for money comparison

The guidelines state that the value for money comparison is carried out *after the selection of the best private sector bid*. It is intended to be a key control element in the process. At a minimum it will assess if the costs to the exchequer of procuring a project by means of a PPP (as represented by the best bid) are below those of procuring a project by means of a PPP (as represented by the PSB). It involves a comparison, over the lifetime of the project, of the exchequer cash flows (primarily the unitary payments but also including any capital contributions, revenue sharing arrangements and tax implications) in the proposed PPP procurement.

Process auditor

All projects or grouped projects being procured as PPPs, where the capital cost exceeds €30m, are required to appoint a Process Auditor.

Issues in implementation

The PPP process is seen as having made a major contribution to infrastructure development schemes such as in the road building programmes in Ireland in recent years. However, attempts to replicate its use in a wider variety of property development settings have had a greater degree of problems. Within the Dublin region, major problems have arisen in 2008 with projects applying the PPP model to social housing regeneration schemes. These often include inclusion of affordable housing and social housing with private housing elements. In such schemes, the city as landowner tries through use of surplus lands and higher densities to achieve mixed-use development to satisfy replacement or refurbishment needs of social stock, which is cross-subsidised by profits on sales of private units on open market. In strong market conditions, it appears that over-bidding occurred on certain sites with difficulties now resulting in a weaker residential market. In effect, competing private bidders to secure access to valuable development sites may enter contractual obligations, which they cannot deliver on if the market weakens. Examples of such risk factors in a social housing PPP include the following:

- construction risk;
- design risk;
- finance risk;
- market risk.

While bidders have been able to manage construction and design risk, both finance and market risks have become a problem in the recent period. Formal PPP process may not suit social housing markets because of uncertainty with housing market prices upon which revenue or GDV estimates are based. The potential to complete social housing elements separately exists; however, this goes against the intention to integrate social, affordable and standard residential units in mixed-use developments. In these cases the PPP may be a cumbersome and expensive process. The clear benefit of PPP can still be had in speed and development and delivery once and when a project is actually commenced as a contractor covers the costs of interest and finance. However, on some projects total time and inputs taken on initiation to and procurement now often exceeds time spent on actual development. In addition, the high levels of expertise, accumulated experience and management time needed to manage such undertakings are not available to many organisations in both the public and private sectors.

This may be particularly so with large apartment-type development schemes that have a heavy front loading of costs. This occurs due to the integrated construction process for such schemes with car parking and landscaping created in advance of each phase of the development compared with the potential for a multi-phase approach to lower-density developments. In practice, the commencements of initial negotiations are informal and no legal agreement or contract exists until a later stage. A small number of larger companies only compete for any housing PPP due to eligibility criteria relating to size and scale of operations required to compete for major PPP housing contracts. Selection criteria include the need for an audited volume turnover over a period of 3 years. The selected panel or shortlist is then invited to bring forward detailed development briefs and a smaller number of specific proposals ,incorporating the basis of bids and projections are considered.

Difficulties can persist after the selection of preferred bidder with some of the steps which follow. These include the need to formally agree and exchange a project agreement. The actual project which is the subject of agreement then has to be processed separately through the formal Planning Development Control process which is not certain in terms of the scale, quantity or design of development. Such issues may in turn be subject of appeal to National Planning Appeals Board with its outcome subject to further uncertainty. Agreements are therefore complex in terms of all contractual and phasing obligations which are linked to the date of obtaining full planning permission.

The costs of preparing, assessing and managing such bids are high for all parties concerned. In turn, funding difficulties can arise in many cases where the financial institution requires title, as in many cases full title is withheld by the public organisation which is landowner pending staged completion of the project. Examples of problems with bank credit committees at the preferred bidder stage are banks requesting scaling down of liabilities or clarifications on detailed termination clauses or agreements.

Professional fees including legal costs can be very high in many types of PPP projects. This occurs also due to issues of tax efficiency where complex transfer structures of completed developments are used to lower costs of stamp duty. Transfer of risk can never really be complete as there is no way to ensure that developers complete developments in a weak market. Particular difficulties may arise once contracts are signed if the private contractor cannot deliver as it may be difficult legally to go to the under-bidder.

The current official guidance states that the overall objective is to ensure that PPP procurement is only pursued where there is a real potential that it can deliver better value for money than the alternatives. For example, it might address whether there are significant transferable risks that might justify the increased cost or premium associated with including private finance in the deal (suggesting a Design, Build, Finance (DBF); Design, Build, Finance and

Operate (DBFO) or Design, Build, Finance, Operate and Manage (DBFOM) structure).

In practice, however, the creation of layers of administration and advisory service requirements that are continually growing can mitigate against the efficiency gains that the PPP process intends to encourage. These begin with the need for government-wide controls, with additional controls and constraints added at each level or layers of delegated authority. The end result can be a large cost on such projects with requirements for buying in of legal and other advice both at each stage of the process and particularly so if changes are envisaged or required. Partnership consortiums in the private sector in turn need to negotiate and agree arrangements. For example, for a major prison complex on the outskirts of Dublin the preferred builder was selected in 2006 but contracts were not yet signed as of June 2008. This issue arises in many projects with the timescale for selected bidder to close often within 1 year even on medium-scale projects. Projects therefore may come towards implementation in a changed market from that in which the original negotiations were conducted. Such contractual agreements can include termination clauses if key phases are not completed by specific dates. While the agreement can be terminated, the difficulties for all parties in failing PPP projects are significant in terms of both actual costs and management time involved.

In practice, with the assistance of the NDFA the task of identification of the principal risks involved in PPP has been facilitated; however, dealing with or mitigating such risks remains more problematical. The NFDA is able to carry out risk analysis across all elements of the project checklist and participants in such projects recognise that such risks are growing in the current difficult market conditions.

Recent and future trends in PPPs

In that PPPs attempt to package and standardise what are complex contractual long-term partnerships, it has been inevitable that serious criticism has emerged of such schemes. Attempts to, in any way, provide a common basis for standard agreement for heterogeneous development projects can be expected to result in both difficulty in negotiations and the resulting outcomes. The suitability for standard road projects of the PPP process has been established by policy reviews. However much debate often centres on value for money in the use of PPPs in other types of development project and the initial premise that efficiencies would be realised is difficult to substantiate. Delays and cost overruns remain in what are admittedly hugely difficult urban development projects whether PPP is used or not.

Initial published examination of specific PPP projects has been critical in many respects. On the first group of schools in Ireland delivered by a modern PPP approach, the cost of this means of delivery was found to be higher than the conventional approach. The report of the Comptroller and Auditor General (2004) found that while these projects had been prioritised and brought forward, the actual PPPP cost evaluated was 8–13% higher than traditional approaches. In addition, critics of this scheme including Hearne

(2008) have pointed to further difficulties involved. Firstly, the long-term viability of this approach was tested in this project as the original developer Jarvis Projects Ltd had financial difficulties in 2006 and was subsequently acquired by another company Hochtief. The original analysis of PPP costs was claimed to be weak as additional costs including treatment of value added tax (VAT) and the costs of conducting the PPP process itself were not included in initial comparisons of the project cost. The other major criticism emerging relates to the difficulties in combining educational uses with income-generating uses, which the private operator of the building might see as desirable or profitable. These impact on or indeed compromise the design, use and adaptation of the school building on an ongoing basis. The government case in favour of the PPP approach remains that the avoidance of initial capital outlay merits the continuation of this approach and that inevitably a learning curve involves adaptation from weaknesses in early schemes.

These types of situations have given rise to Parliamentary PAC enquiries and discussions on the absence of accountability with PPP projects. The PAC published a critical report of the PPP process in 2007. The confidentiality clauses and commercial sensitivity of vital information in PPP project agreements make evaluation and analysis difficult and researchers are reliant on incomplete data from a variety of official reports and media commentaries. In addition, such information is not, even after a period of time, subject to availability under Freedom of Information regulations.

While the public sector agencies can be called before the PAC and subject to scrutiny, no similar obligation extends to private sector participants. In addition, the issue of the commercial sensitivity of information on arrangements entered into makes scrutiny and oversight difficult as these arrangements would be pivotal to any complete value for money assessment. The only overview on behalf of the elected representatives of government and the general public is dependent on the reports of the Comptroller and Auditor General who has access to relevant documentation. Based on such work, the recently retired Comptroller and Auditor General advised against the overreliance on PPP-based solutions for public sector initiatives. Serious deficiencies in corporate governance were highlighted in some examinations of PPP-type deals and in the absence of accountability such concerns will remain in the future.

The generally rising property markets of 1994 to 2006 provided an ideal basis for many land swap-based proposals involving PPP-type arrangements and carried such projects through what may have been complex or difficult agreement processes. Indeed in rising markets delays or weaknesses in such schemes could actually contribute to final success in delivery terms as the rising tide of property values produced major development gains for all concerned. The falling property market in Ireland in 2008 has placed a doubt over many current negotiations for PPPs, which were based on the assumption of stable or rising markets and resulting increasing land values. PPP projects are often based on the land swaps, which can be portrayed as self-financing projects with the sharing of development gains between the private and public sectors. This often suits the public agency owning surplus land assets as the alternative may be to dispose of such lands on the open market and return surplus revenues generated to the general exchequer. Unlocking the potential land value in often centrally located valuable land assets in the recent property boom has been a recurring feature of PPP arrangements.

During May/June of 2008, the viability of a group of social housing PPPs was called into doubt by the withdrawal of a major construction company from a series of major urban regeneration projects including PPP components. Disputes and delays concerning planning and the actual number of units to be developed ended with the developer withdrawing from negotiations. Analysis as to why PPP projects fail or are aborted often results in a welter of conflicting allegations by the parties involved. The recent suspension of protracted negotiations on the delivery of this series of regeneration projects in the Dublin City Council area illustrates this point.

These developments have been extensively reported in all main Irish media outlets in May 2008. In the worsening housing market conditions of 2008, the suspension of a series of key regeneration schemes including Dominick Street in the city centre and St Michaels, a social housing estate, illustrates the difficulties involved. The St Michaels estate is a particular long-term regeneration project for Dublin City Council. Plans for its regeneration had been unveiled in 2001 and evolved since, with working schemes discussed from 1998 onwards. The 14-acre estate was regarded as one of the most deprived areas in Dublin. Earlier plans for its regeneration were rejected by elected members of the council in 2004. The conclusion of planning and community negotiations appear to have come towards fruition at the same time as the protracted housing development boom that made the redevelopment financially attractive had come to an end. The proposal intended to replace a number of older social housing schemes with 1800–2000 new units costing €900m with the development interest selling c.800 of the units for profit as their return on the scheme and the rest being available for use by the city council for social and affordable housing. The development interest stated its reasons for considering the projects as unviable and withdrawing from the process. These included difficulties in obtaining planning permission on a number of sites, the protracted nature of discussions with officials, community groups and others along with weakening market trends. In particular, the amendment of guidelines governing apartment size and energy guidelines was stated to have involved considerable revisions to the scheme. The developer contended that by significantly increasing apartment sizes this effectively reduced the number and profitability of the units available to cover costs and profits on the scheme. While remedies are built into such contracts to compensate private interests where the actions of the planning process result in a reduction in the number of units in such schemes, they do not provide a context for a solution in these cases. This is a particular problem in a falling property market and can be expected to affect a number of similar PPP-based housing schemes in Dublin. In relation to such major setbacks for the new-style PPP process in Dublin it is clear that questions of accountability and scrutiny in terms of PPP projects are to become more intense. Government is currently reviewing

Chapter 5

rules governing the use of PPP in housing contracts with development interests.

Recent concerns regarding availability of finance for PPPs have surfaced in further issues regarding the latest tranche of school projects recently put to tender. Several media sources reported that requests were made by a participating company that the National Finance Development Agency consider full payment be made on completion of the building of the schools rather than receiving payments on a monthly basis over the normal 25-year period. This is the term during which it is expected that the contractor will build and maintain the project buildings. The NFDA maintains a stance that no upfront payments are considered during the duration of the project as the basis of the PPP approach is risk transfer in which the government expects the private sector to take responsibility for managing and dealing with the project risk.

Current experience in Ireland remains that the best areas for PPP development are infrastructure projects where payments are directly from the state or payments are generated by tolls or fares from a proven demand pool of consumers or users. Given the deficits in transport infrastructure, experience to date has been that the primary risk factor in such proposals is the number of customers or users which have tended to exceed targets in examples such as the light rail projects and road projects already undertaken in Dublin.

The current credit squeeze is evidently creating increased difficulties for private companies seeking large-scale credit facilities with even larger banks only willing to underwrite small portions of the total credit required for each project and a greater dependency on debt syndication. This in turn has created uncertainty for the Department of Finance in terms of its capital investment plans which rely on PPPs for a significant element of infrastructure and other development proposals in the NDP. From 2007 onwards, as the advent of an economic downturn became evident, government has prioritised the state-led NDP as an essential component of assisting the economy through such a downturn. Full implementation of such plans has been reiterated as a priority in 2008. However, the implementation of such plan was predicated upon an assumption of economic growth of 4.5% and resulting revenue growth which as the year progresses in no longer guaranteed.

In terms of national accounts some doubts persist as to whether such expenditures can be considered to be totally off balance sheet in terms of public spending so long as issues remain in terms of risk transfer and whether this transfer can actually be considered complete in many of the projects concerned. As the PPP process evolves high costs of policy, compliance with the need to demonstrate transparency and accountability can impact on the ability of any state or local government agency to achieve the full benefit of the intended project spending. Ideologically, many commentators on the PPP process are opposed to the use of PPP for sectors such as social housing and the health care. Equally, proponents of PPP may be ideologically driven to promote PPP in all circumstances as a solution to each and every development need. Given the mixed experiences with PPP some public landowners and agencies in Dublin have chosen alternative routes to make the best use of, or add value to, their property assets by seeking planning permission prior to staged disposal of surplus assets. A more rational long-term approach to both the current use of and potential future use of public land assets would be that PPP should be neither promoted nor opposed on a blanket basis but that it should be among the options considered for state spending on infrastructure and other land development projects.

From experience to date the preference in policy statements for PPP as a preferred procurement option is not borne out as yet by evidence of results of such schemes. This leads to a conclusion that while decision-makers should appraise all procurement options including PPP, the best option should be based on evidence-based decision-making rather than commitments for or against individual options.

References

Central Statistics Office (1986–2008) *Central Statistics Office Data*, Dublin ESRI (various dates) Economic and Social Research Institute Quarterly Economic Commentary, ESRI, Dublin.

Comptroller and Auditor General (2004) *The Grouped Schools Pilot Partnership Project: Report on Value for Money Comparison*, http://www.audgen.gov.ie.

Department of Finance (2006) *Indecon Review of Property Based Tax Incentive Schemes*, Department of Finance, Dublin.

Department of Finance (2008) *Central PPP Unit Reports Including Framework for Public Private Partnerships, Guidelines to State Authorities, Main PPP Guidelines*, Technical Guidance Notes, 2004 Review for Dail/Public Accounts Committee, Dublin.

Department of the Environment and Local Government (2002) *National Spatial Strategy for Ireland, 2002–2020: People, Places and Potential*, Department of the Environment and Local Government, Dublin.

Department of the Environment and Local Government/KPMG (1996) *Study on the Urban Renewal Schemes*, Department of the Environment, Dublin.

Department of The Environment and Local Government (1998) *Review of the Construction Industry 1998 and Outlook 1999–2000*, Department of the Environment and Local Government, Dublin.

ESRI (Economic and Social Research Institute) (1986–2008) *Economic and Social Research Institute, Quarterly Economic Commentary*, ESRI, Dublin.

Hearne R (2008) Public private partnerships in Irish schools. *Journal of Irish Urban Studies*, **4**, (6), 55–69.

Irish Times (2002) 06-04-02 Commercial section reports on Rail Enquiry.

MacLaran A and Williams B (1995) *Residential Development in Central Dublin*, Center for Urban and Regional Studies, Trinity College, Dublin.

McGuirk P and MacLaran A (2001) Changing approaches to urban planning in an entrepreneurial city: the case of Dublin. *European Planning Studies*, **9**, (4), 437–457.

Mullen F (1991) Valuation of tax incentives, *Paper to Annual Conference of the Foundation for Fiscal Studies*, Dublin.

NESC (1985) *Economic and Social Policy Assessment*, The Stationery Office, Dublin.

ODPM (Office of The Deputy Prime Minister) (2003) *Sustainable Communities: Building for the Future*, ODPM, London.

OECD (1987) *Economic Survey of Ireland*, OECD, Paris.

Public Accounts Committee (2006–2008) Reports Irlgov.ie.

Chapter 5

Williams B (1997) Taxation incentives and urban renewal in Dublin. *Journal of Property Tax Assessment and Administration*, **2**, (3), 69–88.

Williams B (2006) Fiscal incentives and urban regeneration in Dublin from 1986 to 2005. *Journal of Property Investment and Finance*, **24**, (6), 542–548.

Williams B (2008) The integration of aspects of enterprise and urban regeneration policies in the development of the IFSC in Dublin. *Journal of Irish Urban Studies*, **4**, (6), 37–53.

Williams B and Shields P (2000) *Acceleration into Sprawl: Causes and Potential Policy Responses*, Quarterly Economic Commentary, Economic and Social Research Institute, Dublin.

Website sources accessed 2007/2008

Ireland Government and Departments of State www.irlgov.ie
International Financial Services Centre www.ifsc.ie
Comptroller and Auditor General www.audgen.gov.ie
Department of Environment Heritage and Local Government www.environ.ie
Department of Finance www.finance.ie
Central Statistics Office www.cso.ie
www.finance.gov.ie

DOE Urban Renewal Legislation

Urban Renewal Act 1986
Urban Renewal Act 1986 (Designated Areas)
The Temple Bar Area Renewal and Development Act 1991
Urban Renewal Guidelines 1999

Chapter 6
Property Funding Partnerships

Introduction

The way in which developers fund property development can be regarded as a form of partnership as there is a contractual arrangement between the parties and both benefit financially from the arrangement. This section explains the various types of funding available for development schemes such as shopping centres, business parks or office buildings. The major emphasis is on public companies quoted on the London Stock Exchange but the overarching rules of finance can be applied to any developer. Neither tax implications nor the project management of the development process are considered in detail.

Although this section concentrates on financial instruments and techniques of funding, it is wise to bear in mind that the security offered for a loan is often the property itself and such matters as lease terms, planning permission, structural integrity, title and design obsolescence will all have to be considered to ensure that both borrower and lender are protected from unacceptable risk. In broad terms, finance for property development can be classified into four types.

1. *Equity* finance is the use of shareholders' funds either in the form of retained earnings from a company or by way of creating more shares in a company, which is known as a rights issue. A private limited company may consider a stock exchange or Alternative Securities Market floatation to generate equity funds. As an alternative, shares may be placed privately rather than offered to existing shareholders through a rights issue. Warrants and options are also available. The former is created by a company inviting investors to subscribe for new shares in the company at some future date whereas the latter will be created by the existing shareholders. Unless the existing shareholder is the company

seeking funds this type of disposal will only benefit the shareholder not the company.

2. *Debt* finance involves the raising of funds from banks and other lenders where the lender will benefit by interest charges and the repayment of capital. None of the equity in the company will pass to the lender although the assets of the borrower may provide collateral for the loan. Finance may be obtained by way of debentures where the debt is secured against all or some of the company's assets. Bonds are similar to government gilts but issued by companies. They offer the funder a higher return than debentures as they are not secured against assets. Some bonds, known as deep discount bonds, offer a very low rate of interest but may be traded by the lender. They are therefore only attractive to lenders if the company is very likely to grow and be successful.

3. *Corporate* finance may be either debt or equity but is raised on the back of a corporate entity, which provides the collateral for a loan or the assets for equity purchasers.

4. *Project* finance may again be debt or equity but is secured on the development rather than the acquiring company. Developer guarantees will be required. An example might be the long-term funding of a completed development by way of a commercial mortgage where debt finance is raised using the value of mortgagor's property as collateral.

Debt or equity?

In choosing the type of funding for a property development scheme, the developer has a choice but rarely a free choice. Whether or not a company can promote a successful rights issue, for example, will depend on how the performance of the company is perceived by the existing shareholders. Similarly the success of a bond issue will depend on how the market predicts the future trading prospects for the company backing the bond. There is, however, one major advantage for companies in using a high proportion of debt finance in any scheme. This is that as the proportion of debt finance in a purchase increases so does the return to the equity in the purchase. This will only be the case if the initial percentage return from the project is greater than the annual percentage interest rate on the debt. In recent times when interest rates have been low and stable this has made development funding by way of debt particularly attractive. Other reasons a greater proportion of debt may be used are if a company wishes to undertake a major scheme, which would not be able to be acquired if only equity funds were used, or if it is funding a joint venture company.

The proportion of debt to equity in the financing of a company, or a project, is known as gearing. In company terms it is known as balance sheet gearing as it compares the percentage of debt carried by the company with the amount of shareholders' funds as stated in the balance sheet. In terms of risk to the company, equity funding is much safer than debt as the only way in which equity shareholders can reclaim the amount of their investment is by selling their shares in the company. Conversely, if a company is in debt to a bank and fails to repay the debt, the bank may call the company for the loan repayment and take legal action in the case of default. The financial strategy of a company undertaking property development will be therefore to increase gearing during boom times when interest rates are low and rental growth is high, but to switch into equity before the peak of the boom is reached and the economy moves into a lower period of growth or even recession.

Lender's risk avoidance ratios

When arranging debt with a bank the borrower will discover that the bank will impose rules that are based on ratios comparing the debt with either the earnings from or the value of the scheme. The loan will first be subject to a loan to value ratio, which ensures that the loan is adequately covered by the value of the investment to be created. Typically this figure will be up to 70%. The bank may also wish to see that interest repayments are well covered by rental income and indeed that the total capital and interest repayments are covered by the total rent roll. For a multi-let development, such as a shopping centre, the lender will also be interested to know at what point of occupancy the debt payments are covered by rental income.

Although the conventional residual appraisal used in some of the examples given later assumes that a developer is 100% debt financed this can never be the case. Any developer who has no equity would be unable to run a viable business. The appraisal is, however, theoretically correct as the opportunity cost of equity would be the short-term rate of interest. In practice, developers respond to market signals and if development appears viable they will seek finance and commence schemes (RICS/University of Aberdeen 1994). As explained earlier, various types of finance will be required. If a developer uses the equity already existing from earnings within the company or raises equity finance through perhaps a rights issue the risk accepted is a great deal less than that involved with debt finance.

A developer's incentive to increase the ratio of debt finance to equity finance in a project is that as the ratio increases so the return to the developer's equity will also increase so long as the interest rate on the debt is less than the return from the scheme per annum. Where the long-term funding vehicle is a sale and leaseback viability is tested by the adequacy of the developer's share of the occupational rent after the fund has taken its return. With long-term debt finance such as a long-term mortgage, it is important that the percentage rate that applies to the developer's long-term debt is less than the percentage return from the property investment created. Example 6.1 illustrates this position. Four scenarios are considered. In Scenario 1, the purchase is relatively lowly geared and the interest rate is assumed to be 6.25% per annum. The same interest rate is used in Scenario 2, but the purchase is less highly geared. In Scenario 3, it is assumed that the interest rate available to the investor has risen to 10% per annum and the purchase is again relatively highly geared. In Scenario 4, the same interest rate is used (10%) but the purchase is assumed to be less highly geared.

Chapter 6

Example 6.1 Debt and equity

A property developer is about to develop a site at a cost of £5m including all on costs and incidentals. The net annual rent from the property will be £400 000 per annum. The predicted initial net return is therefore 8% per annum.

Scenario 1

Assume rate of interest on money borrowed is 6.25%

Development funded by 80% debt and 20% equity

Debt	£5m × 0.8	= £4m
Equity	£5m × 0.2	= £1m

Yearly interest payment

£4m × 0.0625	= £0.25m pa

Net income

£0.4m–0.25m	= £0.15m pa

Initial return to equity

$$\frac{£0.15m}{£1m} = 15\%$$

Scenario 2

Same rate on interest 6.25% but development less highly leveraged

Development funded by 50% debt and 50% equity

Debt	£5m × 0.5	= £2.5m
Equity	£5m × 0.5	= £2.5m

Yearly interest payment

£2.5m × 0.0625	= £0.1563m pa

Net income

£0.4m − £0.1563m	= £0.2437m pa

Initial return to equity

$$\frac{£0.2437m}{£2.5m} = 9.74\%$$

Scenario 3

Assume that the rate of interest available to the investor rises to 10% per annum

Development funded by 80% debt and 20% equity

Debt	£5m × 0.8	= £4m
Equity	£5m × 0.2	= £1m

Example 6.1 Debt and equity (*Continued*)

Yearly interest payment

£4m × 0.10   = £0.04m pa

Net income

£0.4 − £0.4m   = Nil

Project makes nil return

Scenario 4

Assume that rate of interest available to the developer rises to 10% but is less
  highly leveraged

Development funded by 50% debt and 50% equity

Debt   £5m × 0.5   = £2.5m

Equity   £5m × 0.5   = £2.5m

Yearly interest payment

£2.5m × 0.10   = £0.250m pa

Net income

£0.4m − £0.025m   = £0.15m pa

Initial return to equity

$$\frac{£0.15m}{£2.5m} \qquad\qquad = 6\% \text{ pa}$$

No account is taken of the need to repay capital as well as interest in the example given here. If this is included, the difference in the results would be less stark but nevertheless the example shows the reality behind the relationship of developer and bank. In Scenario 1, the developer's bold decision to fund the purchase primarily by risky debt finance has paid off with a healthy return to equity of 15%. Scenario 2 shows how a risk-averse developer using a 50/50 arrangement of the bank and equity finance cuts the return to equity to 9.74%. When interest rates rise, the risk-averse developer makes 6% return to equity (Scenario 3) whereas the developer who chooses a highly geared arrangement makes no return at all with all the rent being eaten up by debt repayment. It is a matter for the developer and the bank to negotiate the terms upon which lending will take place. If a developer is confident that rental growth will be good and there are few inflationary pressures in the economy that might cause a rise in interest rates, a highly geared arrangement will be preferred. This is also the case with private finance initiative (PFI) schemes where a typical arrangement is 90% gearing (HM Treasury).

Corporate finance

Property partnerships are usually concerned with developers' relationships with banks or funds where short-term finance is secured on the site and long-term finance is available to buy the investment away from the developer upon completion and letting. Corporate finance involves the financing of the development company itself where the worth and prospects of the corporate entity provide the security for the loan. Corporate finance in terms of loans can either be recourse, where the lender has recourse to the assets of the company in case of default, or non-recourse, where the loan is not secured by company assets. Corporate equity finance can be sought through a rights issue or, if the company is a limited company, initial public offerings through a stock market listing. Corporate debt can be obtained by debentures, loan stock, and through a variety of bond issues.

Rights issues

A rights issue is a form of corporate equity funding, which has been frequently used by quoted development companies to fund a development programme while reducing balance sheet gearing. If a company is seen as a growth stock and is perceived to be well managed with an investment portfolio in growth sectors, it is likely that it would be able to launch a successful rights issue. It could also probably raise corporate debt fairly successfully as well and if it does so there is the advantage that as the ratio of debt to equity increases so the return to equity increases. Debt, however, is risky where equity finance is not and there may be circumstances where a company board believes that interest rates will rise in the short term, making a loan less attractive and too risky. However, in difficult economic periods the promotion of a rights issue can be seen as a confirmation of weakness and a policy of desperation when a company cannot raise any debt at all.

The mechanics of a successful rights issue is that the company (assumed to be a quoted plc) offers its shareholders a number of extra shares based on the number of shares already held. A 'one to four' rights offer would offer shareholders one share for every four already held and the price quoted would provide a discount to the current share price on the stock exchange. How much discount is offered and the ratio of new to old shares depends on how popular the rights issue is likely to be. The issue will be underwritten by a merchant bank (usually) for a fee. The company is obliged to offer the existing shareholders the opportunity to buy the shares as they have pre-emption rights. If they reject the offer the company can offer them to third parties. In buoyant economic times the rights issue will proceed smoothly with all shareholders taking up their allocation. The shares will dip slightly upon the issue taking place because theoretically there are more shares to divide into any available dividend but later, if the company is a growth stock, the shares should increase in value.

To provide a practical illustration of rights issues two examples are used, both in very different economic circumstances. In 1996 Pillar Properties plc, then a highly regarded quoted company, promoted a rights issue (*Financial Times* 8/6/96). The company had just declared a 4% increase in net assets per share and pre-tax profits had increased by 95% to £6.41m. The rights issue raised £43.9m for a one to four ratio of new to existing shares. The company's gearing fell from 109% to 74% as a result of the issue, which was supported by existing shareholders with the whole issue being underwritten by Kleinwort Benson. As a result of the issue the shares dipped on the stock exchange from 172p per share to 171p before moving upwards again and the money raised was used to fund its development programme in the much favoured retail and leisure sectors. Unbeknown to the company at the time it was operating at the start of a stock market bull run only temporarily interrupted by the dot com problems of the new millennium. During the next 10 years rents would rise, property yields would be stable or drift down, interest rates would stay low and inflation would be negligible. This was not apparent in 1996 and the chairman of Pillar at the time, Raymond Mould, was quoted as saying that the year had been 'exceptionally dull' for the property market. This issue is an example of a well-run and successful property company taking a cautious stance in the face of an uncertain property market and economic conditions.

The above-mentioned example can be contrasted with the attempt at a rights issue by Bradford and Bingley in May 2008 (Bowers and Kollowewe, *The Guardian* 5/6/2008). Bradford and Bingley attempted to raise £300m through a rights issue at 82p per share. Unfortunately the company attempted this at a time when the share price was falling rapidly and a profits warning had been issued. The issue had been underwritten by two banks, UBS and Citigroup, for a fee of £37m but these two companies withdrew from the deal as a result of deterioration in trading conditions. Bradford and Bingley had specialised in buy-to-let and self-certificated loans but mortgage arrears had become unsustainable without additional capital to support the company. The company eventually managed to underwrite the issue at 55p per share but this episode illustrates the perils of attempting a rights issue in turbulent economic circumstances when a company is perceived to be in a risk market.

Categories of project finance

Finance for property development was categorised into four broad types as given in the four scenarios mentioned earlier and is now considered in its various forms. These categories can be described as follows:

1. *Sale and leaseback.* Short-term debt finance and long-term equity finance.
2. *Capitalised sale and leaseback.* Short-term debt finance and long-term equity finance.
3. *Profit erosion with priority yield.* Short-term debt finance and long-term equity finance.
4. *Commercial mortgage.* Short- and long-term debt finance.
5. *Forward sale or forward commitment.* Short-term debt finance and long-term equity finance.

In each case mentioned earlier, any mezzanine finance is classified as short-term finance but may be debt or equity.

Sale and leaseback

Sale and leaseback, as described later, is a method of financing property development schemes where the developer seeks a long-term funder, who will provide capital monies to enable the developer to repay the short-term debt. In property development, sale and leasebacks became popular when rising interest rates in the late 1960s resulted in mortgage funding becoming unviable. A sale and leaseback enabled a developer to retain a long-term lease in a property and enjoy rental growth as a profit rent over and above ground rent payable to the freeholder. Again, as will be seen later, the true sale and leaseback when applied to property development rarely suits the incentives of the parties and has been replaced by capitalised arrangements except in special circumstances.

Sale and leaseback arrangements applied to property development are derived from a long established method of raising business finance (Tipping and Bullard 1994). A business owning the freehold of property is seen to be under-utilising its assets. Received management consultancy advice is for a business owning the freehold of property to find some means of releasing the value of the property into the main business function as it is believed that the return from a core business will be more valuable than property yields over time. Against this argument must be offset the security offered by a freehold property in times of business downturn. A property owning business has a range of methods of dealing with its property assets and the established models are as follows:

1. operational property held within a single business entity;
2. separate property and trading divisions;
3. sale and leaseback;
4. sale and manage back;
5. property outsourcing
   (Tipping and Bullard 2007).

Of the arrangements listed in (1) to (5) above, sale and leaseback and separate property and trading divisions can be regarded as forms of property partnership. In the latter case a business will create two companies within its overall structure. These are often termed *Opco*, which is the operating part of the business, and *Propco*, which becomes the property owning part. This arrangement allows each division to use its particular expertise for the overall benefit of the business with *Propco* acting as landlord and *Opco* as tenant. Sale and leaseback in its simplest form involves the business and property owner selling its operating property to an investor in an arms-length transaction. Where tenant covenant is good and rental uplifts during the term of the new lease can be agreed these vehicles can become attractive investment opportunities. Examples in recent years include the Barclays Bank's sale and leaseback of 15 branches to the Prudential for £85m in 2006 and Debenhams' sale of £495m of property to British Land in 2005 (Tipping and Bullard 1994).

Rent-sharing leases

Rent-sharing leases also have a long history of being used as a vehicle for property development partnerships. When interest rates rose in the mid-1970s developers would seek to agree sale and leaseback long-term funding arrangements with institutions as long-term mortgage funding became unviable. This can be illustrated using a broad-brush practical example. Summarised figures are used so that the various funding techniques can be explained clearly.

Outline residual appraisal

Shopping Centre Project	
Predicted Income	£5m per annum (pa)
YP @ 6% in perpetuity	16.67
Gross development value (GDV)	£83.35m
Costs of disposal @ 5.22%	£4.35m
Net development value (NDV)	£79.00m
Expenditure	
Construction cost + fees on construction including short-term interest, all incidentals and on–costs	£15.00m
Land cost + fees on land purchase including short-term interest and all incidentals	£30.00m
Other costs including short-term interest	£14.00m
Total cost	£59.00m
Developer's profit	£20.00m

Types of rent-sharing leases

Rent-sharing leases are usually sale and leaseback arrangements where a developer will sell a completed scheme to an institution and take a long leaseback. With the monies received for the sale the developer will repay all the short-term capital and rolled up interest and the developer's profit will become the flow of profit rent represented by the difference between the rent from occupational sub-lessees and the rent payable to the freeholder. For the sake of convenience sale and leasebacks are referred to later as simply 'leasebacks'. Three types of rent-sharing lease will be considered:

1. The top slice leaseback where rents are shared on a rent receivable basis
2. The side-by-side leaseback where rents are shared on a rent received basis
3. The reverse leaseback where, typically, a local authority, stands between occupational tenants and fund.

The various arrangements can be looked at in turn by numerical examples based on the outline residual appraisal given earlier.

Top slice leaseback

The top slice sale and leaseback allows the developer to replace short-term finance with long-term finance by selling the completed building to a fund and taking a long leaseback (usually 125 years). The rent under the long lease represents the fund's return. The developer agrees to the terms of the sale and leaseback at the commencement of the project and, if terms are favourable, can borrow all of the short-term monies from the long-term funder as a package deal. The rent from the occupational sub-tenants is received by the developer as head lessee, and the long-term funder's return is usually paid as a percentage of rents **receivable** from the sub-tenants. The rent as a percentage indicates that the leaseback is a **geared** arrangement and the term rent **receivable** shows that whether or not the developer receives rent from the sub-tenants the developer must pay the fund the head rent under the long lease. If the rent reserved under the long lease is **ungeared**, it has no relationship with the rent paid by the occupational tenants but would remain the same throughout the length of the long lease. This circumstance is very unlikely to be acceptable to the fund but it is possible that a semi-geared arrangement could be agreed where the rent paid by the developer is reviewed every, say, 5 years, to a percentage of rent receivable from the sub-tenants. With a fully geared arrangement there is rarely a ground rent review as such. An accounting exercise is conducted yearly and the appropriate rent allocated to the fund.

Using the figures in the residual appraisal given earlier, the financial position of the parties can be calculated.

Example 6.2 Top slice leaseback

Amount of short-term monies lent by fund to developer:	£59m
Initial return required by fund	7%[1]
Initial rental income required by fund	
£59m x 7%	£4.13m pa
Rent from scheme	£5m pa
Developer's profit rent	£0.87m[2]

[1] The arrangement illustrated is a top slice **geared** leaseback. If the leaseback is **ungeared**, the rent of £4.13m per annum remains the same throughout the lease. With a geared arrangement (which is usual) the fund's **share** of the rent paid by the occupational tenants (82.6%) remains the same throughout the lease. It is assumed that the fund would require an initial return of 7% (all risks yield plus 1%) to take account of the risk it carries as a result of its involvement with the development scheme.

[2] The developer's profit rent of £0.87m per annum is 17.4% of the occupational rent and remains the same percentage during the course of the head lease. The developer's leasehold interest is valuable but as the developer is guaranteeing a rent of 82.6% of the occupational rent it would be expected that the profit rent would be valued at a high yield.

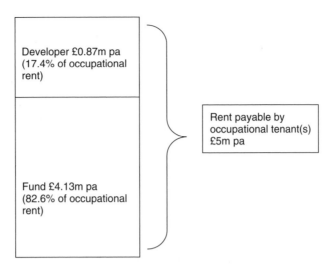

Figure 6.1 Rental shares top slice leaseback.

Side-by-side leaseback

The side-by-side leaseback is similar to the top slice leaseback described earlier but there is one major difference. The rent payable by the head lessee to the fund is calculated as a percentage of the rent **received** rather than **receivable** by the head lessee from the sub-lessees. Therefore if it is assumed the leaseback is geared on the figures in Figure 6.1, the developer, as head lessee, would pay the fund 82.6% of the rent **received** from the occupational sub-tenant(s). Therefore if the sub-tenants did not pay their rent the head lessee is under no obligation to pay any rent to the freeholder. This arrangement is less advantageous to the fund and it would be expected that a higher initial return would be required. In Figure 6.2 it is assumed that the fund would require an initial return of 7.5% rather than the 7%, which was deemed acceptable in the case of the top slice leaseback. The initial ground rent payable to the freeholder will be (£59m x 0.075) £4.425m, which is 88.5% of the rents payable by the occupational lessees. In the case of a geared side-by-side leaseback the developer takes a lease from the freeholder (the fund) and pays 88.5% of the rents **received** from the sub-tenants. The developer's interest is valued at a high yield, as in the previous example of the top slice leaseback, for although no rent is guaranteed to the freeholder, the profit rent is only £0.575m, which is 11.5% of the occupational rent. In reality it is very unlikely that such an arrangement would be acceptable to either the developer or the fund and it is much more likely that the developer's share of the rent would be capitalised with the fund buying out the developer on completion. A fund would resist a ground rent of more than 10% of the rack rent, as its shares of rental growth would be unacceptably low. The developer is also in an unfavourable position with a risky leasehold interest. Example 6.3 illustrates a side-by-side leaseback where the rental

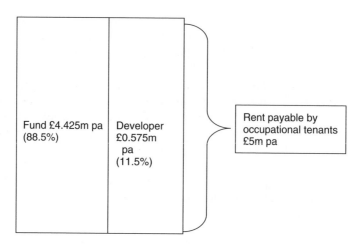

Figure 6.2   Rental shares side-by-side leaseback.

shares are divided vertically to illustrate that if the sub-tenants do not pay the rent due, the fund and developer are both disadvantaged according to their rental shares.

Example 6.3 Side-by-side leaseback

Amount of short-term monies lent by fund to developer	£59m
Initial return required by fund	7.5%
Initial rental income required by fund	
£59m x 0.075	£4.425m pa
Rent from scheme	£5m pa
Developer's profit rent	£0.575m

Reverse sale and leaseback

The reverse sale and leaseback has been used in the past by local authorities when faced with promoting development of buildings that are not normally institutionally acceptable. It may also be used as a means of allowing a developer to own a valuable interest rather than a virtually unsaleable, highly geared leasehold. For example, a developer could be appointed to develop a local authority owned site. During the development period, the developer occupies the site under licence and carries out a development using short-term monies borrowed from a fund. Upon completion, the local authority sells the freehold of the land to a fund and takes a long leaseback. The rent payable under the long lease becomes the fund's return as freeholder and the developer departs with a lump sum profit that forms part of the short-term finance. The local authority is the head lessee and the competent landlord for the tenants occupying the buildings on site. The rental shares are agreed on a side-by-side or a top slice basis but the latter is more likely as the fund would require the local authority to be responsible for its return.

A variation of the case mentioned earlier is where a long lease is granted to a fund at a peppercorn rent during the development period and a developer (the freeholder) carries out the development for a fee, which might be a capitalised share of income. The fee is part of the development cost lent by the fund to the developer. Upon completion the fund takes its rent as a priority calculated as a percentage of the occupational rent. The developer as freeholder receives a top slice rental income when the fund's share has been deducted from the occupational rent.

Documentation for profit sharing leases

There are three documents that are agreed between fund (landlord) and developer (tenant) in a rent-sharing lease. These are the joint venture agreement/agreement for lease, the lease and the draft underlease (Darlow *et al.* 1994).

The joint venture/finance agreement

In this document the developer covenants to complete the development and the fund agrees to provide finance. The timing of the sale and leaseback is stated and this will be either immediately or at the completion of the development.

The lease

This sets out the terms agreed by landlord and tenant including the rent reserved, the way it is shared, approval of sub-tenants and a general letting policy. This is dealt with in detail under the section titled 'Rent-sharing leases – terms, risks and responsibilities'.

The draft underlease

The fund will have a draft lease, which it finds acceptable for the type of development proposed, and this will form part of the agreement between the landlord and the tenant. It may be that some flexibility will be sought by the developer to reflect market conditions. For example, funds have been obliged to come to terms with the market reality of tenants demanding shorter leases than the standard 25-year term, which once was an essential institutional requirement.

Rent-sharing leases – terms, risks and responsibilities

Top slice, side-by-side and reverse sale and leasebacks, collectively known as rent-sharing leases, are sometimes subject to minimum rental payments to

Chapter 6

the landlord although, in the examples cited earlier, this is assumed not to be the case. There are a number of important matters that have to be addressed in the leases, which are agreed between the landlord and lessee.

The timing of rental payments to the landlord

The rent reserved to the landlord will often be subject to an end-of-year accounting exercise when all the rent from the scheme is summated and the relevant proportion paid as ground rent. In the case of a top slice leaseback, this would, of course, be a percentage of rents receivable but even in this case what should be receivable would need to be calculated by the definition in the ground lease. If a tenant receives rent from the occupational sub-lessees on the usual quarter days there may be some cash flow advantage if the ground rent is not paid until the end of the financial year. This advantage to the developer tenant should be reflected in the terms of the original deal when it is struck. Alternatively if a number of occupational tenants are late in paying rent this may be to the disadvantage of the sub-tenant as payments may have to be made to the landlord without funds being available.

It is preferable for the rent from the occupational sub-tenants to be receivable before the ground rent is payable to the landlord. If the parties find that the timing of rental payments is a point that is preventing the sale and leaseback being finalised the rental income can be paid into an interest bearing account with interest being treated as part of the rental income. If the landlord is concerned that rents received from sub-tenants after the quarter day (in the case of a side-by-side leaseback) will not count for sharing purposes it is possible for the calculation to include all those rents that have been received after, but should have been received before the day.

Management during the term of the lease

The lease to the developer tenant will contain clauses that emphasise the importance of maintaining the property and maximising returns to both parties. Typically the tenant will covenant to maximise the rental income from the sub-tenants (backed up by a reasonable endeavours clause) and to always ensure that the property is occupied by sub-tenants with an arms-length relationship with the tenant. If the developer tenant, or a closely associated company, was to be allowed to occupy it may do so at a concessionary rent. It would be expected that the fund, as landlord, would approve the present managing agents and any change in the managing agents, and the tenant would also covenant to submit quarterly income and management reports to the landlord.

Letting policy

The fund would be concerned that the terms of the occupational tenancies complied with its requirements. The fund and the developer would therefore agree on a formal policy, which would cover such items as the length and terms of the occupational tenancies, rent reviews, rent-free periods, and service charge provisions together with annually agreed service charge budgets.

Underletting of part or whole

It would be usual for the tenant to be able to assign its interest in the property as it may be needed for financial reasons. This might be a major problem for the fund as the landlord, as an unsuitable assignee might downgrade the property. Rights would be reserved to approve the assignee so that only substantial and experienced companies could be considered although the risk to the landlord can never be completely eradicated. Underletting of the whole is normally prohibited unless it is with no premium and at an open market rent. The landlord would not want a complex structure of further rent-sharing leases to be created as its management powers would become diluted. Underletting of part is normally allowed.

With a sale and leaseback the lease to the developer will be a long one of up to 150 years. This brings it within the scope of the Landlord and Tenant Act 1927, for if the term of a 'building' lease is for 40 years or more the tenant is able to underlet without the consent of the landlord except in the last 7 years of the lease. The conditions are contained in Section 19 (1) (b) of the 1927 Act and it is therefore prudent for the landlord to insert clauses in the lease that would require the developer to comply with an underlettings policy or impose a criterion to define an acceptable underlessee.

Rent under the lease

In the case of a top slice leaseback the tenant will be guaranteeing the return to the landlord on the basis of a percentage of rents receivable. A bank account would be opened in the names of both landlord and tenant and all rent would be paid into it. Depending on the definition of rent in the lease, the landlord's rent (subject to agreed deductions) will be paid and what remains would be paid to the tenant. The rental income payable to the landlord would normally include rents, licence fees or interim rents paid by any sub-tenant together with any sums received by the tenant in respect of surrenders, rent insurance, damages and interest on late payment of rent. Any charges made by the tenant for the management of the property would not be included in the definition of rental income.

If a fund, as landlord, has the benefit of a long lease and is receiving rent as a percentage of the rent received or receivable by the tenant, it is important that there is no uncertainty in the figure to which the percentage is applied. There are a number of events that would be covered in the lease and that would require an assumed rent to be substituted for the passing rent. The most likely occurrences are if the tenant lets part of the property for a premium at a low rent or if for some reason the tenant lets at a figure below market rent. Should the tenant agree to a concessionary rent to a sub-tenant or if a rent review is missed and time is deemed to be of the essence, a market rent would normally be substituted and this would be an option available to the landlord. It is possible that the rent payable is above prevailing market rents and if the landlord is restricted to the latter there would be a loss of rental income.

Major refurbishment or redevelopment

With a lease of up to 125 or 150 years, redevelopment or refurbishment will become an issue. Major expenditure is very much a live issue with rent-sharing leases and where a local authority is the ground landlord and a fund is the long lessee, the local authority will be unable to contribute to the refurbishment costs. This situation is dealt with in Chapter 7. With a rent-sharing lease where the landlord is a fund and the long lessee a developer, it is unusual for any partner to be obliged to contribute to the costs of redevelopment. The lease will normally provide for the partner making the financial contribution to benefit by additional rental income from the property. If it is assumed that the fund chooses not to contribute to the redevelopment expenditure, the new percentage of rent payable to the landlord could be calculated by the following formula.

New percentage

$$= \frac{\text{Value of the landlord's interest in the undeveloped property}}{\text{Value of the undeveloped property} + \text{development costs}} \times 100$$

If a number of refurbishments or redevelopments take place, there is a possibility that the landlord's rental income will become progressively lower – it is therefore usual for there to be a minimum rent below which the landlord's rent cannot fall. The redevelopment clause is likely to be lengthy as it will have to cover all the terms used, such as development cost, as well as providing a means of arriving at a fair valuation of the undeveloped property and the landlord's interest. An arbitration clause will be required if the parties fail to agree to these important provisions.

Capitalised sale and leasebacks

Sale and leasebacks as described earlier have tended to be replaced, except in special situations, by capitalised arrangements where a developer will carry out a scheme and depart with a lump sum profit rather than retain a leasehold interest and take a flow of rent as profit. This has advantages for both developer and fund. The developer is not left with an unsaleable leasehold interest and the fund has control of the building and its tenants as a competent landlord and can enjoy all the rental growth in the future.

Using the figures from Example 6.2, the financial position of the parties can be summarised in Example 6.4. The developer's share of the rent is capitalised at a higher rate in comparison with the all risks yield. This reflects the highly risky nature of the developer's position should the fund not take a surrender of the ground lease with its small profit rent when compared with the rent guaranteed to the freeholder. It is assumed that the fund would require an initial return of 7%, which is the same as that used for the top slice leaseback although it could be argued that the fund is in a more favourable and less risky position in comparison with the top slice leaseback and a slightly lower yield could be used. The developer's share of the rent is calculated as a top slice. In reality it is likely that the developer would be able to negotiate an additional guaranteed fee for managing the project during the development period.

Example 6.4 Capitalised leaseback

Amount of short-term monies lent by the fund	£59m
Initial return required by fund	7%
Initial rental income required by fund	
£58m × 0.07	£4.06m pa
Rent from scheme	£5m pa
Developer's profit rent	£0.94m pa
Fund purchases developer's rental share @ 8% perpetuity	12.5
Capital profit for developer	£11.75m
Fund's final position	
Short-term monies lent	£59m
Purchase of developer's share of rent	£11.75m
Total cost to fund	£70.75m
Rental income from scheme	£5m pa
Initial return to fund	7.06%

Theoretically the developer has surrendered a leasehold interest for a consideration of £11.75m in Example 6.4. In reality the developer has acted as project manager for the fund and has earned a fee for doing so. It will be noted that the fee is 19.91% of the total development cost. Any smaller percentage than this would be unlikely to commend itself to the fund when the financial deal is being negotiated as the developer's profit would not be great enough either to form a proper incentive or to give the fund much protection from the risks of being involved with a development scheme. In any case, 19.91% is marginal. The scheme must be profitable enough to allow the fund to achieve its minimum acceptable return and provide the developer with a reasonable profit, usually taken to represent 20% of the cost. It is this profit that would be used first if problems are encountered with the project and extra costs are needed.

Profit erosion with priority yield

The relationship between long-term funder and developer where the developer's rental shares are capitalised has evolved into a method known as 'profit erosion with priority yield'. The developer becomes the facilitator of the scheme and effectively acts as the project manager for the fund. If

Chapter 6

the developer achieves a rental income from the occupational tenants that exceeds the minimum return demanded by the fund (the priority yield) the extra rent is capitalised and some of the extra capitalised profit will be paid to the developer. The level of the fund's priority yield will depend upon the fund's perception of the quality of the scheme and the risks it will carry, the status of the developer, and wider matters such as macro-economic conditions. The developer will normally be paid a guaranteed fee, which is regarded as part of the development cost in addition to the incentive fee based on a capitalised rental top slice. All these matters, together with the way in which the top slice rental income is to be capitalised, will be negotiated between the parties and their respective advisers. Although the funding transaction will provide both short- and long-term funds for the developer, and is done at arms length, the fund is only likely to wish to enter into this sort of financial arrangement with a developer who is both known and trusted.

The developer is incentivised to produce the highest rental income possible from the occupational tenants. If the property is 100% pre-let before the funding is in place there is little opportunity for the developer to exercise letting skill to maximise rent. Profit erosion with priority yield is best suited to shopping centres in a rising market where a developer can achieve high rents having agreed a priority yield with the fund. A developer involved with a typical shopping centre will pre-let the anchor stores and let the remaining shop units during the course of the development. If there is strong rental growth this type of scenario is suited to profit erosion priority yield. The outline residual appraisal that has provided the basic information to illustrate the funding calculations in Examples 6.1 to 6.4 is a fairly realistic example of a scheme that would be funded by profit erosion with priority yield and can be used to theoretically illustrate the use of this type of funding.

Example 6.5 Profit erosion with priority yield

It is assumed that the rent achieved from the scheme is £5.85m per annum although when the funding arrangement is agreed, the estimated rental value was £5m per annum. The developer can negotiate a guaranteed fee as part of the deal and it is assumed that the guaranteed profit is £5m. The fund will probably acquire the freehold of the land early in the project on the assumption that the developer has acquired the site. In this case the guaranteed profit would represent the price paid by the fund for the land. As this is regarded as a part of the short-term funds drawn down by the developer from the fund, the lower it is the higher will be the incentive fee payments when the whole of the building is completed and let. This type of arrangement requires many items to be negotiated. The developer, having agreed the amount of the guaranteed fee, will also have to negotiate the way in which the income over and above the fund's 'priority yield' is capitalised. The fund will state its 'priority yield', which is its minimum acceptable level of initial return and should properly be regarded as a priority return. The usual method of capitalising the developer's rent above the fund's priority return is to calculate it in a series of tranches. As the developer produces higher and higher rents so the incentives are

Example 6.5 Profit erosion with priority yield (*Continued*)

increased. The outline residual appraisal will be used with the rent altered to reflect the rental growth that is assumed to have occurred in the development period. For the sake of simplicity all figures other than rent have been left as the original example. It is assumed that the fund's priority yield would be 1% above the all risks yield used in the appraisal to reflect the risk involved with its involvement with a development scheme.

Amount of short-term monies lent by the fund	£59m
Add developer's guaranteed fee	£5m[1]
Total monies lent by fund	64m
Minimum rental return required (priority yield)	7%[2]
Minimum rent required (£59m × 0.07)	£4.48m pa
Rent from scheme	£5.85m pa

[1] The developer's guaranteed fee is put at £5 000 000 and this is negotiated between the developer and the fund. It is often the land cost if the developer has already purchased the site and now sells it to the fund. If the developer is confident about achieving rental levels above those stated in the original appraisal, this fee will be lower as a result.

[2] The fund's priority yield is put at 7% as it is assumed that the fund would require a margin of 1% above the all risks yield. The extent of the margin will depend upon the fund's opinion of the risks it is carrying in comparison with the purchase of a standing investment. The fund will wish to see the developer with a healthy profit from the scheme as it is the developer's incentive fee payments that effectively hedge the risk for the fund.

Additional profit to developer is calculated in tranches of rent and then capitalised.

Tranche 1

50% of the amount by which net annual rent[3] shall exceed 7% but not 8% of the fund's expenditure

$$8\% \times £64m = £5.12m$$

$$7\% \times £64m = £4.48m$$

Excess rent £0.64m

Take 50% × 0.5

Tranche 1   £0.32m

[3] The various tranches of additional rent above the fund's priority yield are shared between the fund and the developer but as the rents increase the developer is awarded an ever-growing share. The top tranche of rent above 9% of the fund's short-term financial commitment is awarded in its entirety to the developer and then capitalised. The term 'net annual rent' will be precisely defined in the agreement between the fund and the developer. It will normally ignore any rent-free periods or concessionary rents.

Chapter 6

Example 6.5 Profit erosion with priority yield (*Continued*)

Tranche 2

75% of the amount by which net annual rent shall exceed 8% but not 9% of the fund's expenditure

$$9\% \times £64m = £5.76m$$
$$8\% \times £64m = £5.12m$$

Excess rent	£0.64m
Take 75%	× 0.75
Tranche 2	£0.48m

Tranche 3

100% of the amount by which net annual rent shall exceed 9% of the fund's expenditure

Net annual rent	£5.85m pa
9% × £64m	£5.76m pa
Excess rent: Tranche 3	£0.09m pa

Total incentive fee payments

Tranche 1	£0.32m
Tranche 2	£0.48m
Tranche 3	£0.09m
Total	£0.89m
Capitalised at 6%[4]	16.66
	£14.82m
Fund's final financial position	
Amount of short-term monies lent	£59m
Developer's guaranteed fee	£5m
Developer's incentive fee payments	£14.82m
Total expenditure by fund	£78.82m
Initial rental income to fund	£5.85m pa
Initial return to fund	7.42%

[4] The rate at which the tranches of rent are capitalised will be negotiated between the developer and the fund. The figure of 6% is used as it is the all risks yield and as such reflects the capital value of the slice of income. As the tranches are effectively top slice income, the developer might argue that they should be capitalised at a lower rate to reflect the willingness of the developer to accept the risk involved by reducing the guaranteed fee. This becomes even more convincing when the capital value of the scheme is calculated using the new rental income of £5.85m per annum. At an all risks yield of 6% the gross development value (GDV) is £97.52m (YP 16.67 × £5.85m) and conventionally a developer would expect a development profit of 20% of GDV, which in this case is £19.50m. In Example 6.5 given earlier, the developer earns a total of £19.82m (£5m + £14.82m), which effectively means that £0.32m of profit is accepted for the risk of carrying a substantial top slice, which is then capitalised. A good case for additional development profit could be made although the fund is only receiving 0.42% over its priority yield. The solution here may be to increase the developer's guaranteed fee payment.

There are many alternative methods of calculating the developer's incentive profit. One such alternative method of calculating this profit is as follows.

$$(M \times (N \times P) + (M \times \tfrac{1}{2}(Q \times P)) - R$$

where

$M =$ the capitalisation factor; in this case, 16.66 reflecting a yield of 6%

$N =$ the rental income from the premises divided by the net internal area (assumed to be 3622 m^2) up to the amount of the fund's priority yield

$P =$ the net internal area of the building assumed to be 3622 m^2

$Q =$ the rental income per square metre above the fund's priority return

$R =$ the development cost

Putting the figures from Example 6.5 into the formula gives the following result:

$$16.66 \times (£1,237 \times 3,622) + (16.66 \times \tfrac{1}{2}(£378 \times 3,622)) - £59m$$

$$16.66 \times £4.48m + 16.66 (0.5 \times £1.37m) - 59m$$

$$£74.63m + £11.41m - 59m = £27.04m$$

The fund's financial position is as follows:

Amount of short-term monies lent	£59.00m
Developer's fee payments	£27.04m
Total cost	£86.04m
Rent from scheme 5.85m	

$$\text{Initial return to fund } \frac{5.85}{86.04m} = 6.80\%$$

By multiplying rent producing areas of the building by firstly the rent that reflects the priority yield, and secondly the rent over and above the priority yield the developer is obliged to produce the net floor area that the parties have agreed. If the building is smaller than agreed the developer's profit will be lower as a result. In comparison with the previous method of calculating a profit erosion arrangement this method brings rent producing areas into the formula rather than relying on lump sum rental income. Neither is the developer's profit adequate nor is the fund's return. In this case, as in the previous example, the developer's incentive is very crude. Investment quality, a vital factor for fund investment, does not depend only upon maximising initial rent and net internal area.

Timing

The profit erosion priority yield arrangement discussed earlier will only be legally concluded when the development scheme is complete. Initially the developer will prepare a business plan that will be considered by the fund and its advisers. This will propose criteria for the provision of short- and long-term funds with the developer usually putting in some initial equity. The business plan will include a development appraisal, which will contain an estimated rental value as well as dealing with such matters as concessionary rents for major anchor tenants.

The developer will usually seek a 'package deal' with the fund with short- and long-term monies provided at an agreed rate. Short term in this context refers to funds used for site purchase, development and letting whereas long term is the rate at which the fund will capitalise the developer's rental share to arrive at a capital profit. In the case of profit erosion priority yield, there are a number of matters to be negotiated and agreed. The amount of the developer's guaranteed fee, the short-term rate of interest and the way in which the rent above the priority yield is shared and capitalised will all have to be decided. During the development period the developer will be the contracting employer but the design team and the contractor will sign collateral warranties with the long-term funder. The fund may well take possession of the site early and the developer will occupy it during the development period under licence. When the project is completed and let the fund will take formal possession of the property as landlord and the developer will depart with a guaranteed and incentive fee, so long as rents have exceeded original expectations.

Funding structure

Where an institution is involved with a profit erosion/priority yield arrangement with a developer it is usual for the developer to provide some equity that is spent early in the project. The remainder of the development finance is provided by the fund and attracts interest as it is drawn down. The interest payments are usually calculated using quarterly rests.

Although the primary categories of development funding are equity and debt, there is also a further category sometimes known as junior debt or mezzanine funding. The senior lender would take a first charge on the site and the mezzanine lender a second charge with the developer providing some equity. If the project did not let, for example, the development funding agreement would not be completed, the developer would not receive the incentive payments and the developer's equity would be eroded first. With a development scheme the developer's equity is therefore most at risk, the mezzanine funder next at risk and the senior debt at least risk as it is protected by the first two if and when profit is eroded. A typical funding structure can take debt up to 95% of cost (Isaac 1993) and there are distinct advantages for developers to increase the ratio of debt to equity when markets are favourable with rents increasing, interest rates low and

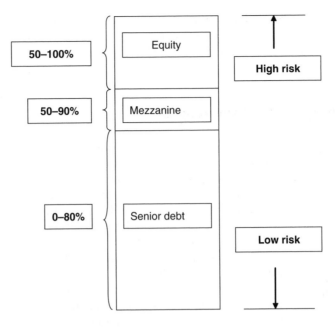

Figure 6.3 Funding structure.

stable and yields falling. A typical funding structure for a project is seen in
Figure 6.3.

Return and yield

The terms return and yield are often used synonymously in the context
of property investment and development. In some cases they are synonymous. For example, if an investor purchases a standing commercial property
investment for £20m less all incidental costs and the net rental income
is £1.2, the net annual return is 6%. A valuer using this transaction as
a comparable would regard 6% as the all risks yield as applied to this
type of property and would value other properties accordingly. However
in the case of a fund becoming involved with a property development,
the terms are not synonymous. With a profit erosion priority yield structure, as described earlier, the fund's 'priority yield' is in reality a priority
return. It is the minimum return on capital employed that the fund is
willing to accept and may well be related to the all risks yield of 6%. In
the example, it is 1% above to reflect the additional risks involved in a
development scheme compared with the purchase of a standing investment.
As the scheme progresses, and eventually completes, the fund will wish
to see the yield applied to the property decline. Indeed when the scheme
is completed and let, the fund would be pleased if the yield applied to
the property for valuation purposes was 5.5% rather than the 6%, which
was the all risks yield at the start of the scheme. The total return, which
includes both capital growth and rental receipts, would increase as a result.

Chapter 6

It can be said therefore that when a long-term equity funder becomes involved with a development scheme the incentive is to maximise return from the scheme and minimise the yield applied to the investment eventually created.

Mortgages and debentures

A commercial mortgage can be secured on the property to be acquired and the mortgage payments to the mortgagee (the lender) will be met by the rental payments made to the mortgagor (the borrower) by the occupational tenants. It is also possible to arrange an interest-only mortgage with capital being repaid at the end of the term as a 'bullet' repayment. This is advantageous if there is an insufficient margin between property returns and interest rates. Some major borrowers will accept, and will find a lender, for deficit funding up to the first rent review when (it will be hoped) increased rental receipts will allow a cash surplus over the mortgage repayments. Any interest payments that are made in respect of debt amortisation (i.e. payments to repay capital borrowings) will be tax deductible but any direct repayments of capital are not. This will influence the borrower's decision whether to seek interest-only or fully amortised debt where capital is repaid during the course of the loan. Other debenture issues will be secured against other assets of the company and in some cases it may be possible to negotiate an equity participation or convertible mortgage where, in return for a reduction in interest rate, the lender will participate in increased capital values of the investment property. The commercial mortgage arrangement can be illustrated by using the outline residual appraisal given earlier.

Example 6.6 Long-term mortgage funding

In this example, it is assumed that the property has let for £5.85m per annum and the all risks yield is 6% (16.67 YP in perpetuity) as stated in the original outline residual appraisal. The GDV would therefore be £97.52m (£5.85m capitalised at 16.67 YP in perpetuity).

Total short-term debt   £59m

Gross development value   £83.35m

Loan to value ratio $\dfrac{59}{83.35} \times 100 = 70.78\%$

The loan to value calculation is important as banks will wish to see a ratio of no more than 70% for the mortgage to be considered (Isaac 1996). In this example, it is assumed that the mortgagee (the lender) is willing to provide funds based on a first charge on the property, which is valued at £83.35m.

Short-term debt   £59m

Assume 20-year mortgage at 9% pa

Example 6.6 Long-term mortgage funding (*Continued*)

Repayments of capital and interest using Parry's

Valuation and Investment Tables (Davidson 1987, p. 154)

Amount in pounds per month to redeem £100 borrowed 1.0338

Yearly repayment of capital and interest

$$\frac{£59m}{100} \times 0.9129 \times 12 = £6.46m \text{ pa}$$

As can be seen, the mortgage repayments per annum exceed the rent from the property even with a term of 20 years. The mortgagor (borrower) can consider two options to deal with this problem of deficit cash flow. An interest-only mortgage can be sought from the mortgagee or the deficit cash flow can be accepted for the first 5 years of the mortgage until the first rent review of the occupational leases results in the passing rent from the property exceeding the mortgage repayments. Figure 6.4 explains these arrangements.

In Figure 6.4 the mortgage repayments over a 20-year period are shown by a dashed line. It is assumed that the mortgage rate stays the same throughout the term although this is very unlikely. A floating rate is probable or the mortgagee can consider the purchase of a financial instrument such as a cap or collar. The conventional mortgage repayment exceeds the rent from the property up to the first rent review (5 years) but is then exceeded by the rent. The required rental growth per annum required for

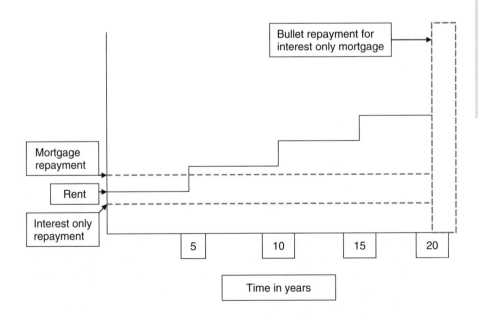

Figure 6.4   Mortgage funding.

the rent to equal the mortgage repayment after 5 years can be calculated as follows:

Rent required	£6.46m pa
Rent at first letting	£5.85m pa

$$\text{Growth factor: } \frac{6.46}{5.85} = 1.104$$

The multiplier of 1.104 reflects a rental growth rate of 2% per annum (Davidson 1987, p. 94). Such a growth rate for a well-located retail investment in stable economic circumstances cannot be regarded as excessive and substantial investors may elect to accept the initial deficit cash flow in the expectation of future growth in rents. Alternatively the mortgagee may seek an interest-only arrangement with a bullet repayment of capital when the mortgage term is complete. As shown in Figure 6.4, this may allow a positive cash flow from the start of the mortgage. In Example 6.5, the repayment for an interest-only mortgage would be £5.31m per annum (£59m × 0.09), which is exceeded by the rent of £5.85m per annum. The capital of £59m would be repaid at the end of the mortgage term but by this time the rent, at a modest 2% per annum compound rental growth, would have risen to £8.69m per annum. At this time the mortgagor would raise another mortgage on a conventional basis and the rent is likely to comfortably exceed the mortgage repayments. The success of such arrangements does, of course, depend on mortgage rates (very much dependent on the level of minimum lending rate) remaining low and stable and the property remaining popular with tenants and not suffering from rent-losing obsolescence. This can be a particular problem with shopping centres and a good example is St Martin's Property Corporation's Drummond Road shopping centre in Croydon. This centre, in spite of its excellent location in Croydon, was redeveloped as Centrale some 24 years after its original opening and this was mainly due to the obsolescence of the design together with local opportunities for an extension.

Profit-sharing mortgages

In the case of mortgage funding described earlier, the mortgagee does not participate in increases in capital value but only receives debt repayment. The developer will therefore enjoy all the capital gains consequent on rental growth over time. A profit-sharing mortgage allows the mortgagee to receive some benefit from increases in capital value. There are two types of profit sharing mortgage, which can be considered (Darlow *et al.* 1994). A participating mortgage will pay a fixed sum to the mortgagee, which will be a percentage of the rental growth of the property. A convertible mortgage allows the mortgagee to convert some of the loan into an equity interest in the property. From the developer's point of view a profit-sharing mortgage means that ownership of the property can be retained with a loan made available at a concessionary rate, and may also mean that the lender will consider granting the mortgage at a higher loan to value ratio than in the case of a conventional arrangement. The documentation will consist of a mortgage deed, which will record matters such as the interest payment on the loan and the conditions upon which the loan is made. There will also be a separate document that will record the percentage increase in value of the property to which the lender becomes entitled and when. A convertible mortgage will state the percentage of the loan that becomes convertible and the way in which the conversion is calculated.

Profit-sharing mortgages have attractions for developers in times of economic slowdown when interest rates may be too high for development to be viable. A concessionary rate for borrowed funds may be sufficient for a developer to survive a downturn on the presumption that property values will rise in the future.

Default by mortgagor

An unusual remedy is available to mortgagees should a mortgagor fail to meet the repayments required by the mortgage deed. This is the appointment of a receiver under the 1929 Law of Property Act (LPA). In the case of default by the mortgagor, the mortgagee would normally be able to take steps to repossess the property against which the charge is held. There may be circumstances, however, where this is not an attractive prospect. The property may require intense management, tenants may be in rental arrears and there may be illegal occupation. A mortgagee faced with these problems may not wish to take direct responsibility and the appointment of a Law of Property Act Receiver (LPA Receiver) as the role is known, is a method of passing management responsibility to a third party (which the mortgagee can nevertheless control) while ensuring that legal responsibility remains with the mortgagor.

Three documents are important in the appointment of an LPA receiver. Firstly the 1929 Law of Property Act, secondly the mortgage deed and thirdly the deed of appointment of the receiver. The powers of the receiver are covered in Section 109 (3) of the 1929 Law of Property Act. The receiver has a general duty to assume control of the property and to safeguard it but is in the unusual position of being appointed by the mortgagee to act as agent for the mortgagor. As such he or she may seek and receive instructions in writing from the mortgagee but must always act in the financial interests of the mortgagor. In effect this normally means carrying out those actions that any prudent property manager would carry out and paying the rental income from the property to the mortgagee until the mortgagor's debts are repaid. Section 109 of the 1929 Law of Property Act is specific about the way the receiver deals with rental income, or indeed any income, received from the property. This must be applied in the following order:

1. to pay outgoings;
2. payments under prior mortgages;

Chapter 6

3. payments of the receiver's own commission on insurance policies payable under the mortgage and the cost of carrying out repairs if required by the mortgagee;
4. interest payments due under the mortgage;
5. paying off principle under the mortgage if required by the mortgagee;
6. paying any residue to the mortgagor.

Receivers may be given further powers by the mortgage deed. These would normally include a 'catch all' clause such as empowering the receiver to 'make any arrangement or compromise that the receiver or the bank (mortgagee) shall think fit'. The receiver would also be able to 'sell, let or lease' the mortgaged property.

The receiver's powers are personal and the appointment (by the mortgagee to act for the mortgagor) would not be to a firm although the receiver would normally be a Chartered Surveyor in a senior position. It is normal practice to appoint joint receivers, typically two partners or directors of the same firm.

An LPA receiver is not at all the same as an administrative receiver and those who are appointed as LPA receivers have to be careful that they do not, unwittingly, become administrative receivers. The problem arises in the case of a single asset company, with a property as the asset, with an LPA receiver appointed to administer the sole asset. In this case the receiver may become the receiver for all the assets of the company and therefore unwittingly become an administrative receiver. A receiver would decline an LPA appointment in this type of case unless the matter was specifically dealt with in the Deed of Appointment. The receiver's fees are covered in the LPA 1929 Section 101 and are stated to be 5% of the gross monies received but the appointment deed may vary this arrangement.

In recessionary periods the appointment of LPA receivers tends to increase for obvious reasons and those appointed have to use keen judgement in undertaking the role. The mortgagor is likely to be in a dire financial position, especially because he or she is an individual rather than a company, and will not be best pleased to be informed that a receiver has been appointed by the lender to manage property on his or her behalf and then pay receipts to the lender. Various ploys may be expected to frustrate the LPA receiver such as accusations made to the mortgagee about maladministration or changing locks that the receiver has just changed. Tenants may be verbally instructed not to pay rent to the receiver. These types of problems may be expected and the receiver must be sure to advise the mortgagee that administration will come at a cost. Legal action may need to be threatened and in some cases action by the court may be necessary. Instructions from the mortgagee may be difficult to elicit, particularly with regard to fees. Neither must it be forgotten that in the absence of anything to the contrary in the deed of appointment the 5% fee stated in the LPA will apply if the receiver is instructed to dispose of a property that is of somewhat higher rate than the fee that could be expected in a normal agency arrangement.

Forward sale or forward commitment

A forward sale allows the developer to secure a commitment to long-term equity funding before a development has been started. It is similar to the profit erosion priority yield structure but is simpler in the sense that the developer is not directly incentivised to maximise rental growth. However in the sense that the higher the rent the higher will be the developer's profit the incentive is still there. The developer would agree a forward sale with a long-term funder perhaps before a site has even been acquired. A business plan would identify the purchase and would include full details of the scheme envisaged. For this type of arrangement to be considered by a fund the property would have to be completely or substantially pre-let and this, of course, restricts or prevents the developer from taking advantage of rental growth in the development period. It is sometimes possible for a pre-let tenant to agree to rental growth increases during the development period based on a mutually acceptable index but the point is that the eventual rent can be predicted with a fair degree of certainty. The long-term funder would be expected to require a return that exceeds the all risks yield applied to the type of property as in the case of profit erosion, as more risk is involved than in the purchase of a standing investment. The developer will require short-term debt finance, and perhaps some mezzanine finance, and may negotiate this with the long-term funder to find an alternative source.

There are therefore two main methods of forward sale and normally these are referred to as forward commitment and full funding with interim finance. The former excludes the provision of interim (short-term) finance whereas the latter provides the developer with interim finance as well as a commitment to acquire the property upon letting. The procedure will require the fund to acquire the site upon completion of the funding contract with the developer, the receipt of full planning consent and the completion of all preliminaries. The developer will then drawdown monies from the fund and these payments will attract interest at the rate agreed. It is sometimes the case that the fund will wish to see architect's certificates during the development period before advancing monies as it is possible that the developer could benefit by drawing down money early and then placing it on deposit. Depending on the interest rate agreed with the fund and rates available in the market the developer could obtain a monetary benefit from a short-term deposit especially if interim finance has been agreed at a concessionary rate. When the scheme is completed, as defined in the funding agreement, the total development cost will attract interest until lettings are complete. At this time the developer will be paid the development profit, which will be the capital advanced by the fund as interim finance, plus rolled up interest, deducted from the capitalised rent from the building at the agreed rate. There is a detailed discussion of the relationship between fund and developer particularly in term of finance, in a later section dealing with documentation.

By entering into a forward commitment the developer will not benefit from any favourable yield movements in the development period. If yields fall in this time no extra profit will accrue to the developer. Using the example of the conventional residual appraisal a forward sale or forward commitment arrangement can be illustrated. It is assumed that the fund would require an initial return of 7% to reflect the risks involved with a development scheme.

Example 6.7 Forward sale

Predicted rent	£5m pa
YP @ 7% in perpetuity	14.29
Purchase price from developer	£71.45m
Sale and acquisition costs (to be met by developer) at 5.2%	£3.72m
Net sum to developer	£67.73m

$$\text{Return to fund} \quad \frac{£5m}{£67.73m} = 7.38\% \text{ pa}$$

Total development cost of scheme	£59m
Developer's profit	£8.73m

$$\text{Percentage return to developer} \quad \frac{£8.73m}{59m} = 14.80\%$$

On the figures given earlier, it is unlikely if the fund would consider the developer's profit adequate to protect its return unless there were particularly favourable economic circumstances with rents rising strongly.

Debt structure

As stated earlier, in certain stages of the economic cycle it will be to the advantage of the property investor to increase gearing. However, it may not be possible to raise sufficient funds to purchase an investment by using senior debt (which will have a first charge on the rental income from the property) and the borrower's equity in the scheme. In these circumstances further funds are obtained using mezzanine finance, which is more risky than senior debt as there is no charge on the property in the case of default. Most property investments will have an element of mezzanine finance as lenders of senior debt will only wish to provide 70–80% of the value of the property as a loan. Therefore, mezzanine finance will typically impose a higher interest rate on the borrower and the annual percentage rate will also be high as a result of fees charged to the borrower. There may also be an arrangement whereby the mezzanine lender will participate in the future returns from the property either as capital or rental value.

A typical arrangement for debt structure is as follows:

Equity	10% of total development cost
Mezzanine	15% of total development cost
Senior debt	75% of total development cost

Interest rate hedging techniques

A borrower will frequently wish a development to be held in a Special Purpose Company (or Vehicle (SPV)), perhaps as a joint venture with other companies. It will obviously be to the borrower's advantage for the lender only to have recourse to the assets of this SPV in the case of default. It is possible to arrange a fixed interest loan but this will be substantially more expensive than a variable rate loan. Obviously if interest rates should fall during the course of the loan the advantage of the fixed rate is negated.

Caps

A cap is a financial vehicle that can be purchased in the form of an insurance policy. The payment of a premium, in effect the purchase of a policy, gives the borrower an assurance that short-term interest rates will not rise above a certain rate during the course of the loan.

Floors

A floor can be used in connection with a cap and may reduce its cost. The lender is provided with a minimum lending rate below which the interest rate charged to the borrower will not fall.

Collars

A collar is a combination of a floor and a cap where the interest rate charged to a borrower will only move between a maximum and a minimum interest rate.

Swaps

A swap arrangement allows one borrower to swap interest rate obligations with another borrower. Typically variable rate may be exchanged for fixed rate if it is in the interest of the parties to do so. A 'Swaption' is an arrangement where, upon payment of a fee, the holder of an option can switch borrowing obligations with another party in the future.

Chapter 6

Drop locks

> This vehicle allows the borrower to lock into a prevailing rate of interest during the course of a variable rate loan. A borrower might, for example, take a loan on an 8% per annum variable rate but the drop lock will be triggered when the prevailing rate falls to 6% at which point the new rate will become fixed for the remainder of the loan.

Bonds and junk bonds

> The issue of a bond is particularly useful for substantial property companies and it is, in essence, a long-term loan. If the company seeking the loan is well managed and funded with a property portfolio in growth sectors, investors may be willing to buy bonds at a discount on the prevailing interest rates with a view to benefiting from a high redemption figure in the future. Deep discount bonds pay low returns to the purchaser in the early years but allow high returns on maturity or some participation in rent review rises for a property investment.
>
> Junk bonds are purchased by investors who are willing to take a high risk with the prospect of big rewards in the future either in the form of high yields during the term of the bond or at redemption.

Other corporate lending

> Apart from the matters considered earlier, other options are available for the property developer wishing to fund a development.

Unsecured and convertible loan stock

> Unsecured loan stock depends upon the attitude of the lending market to the borrower and how highly the borrower's credit rating might be as no security is provided other than the strength of the borrower's covenant. Convertible loan stock (CLS) allows for a debt to be transformed into shares at times predetermined in the loan agreement.

Other investment vehicles

> Some mention should be made of some of the other vehicles available for investors in commercial property.

Property unit trusts

> These trusts are regulated by the Securities and Investment Board and they enable investors to participate in property investment as part of a managed package. There are certain tax advantages for investors in these trusts such as the lack of CGT (capital gain tax) on the disposal of a property.

Real estate investment trusts

Real estate investment trusts (REITs) are available as tax transparent property investment vehicles for investors. Companies can convert to REITS from 1/01/07 and many UK property companies have done so including Brixton Estate, Slough Estates (now Segro) and Hammerson. The attraction of REITs is that almost all of the profits are passed to the shareholders and the REIT behaves almost the same as a property investment company while avoiding the double taxation imposed on investors in property company shares, namely, that tax is paid by the company in terms of corporation tax and again by the shareholder as income tax. A REIT must pay out at least 90% of its rental income as dividends and it must take 'reasonable steps' to ensure that it does not pay a dividend to a shareholder owning more than 10% of the REIT. To convert to a REIT, a company must pay a charge of 2% of the gross market value of its properties.

Limited partnerships

Limited partnerships (LPs) are those that are tax transparent and invest in property. Each partner has liability capped at the amount of investment into the LP and they allow a pooling of resources to purchase substantial investments that would not otherwise be available.

The charge to interest

A loan to a developer whether it is short- or long-term debt from a bank or from an institution as a 'package deal' with long-term finance will attract interest. The most common method of charging interest is by calculating interest each quarter on a compound basis. This means that a developer will take loan with 'quarterly rests' although sometimes banks will calculate interest daily. If a developer takes a loan at a quoted interest rate of 10% per annum charged at quarterly rests, the quarterly compound rate will be 2.4%, calculated as follows:

$$[\sqrt[4]{(1.10)}] - 1 \times 100 = 2.41\% \text{ per quarter}$$

To take a simple example if a developer agrees a loan of £5m with a bank at a quoted interest rate of 10% per annum and draws down £1m in the first month, £2m in the fourth month and £2m at the end of the ninth month, the interest calculation will be as follows:

Drawdown	Total debt	Interest charge at 2.4%	Accumulated debt
£1m		£0.0240m	£1.024m
£2m	£3.024m	£0.0726m	£3.097m
£2m	£5.097m	£0.1223m	£5.219m

Over a 9-month period, the developer has therefore accumulated a total of £0.219m of debt with interest charged at 2.4% per quarter. The calculation given earlier does not, of course, include such items as arrangement fees or other costs that the developer may have to meet as a condition of the loan.

Profit erosion with priority yield documentation

This form of development funding involves the long-term funder providing short-term monies for the development to be carried out and, upon completion, the developer departs with a development profit. Part of this profit will be in the form of a capitalised share of the rent above the fund's 'priority yield', which, as explained earlier, is really a priority return. Profit erosion has many advantages for the fund. It is possible (theoretically) to control the activities of the developer by means of a funding agreement designed to wrap the developer in a straight jacket of legal requirements. The fund becomes the unencumbered owner of the freehold interest save for the rent paying tenants and the developer has an incentive to charge the highest possible rents and this will benefit both parties. Finance agreements come in many different forms, depending on who the fund instructs as legal representative, but all have certain features in common. The fund's rights must be stated with clarity and there must be no ambiguity when calculating the developer's profit or other matters that influence the fund's interest.

The funding agreement between the parties will normally deal with the following matters. Commentary is added as alternatives are often available.

Guarantor

A developer's guarantor is usually included unless the developer is of undoubted covenant.

Approved plans

The agreement defines the important documents that substantiate the relationship between developer and fund. The 'approved plans' are listed in a separate schedule and are evidence of what the developer has contracted to build. At the time of signing the agreement the development will be at a preliminary stage and the definition may be added later when design has progressed. However, it is not possible to have a contract to agree and the design of the building is one area of uncertainty. It is very unlikely that the building will be designed in any detail before the funding agreement is signed.

There will be a procedure within the agreement for further plans, elevations and specifications to be approved by the fund when details are available but the questions that arise are – to what level of detail does the fund approve and how is this approval evidenced? If the fund approves by a representative initialling drawings it must be recorded that this does not imply any technical approval as the integrity of the design is a responsibility that remains with developer, architect and design team. A separate schedule in the agreement will contain all the approved plans and so on, and will also record the fund's approval to all changes sought by the developer. The fund will retain the right to prior written approval to any changes in plans or specifications but this is normally subject to the approval not being unreasonably withheld. As with many aspects of funding agreements the apparent legal protection offered by rights of approval is to a large degree more theoretical than practical.

Development cost

As this type of agreement will provide incentives for the developer if the fund's minimum acceptable is exceeded, the development cost is defined in detail.

The development cost will usually consist of the following:

1. the amount that the fund will pay the developer for the scheme upon completion;
2. construction cost and all professional fees associated with construction;
3. the fund's solicitors' costs both in relation to the property transactions and in respect of general advice given during the course of the development. The developer would be expected to require some sort of cap placed on this figure;
4. marketing and letting fees and the fund's investment surveyor's fee, which will normally be a percentage of the acquisition cost;
5. interest payments calculated with quarterly rests on all development costs but the interest charge will be reduced by any rent received during the development period;
6. any VAT (value added tax) or other tax expended and there will also be a 'catch all' clause referring to any sums expended, which do not come within the categories mentioned earlier.

Maximum short-term finance

There will be a statement of the maximum commitment that the fund will make to enable the developer to build and let the scheme. This will be stated as a sum in pounds sterling. The maximum commitment will not necessarily be the same as the development cost as the developer may be able to negotiate some contingency to offset any potential problems as the scheme progresses.

Building area

The plans and specifications referred to earlier will provide comfort to the fund as it will know what it is committed to take over on completion from the developer. There will also be a statement of the gross and net floor areas of the building to be purchased as a form of insurance for the fund that it is not accepting a building that is smaller than the developer's business plan predicted. There will be a provision for the building to be measured on completion and a full set of 'as built' drawings to be provided to the fund.

Monitoring surveyors

The fund will be represented by a firm of surveyors in all its dealings with the developer and the fees of this firm will form part of the development cost and thus attract interest until completion. When the building is practically complete the architect as supervising officer under the building contract will issue a certificate to the building contractor signifying that all the works required have been completed. The contractor will undertake 'snagging' work in the remedial period (previously known as the defects liability period) and there will be a retention of typically 5% of the construction cost to cover this.

Settlement date

The settlement date is an important time for the developer as it determines when the final developer's profit is paid by the fund. This date will be defined usually as the latest of three dates: the date of practical completion, the date when all the building is let or the date when rent starts to flow from the occupational tenants. The payment to be made to the developer at this time will be calculated on an incentive basis as in Example 6.5 and may or may not include a guaranteed fee. This fee will have been drawn down as a development cost during the development period.

Practical completion

In the standard form of JCT (Joint Contracts Tribunal) fully billed lump sum building contract, the architect as supervising officer certifies that the building has been completed. The funding agreement will make this subject, in terms of the agreement but not the building contract, to the approval of the monitoring surveyor acting for the fund. There will be an arbitration provision usually to an independent architect acting as expert.

Development cost drawdown

The agreement provides the developer with a facility for the drawdown of monies to pay the contractor and others. There will be a procedure for the developer to drawdown the required funds, and the architect's certificate stating that the contractor has carried out the work relating to the cost drawdown will be required. Older types of funding agreement did not contain this provision and there was the danger that the developer would drawdown monies ahead of paying the contractor and gain a monetary advantage by placing the funds on deposit. Modern agreements will often allow for payment direct from fund to building contractor.

There is also a multiplicity of rights reserved for the fund in the standard agreement. These would include rights to approve the following although those marked with an asterisk would include a 'consent not to be unreasonably withheld' condition.

1. all drawings and specifications relating to the development;*
2. any variation to the approved plans* (The 'approved plans' would be signed by the parties and identified as 'approved');
3. the terms of appointment of the architect, quantity surveyor, structural engineer and services engineer* (with any other appointments known as the professional team);
4. the receipt of collateral warranties from each member of the professional team;
5. the sum insured in any professional indemnity policy held by the professional team and the terms of the policies;
6. the main building contractor and terms of the building contract;*
7. the form of building contract (likely to be specified as the standard form of JCT contract lump sum with full Bill of Quantities) and the amount of retention;*
8. collateral warranties and duty of care from building contractor and sub-contractors;
9. date of contract commencement and practical completion. The fund would also approve any extensions of time. The developer would be able to claim an extension of time if the building contract provides one for the contractor but will be obliged to use 'best endeavours' to mitigate the loss of time;
10. the terms of the property insurance and consequential loss insurance;
11. the fund's monitoring surveyors will be provided with rights to inspect the scheme at any time to check for matters covered in the agreement;
12. attendance at site meetings, which will be held at least at monthly intervals;
13. the monitoring surveyors will be provided with all documents relating to progress and site meetings minutes and also all architects' instructions;
14. the right to instruct consultants (in addition to the monitoring surveyors) to inspect or check any part of the scheme. The cost will form part of the developer's short-term borrowings;
15. the developer will remedy any latent defects within a specified time period;
16. developer's marketing proposals and identity of letting agents;*
17. the right to appoint letting agents to act jointly with developer's agents;
18. letting terms. Some older agreements specify that leases will be 25 years but with modern market realities, this is now usually omitted;
19. terms of the lease. A standard form of lease will be appended to the agreement;
20. any general dispute between the parties will be determined by an expert but any dispute relating to the building contract will be determined by an arbitrator;
21. there will be a confidentiality clause binding on both parties;
22. there will be a number of additional minor matters such as the fund's ownership of any items of antiquity found on site and the right to the fund to approve the sign board and its contents.

Chapter 6

Management reality and conflict of objectives

The relationship between developer and fund, as evidenced by the funding agreement, is that the developer effectively project manages the scheme so that the fund takes over a completed building that complies with all the fund's investment requirements. The developer's interest is concentrated on the life of the project and the 'settlement date' will be the end of the project. For the fund, however, the real project (the management of the investment) is just beginning. During the course of the scheme most checks in the funding agreement to protect the fund's interests are subject to the test of reasonableness, such as design changes. The fund's consultants will rarely have cause to deny the developer's request particularly if it is at the behest of a pre-let tenant. In this context the many clauses in the agreement devoted to the approval of changes (all subject to a test of reasonableness) are seen to be little more than an information gathering exercise to the fund and a chore for the developer's consultants.

The developer has an incentive to maximise the rent from occupational tenants and, as stated earlier, this might be to the long-term detriment of the investment. The developer's incentive fee payment, which is received shortly after the settlement date, is built into the agreement and the protection offered to the fund by rights to approve is essentially defensive and subject to the test of reasonableness.

Some clauses in the funding agreement are drafted in absolute terms such as the maximum borrowing limit and the time limit that binds the developer to achieve practical completion by a certain date. If the developer exceeds the cost limit, or is in delay for some other reason than those that the contractor could normally claim for, the agreement will make provision for the developer to be charged with interest calculated on a daily basis on the outstanding sum and other serious measures. The developer, however, is always highly geared with a development scheme. Although there will be an element of developer's equity in the finance structure the bulk of the short-term monies will come from the fund. It is difficult to see what advantage would accrue to the fund if it forces the developer into bankruptcy or seeks to determine the agreement should the developer exceed the cost limit or default in some other way. The fund would then be in a position to take over the development before it is complete and with outstanding commitments to tenants, statutory undertakers and others. For pragmatic reasons it is usually advisable for the fund to allow the developer to complete the scheme rather than take pre-emptive legal steps. If the funding structure has been carefully managed, the developer's incentive fee payments should act as financial protection for the fund as it is the developer's profit that is eroded first should costs increase during the project.

References

Darlow C et al. (1994) *Property Development Partnerships*, Longman, London.
Davidson AW (1987) *Parry's Valuation and Conversion Tables*, Estates Gazette, London.

Isaac D (1993) *Property Finance*, Palgrave Macmillan, Basingstoke.

Isaac D (1996) *Property Development Appraisal and Finance*, Macmillan, London.

Tipping M and Bullard RK (2007) Sale and leaseback as a British real estate model. *Journal of Corporate Real Estate*, **9**, (4), 205–217.

University of Aberdeen and IPD (1994) *Understanding the Property Cycle: Main Report Economic Cycles and Property Cycles*, RICS, London.

Chapter 6

Chapter 7
Development Partnerships and Landowners

This chapter discusses methods for landowners to participate in property development and benefit in a variety of ways. A local authority may own the freehold of a central site where a partnership with a developer would regenerate the town centre. A major retailer may similarly own the freehold of an old-fashioned department store. Lack of funds may preclude a redevelopment but a partnership with a developer may result in a new store as anchor tenant in a new shopping centre. The retailer might benefit from freeing monies tied up in property to invest in its core business and would be able to participate in the development profits from the scheme. With residential or mixed-use development, multi-owned sites will require an equalisation agreement to allow development to take place. Planning Policy Statement 3 (PPS 3) encourages a higher intensity of land use and, in a rising housing market, sites occupied by perhaps one dwelling may be acquired and developed more intensively. The original landowner can again benefit from the development profits created. When discussing the relationship between institutions, developers and local authorities, the emphasis is placed on retail development as this offers the best example of the use of profit erosion with priority yield funding where the developer is incentivised to produce the highest possible rent. The usual way in which shopping centres are funded in the United Kingdom is by a partnership between the three parties mentioned earlier to their mutual advantage. 'If such a thing as a "typical" UK shopping scheme exists, it would probably have a local authority partner providing the site on a ground lease, a major institution providing forward funding and a specialist property company as partner/developer' (Cushman and Wakefield, Healey and Baker 2004).

Methods of site purchase

The simplest and easiest way of purchasing development land is by an outright purchase at an agreed price. The landowner will sell and all the risks of the development will be borne by the purchaser. In another sense, if the land has not been thoroughly investigated by the purchaser and planning consent has yet to be achieved, the landowner sells at the time of greatest risk to the purchaser and the price will be lower than it would have been if the risk had been managed out. The purchase of a site can form the start of a partnership between developer and landowner and can allow the landowner to participate in development profits or receive further monies as land values rise. From the developer's viewpoint any way of pushing the cost of land purchase back in the development programme will be welcome. Most developers are highly geared and short-term interest liabilities will be reduced if the payment of capital monies can be delayed. A number of techniques can be considered to delay site purchase while securing the site to allow preliminary development work to commence.

Options

An option is an agreement between two or more parties to sell land at a future date. The purchaser, usually a developer, has the option but not the obligation to acquire the site up to a future deadline. The option can last for any time but somewhere between 2 and 20 years is usual. The landowner is precluded from disposing of the site during this period and the option is registered on the title, which will prevent further encumbrance of the interest. The option can be related to the discharge of a condition or may be unconditional and the price the developer pays the landowner for entering into the option can be agreed at the start or can be subject to a formula. This formula, if adopted, must be unambiguous, clear and incapable of misinterpretation. The fee increases the longer the option period lasts because, of course, the landowner's actions are severely restricted. If a price is agreed for the land, for example, and land values rise, the landowner will be unable to benefit. In this case it would be expected that there would be a formula for allowing increases in the eventual purchase price.

The option will include the form of land purchase contract so both parties are clear about all the conditions of sale and purchase. If the option is not by deed, money must change hands, and the option will be exercised in writing before the option deadline. Time will be of the essence. The developer entering into an option will require a licence from the landowner to enter the land and there will, of necessity, be a side arrangement to allow both parties to fulfil their various functions during the course of the option. The landowner may wish to enjoy the benefits of ownership while the developer will wish to carry out site investigations and, perhaps, planning and design.

Conditional contracts

A conditional contract obliges a seller to sell and a buyer to buy when a condition precedent is met. As in any normal land purchase all the terms are agreed and inserted into the contract but the land sale is not completed until the condition is met. It is possible to have more than one condition and these may be contracted to be satisfied individually or in sequence. There is a wide range of conditions that can be used including the receipt of outline planning permission, approval of reserved matters, the release of a restrictive covenant, the signing of an agreement to lease for a major occupational tenant, site assembly issues, or the achievement of vacant possession. Some conditional contracts seek to impose the condition of financial viability and this can pose problems as the definition of viability must be unambiguous and understood clearly by both parties. Some consideration will pass from developer to landowner for the landowner to enter a conditional contract and it is possible to have a time limit on the condition being exercised. Time in this case would be of the essence. As the condition to be satisfied is rarely in the developer's control, a strict time limit would be unacceptable but a landowner would require a 'best' or 'reasonable' endeavour clause in the contract so at least the developer will be obliged to make speedy progress to satisfy the condition.

Overage and clawback

These arrangements are discussed in detail later with examples. Some financial deals fall between the two definitions but overage implies that the landowner will benefit from future development profits where these exceed some previously agreed formulae. Clawback allows the landowner to benefit from future rises in land value as a result of the development scheme to be constructed.

In addition to the relationships discussed earlier, the landowner and developer can form a development partnership either by the developer taking a long lease where returns to the landowner depend on rental income from the scheme or a joint venture company can be formed with both parties contributing to its finances. Again these types of relationship are discussed in more detail later.

Partnerships with local authorities

Local authorities form partnerships with developers for a variety of reasons. In some cases local authorities may use developers to achieve the refurbishment of publicly owned housing as with the Haddo Estate in Greenwich, London. This section, however, focuses on local authority relationships with private sector developers and funders in respect of a town centre sites in the ownership of local authorities. Opportunities to create viable commercial development schemes for the benefit of both parties exist.

Local authorities are able to dispose of land and may do so even if the disposal proceeds are less than the full market value of the land. Where the difference between the market value and the disposal proceeds does not exceed £2m the local authority is not required to seek any further consent but if it does, consent is required from the Department for Communities and Local Government (Fisher *et al.* 2006). In some circumstances, but rarely, as land transactions are excluded except under special circumstances, the proposal must be advertised in the Official Journal of the European Union (OJEU). A local authority can dispose of a freehold but the usual vehicle for land disposal is a 125-year lease (Fraser 1993). By this method a local authority can benefit from development profits and has a vehicle to control the developer.

Process

Having identified a site for disposal, expressions of interest are sought from potential development partners. Current practice is for the number of eventual bidders to be limited to four or five (Fisher *et al.* 2006) to maintain competition, give each bidder a reasonable chance of success and ensure that bidders remain, if one or two should withdraw. Local authorities will usually select a closed tender list based on the credibility of those expressing interest. Potential tenderers should be able to demonstrate financial capability and a developer with an established source of institutional finance will be sought. Experience of similar schemes will also be important as will the experience of working in partnership successfully with the public sector in the past. Following completion of a tender list, bidders are issued with a development brief and the invitation to tender for the scheme. The local authority may interview the developers at this stage and there may be a further interview following the tender submission date and developers may be invited to resubmit. The preferred developer will be identified following the submission (or resubmission) of a financial bid and proposed sketch design for the scheme. At some stage in the process but before a final decision is made on a preferred bidder, the public may be invited to comment on the developer's proposals. This invitation takes place in the context of the council's four main incentives for becoming involved with a development scheme. These can be listed as follows (Dubben and Sayce 1991, p. 237):

1. planning and design incentives;
2. maximisation of rate income;
3. monetary profit in the form of a premium and/or ground rent;
4. civic pride and political popularity for the ruling party.

The involvement of the public in commenting on the proposed design of a scheme may or may not influence the eventual decision on which developer to choose. In the case of the Brooks shopping centre in Winchester (a 1980s scheme) the design least favoured by the public was eventually chosen (Dubben and Sayce 1991, p. 237). It must be said, however, that today the Local Development Frameworks, proposed by the Planning and Compulsory Purchase Act 2004 and currently being completed by local authorities, provide explicit statements of community involvement although it is not yet clear whether this will lead to any real influence over the form of the built environment. The process of selecting a development partner is summarised in Figure 7.1 (adapted from Fisher *et al.* 2006, p. 387).

Chapter 7

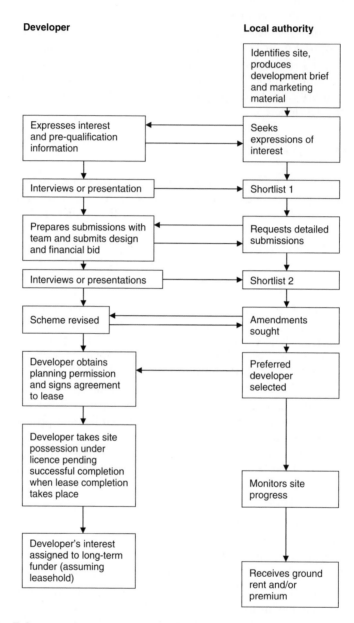

Figure 7.1 The disposal of ground lease on local authority-owned site (*Source*: Adapted from Fisher *et al*. 2006, p. 387).

The development brief

The development brief, issued to those firms selected for the tender list, is an important document as it states the authority's intentions and aspirations for the site. It must be remembered that the development brief will eventually become the agreed design for the scheme, after modification, and will have been produced after extensive consultation within the local authority and will also involve other stakeholders such as English Heritage if historic buildings will be affected by the scheme. The development agreement, when eventually signed, will enable the local authority to control the developer to a far greater extent than a planning consent. A planning consent deals only with planning matters although it is possible to make provision for peripheral planning gain through a Section 106 Agreement under the 1990 Town and Country Planning Act. A development agreement, in reality a contract, will bind the developer to follow an agreed design and is much more powerful as a result. Both brief and development agreement will, however, incorporate flexibility and freedom for the developer to change the scheme usually with the consent of the freeholder not to be unreasonably withheld. This is mainly due to reasons of commercial practicality as developers must react to market realities when it comes to letting and income generation.

Extensive advice to local authorities on the form and content of planning briefs is available through *Planning and Development Briefs: A Guide to Better Practice* (Department of Communities and Local Government, 1997). This publication sees planning briefs bridging the gap between the development plan and a planning application but there is confusion among local authorities about what is necessary and required. A total of 21 different titles are identified. It is noted that in some circumstances, perhaps where a local authority has no firm plans for a site or the existing development plan is sufficient, a planning brief is not required. This is unlikely to be the case with the disposal of a local authority owned town centre site, which is important to all users of the town centre including retailers. The role of the brief in stimulating developer interest distinguishes promotional briefs that emphasise developer interest and planning briefs that state planning policy. A feature of the former is the recognition that there may well be conflict between the 'requirements of the brief and the financial expectations of the local authority' (*PDB* 3.5). A local authority will only be able to dispose of land if it obtains the best consideration available, unless it obtains dispensation from the Secretary of State, and the brief will influence the value of the land and the level of bids received from developers.

The guidance promotes market-based private sector solutions, which are similar to those noted elsewhere in the field of public–private sector relationships. It is reason on its own for preparing a planning brief. The guidance continues to advise that if there is 'healthy demand' and there are no other grounds for a brief to be prepared, the disposal should be an entirely commercial matter. It is noted that market considerations are rarely addressed in briefs but it is also stated that 'planning briefs should not always defer to the local property market' (*PDB* 6.5). Local authorities are advised to use specialist help where, for example, there is intense developer competition for a site or where there is conflict between market conditions and planning policy. In practice, a developer may present design proposals and a form of planning brief with the eventual tender. What may not be present is the strategic control that the local authority can exert before tenders are sought, other than through existing planning documents.

Reasons for preparing a brief may be where higher building densities are sought, or to enable control of general layout and height, scale and massing. Urban design in terms of managing the space between buildings is mentioned with an emphasis on the importance of conservation areas.

Content

If a brief is prepared the content would normally include the following (adapted from *PDB*, Chapter 4):

1. site plan and area of site;
2. reason for preparing the brief and objectives of the brief;
3. status of the brief;
4. existing planning consent; planning status within RDF (Regional Development Framework) and LDF (Local Development Framework);
5. national planning policy guidance, supplementary planning guidance, other area based initiatives, adjacent local authority policies where relevant;
6. physical context (topography, roads, public transport);
7. previous site uses and planning history;
8. ownership, rights of way, restrictive covenants, easements and way leaves;
9. site description (vegetation, configuration, buildings, access and egress);
10. conservation areas, listed buildings, SSSIs (sites of special scientific interest);
11. areas and features to be protected from development;
12. ground conditions, underground service media;
13. possible contamination;
14. access limitations;
15. sensitive uses or buildings on site or adjacent.

In addition to these, guidance would be provided on design factors that had an impact on market demand and viability. A timetable will inform developers of the appropriate response to the brief, which may be a full planning application if the brief is provided in sufficient detail. Details of the range of organisations and individuals who the developer may wish to contact will also be provided when drawing up development proposals. It is also important that local authorities analyse developers' response to the requirements of the brief when tenders are received and it is recommended that the consultants (in-house or out-house) who originally developed the brief should carry out this service.

Chapter 7

The disposal documents

The development partner, when eventually selected, will be invited to sign a development agreement and a ground lease with the local authority. The development agreement will, in many cases, mirror the agreement between developer and fund described in Chapter 6, as the rights of a party remote from the development will be protected.

The development agreement and ground lease

The development agreement and ground lease will, in summary, provide the following definitions, rights and covenants. Terms will vary depending upon circumstances and the nature of the parties, but the following is derived from an actual agreement for a town centre retail development and the matters covered can be regarded in most areas as typical.

1. There will be a number of definitions at the start of the document where such matters as 'approved plans' and 'architect' are defined.
2. The date of ground rent commencement will be defined. Definitions vary depending on the result of discussions between the developer's legal team and the authority's team but a typical definition is the earlier of (a) the completion date of the development ('completion' will be defined) and (b) a calendar date. There will be a multiplicity of caveats attached to the calendar date, which may be extended as a result, typically, of *force majeure*, delays in Compulsory Purchase Orders, redesign necessitated by the requirements by an under tenant, or any other delay occasioned by the local authority.
3. The developer will be obliged to use 'best endeavours' to pre-let the largest units. In the case of the agreement used as an example, the developer was able to terminate the agreement if pre-lets were not achieved by a certain date. This type of clause is wholly unusual and it reflects both the vitally important nature of pre-letting to schemes and perhaps the weakness of the letting market at the time.
4. The developer will occupy the site under licence during the development period and shall proceed to employ a building contractor to carry out the works. There will be the usual rights for the council to approve redesign of the works or change the contractor or member of the design team but these approvals will always be subject to a 'consent not to be unreasonably withheld' clause.
5. The developer will insure the works to the council's approval and will covenant that any archaeological finds belong to the council.
6. The developer may assign for the purposes of raising finance and this would include assignment to an institution.
7. An estimated development cost is included in the agreement and the developer must notify the council if this is likely to be exceeded. This will be important if the council will benefit by a share of the rent higher than a certain return on costs to the developer.

Chapter 7

8. The council will have rights to inspect the works for all reasonable purposes.

9. During the development period when the developer occupies the site under licence the council will receive the 'minimum ground rent'.

10. The ground lease will be granted upon completion of the development and the actual date of completion will be inserted in the ground lease. What is implied here is that when the completion date is known (as defined) the date is inserted but this will not be done at the start of the scheme.

11. There will be the usual clause in the ground lease regarding the service of notices and the manner of council consent. The developer will also covenant to keep the premises (the retail development) in 'good and tenantable repair' as well as remedy all defects. The developer's covenants here mirror the covenants that the developer will impose on the occupational sub-tenants and are evidence of the importance that the council places on the quality and condition of the premises.

12. The lease used as an example contains a lessor's pre-emption clause, which may be regarded as unusual. The council retains the right to buy the developer's interest if the developer wishes to assign the ground lease by any other method than by mortgage. The developer states the price required and the council has a period during which to acquire the interest. If the council declines, the developer can deal with a third party but for no less consideration than the offer to the council.

13. There will be the usual lessee's covenants regarding management, cleanliness and refuse disposal and all these areas will again be mirrored in the occupational sub-leases.

14. The council will reserve rights of re-entry and eventual forfeiture of the ground lease should the developer not pay the ground rent (as defined) within a stated period.

15. The rent reserved to the local authority will be subject to a minimum payment. This will be calculated in a variety of ways but in the lease used as a practical example, it is arrived at in a particularly complex way, which is not the case with most leases. The minimum ground rent, in the example used, is the amount payable by the developer during the licence period and will be calculated by the agreed estimate of annual rack rent less the developer's minimum acceptable return from the scheme. The minimum ground rent will be a percentage (to be negotiated but 80% in the example used) but no lower than a backstop figure, which is also negotiated. There will also be a formula for the lessee to benefit from any rent paid by the occupational tenants, which exceeds the estimated annual rack rent. The formula will allow the developer and the council to share in these uplifts on a pre-agreed negotiated basis.

With a town centre retail scheme it is usually essential, as in the example given earlier, for the anchor stores to be pre-let. The pre-letting of a unit

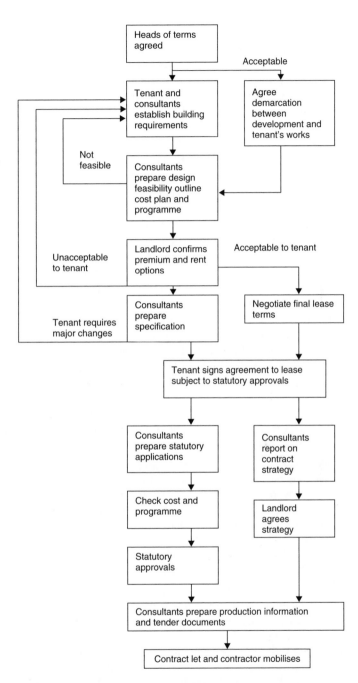

Figure 7.2   Typical procedures for agreeing on the pre-let. Adapted from an original diagram by Colin Mansbridge.

is a time-consuming and complex task especially when the unit is part of a new shopping centre where late changes may impact on the design of the centre. The first step is for the commercial agents acting for the landlord and the tenant to agree heads of terms. These will cover matters such as length of lease, timing, approvals, rent reviews, rent-free periods, service charge contribution and signage. The agreement on the rent to be paid may well be delayed until all the implications of the store design are known and it is therefore imperative that the pre-let process proceeds speedily. Figure 7.2 illustrates typical procedures for agreeing on the pre-let.

It will be appreciated from Figure 7.2 that the pre-let process can be involved and complex as the landlord and tenant negotiate an acceptable specification and lease terms. The developer's consultants will be briefed to provide speedy cost and time implications of the pre-let tenant's requirements, which will naturally be easier to accommodate into the scheme if they are fully agreed before construction commences. As funding may depend on a successful outcome, the tenant is often in a strong position to negotiate a very favourable rental payment but the landlord would be mindful that nothing must be agreed that would reduce the attractiveness of the scheme to an institutional investor.

Example 7.1 sets out one method of a partnership scheme involving developer, local authority and what is assumed to be a pension fund or life assurance fund (the fund). The example can, however, be applied to the relationship with any long-term funder. The figures used then form the basis of further examples.

Example 7.1 Retail development with local authority ground landlord

Firstly a broad-brush developer's appraisal provides the basis for the calculation. It is assumed that the developer is funded by profit erosion priority yield and the development is in a town centre location with recent buoyant rental growth although there are signs of a cooling of the market and it is proving difficult to pre-let the main anchor stores. In a conventional residual valuation the developer's profit is normally taken at 20% of GDV (gross development value) and this is used in the appraisal. Some figures have been rounded up for the sake of clarity.

	£
Rental income	3.50m pa
YP @ 6% in perpetuity	16.66
GDV	58m
Costs of disposal 5.5% GDV	3m
NDV	55m
Construction cost including all short-term interest and fees	25m
Land value including all short-term interest and fees	13.4m
Other costs including short-term interest	5m
Developer's profit	11.6m

Example 7.2 Conventional ground rent calculation

A conventional ground rent valuation calculates the return required by the developer and fund and deducts this amount from the rent from the scheme. The resulting residual is the ground rent for the local authority.

	£	£
Rental income		3.5m pa
Construction cost, etc.	25m	
Other costs	5m	
Total cost	30m[1]	
Development yield		
7% for fund[2]	0.07	
2% for developer	0.02	
Total development yield	0.09	
Rent required for developer and fund		2.70m pa
Residual as ground rent		0.80m pa[3]

[1] The total cost of £30m excludes the land cost as the local authority will receive the land value as a ground rent. Land cost is, therefore, not part of the finance that the developer will have to find to carry out the scheme.

[2] The fund's development yield of 7% can be regarded as a priority yield. It is 1% more than the all risks yield used to capitalise the income in the outline appraisal to take account of the long leasehold interest and the risks of becoming involved with a development scheme. The developer's yield is taken at 2%, which broadly equates to 20% of cost as a lump sum profit. This will of course, in reality, depend on a number of factors–the length of the project, the strength of the developer's position and the buoyancy of the letting market. The developer's rental share would be capitalised into a lump sum profit and paid as such by the fund.

[3] The ground rent of £0.80m per annum is 22.86% of the rack rent of £3.5m per annum. This would be unacceptable to the fund in current market conditions as it would not enjoy sufficient rental growth in the future nor would it receive an acceptably high share of the rent from first letting.

Example 7.3 Ground rent with premium

Funds regard ground rents higher than 10% of rack rent unacceptable and therefore the local authority's excess rent of more than 10% of rack rent is paid as a lump sum premium. It is likely that there would be a guaranteed ground rent to the authority, which would be expressed in money terms, and a percentage of the rent receivable or received by the fund (with the departure of the developer the fund would be the long lessee). Whether the ground rent higher than a minimum is expressed as a percentage of rents received or receivable depends upon the bid from the developer and the relative strength of the party's positions if it comes to an eventual negotiation with a 'preferred bidder' after initial bids have been received. The calculation shows the position with ground rent payable to the local authority in addition to a premium.

Example 7.3 Ground rent with premium (*Continued*)

	£	£
Residual ground rent (from Example 7.1)	0.80m	
10% of rack rent £3.5m × 0.10	0.35m	
Rent to be capitalised	0.45m	
YP @ 10% in perpetuity	10[1]	
Premium	4.5m	
Developer's share of rent from Example 7.1	0.6m	
(2% × £30m)		
Capitalise @ 8% in perpetuity	12.5	
Developer's profit	7.5m	
Funds final position		
Costs		30.00m
Premium to local authority		4.5m
Developer's profit		7.50m
Total cost		42.00m
Rent from scheme		3.5m pa
Ground rent		0.35m pa
Net rent to fund		3.15m
Initial return to fund	$\dfrac{£3.15m}{£42.00} =$	7.5% pa[2]

[1] The excess ground rent to the local authority is capitalised at 10%, which is 1% above the development yield and reflects the returns required from fund and developer. It could be argued that this rent, which is well secured, should be capitalised at a lower yield but this would not take into account the risky development scheme that produces it. The ground rent may well be valued at a lower yield in a conventional valuation but the 10% reflects not a valuation but a development deal based on a risky development scheme. The developer's profit of £7.5m is 25% of the costs of £30m but falls considerably short of the £11.4m profit shown in the outline appraisal on which the figures are based. It is customary, for a scheme to be considered viable, that the developer's profit should be 20% of the total cost, including land cost and short-term interest. Whether or not this level of profit is acceptable depends on the negotiation between developer and fund at the signing of the funding agreement and would be decided on the respective negotiating strengths of the parties and any other incentives that the fund could offer the developer to increase the overall profit. With profit erosion the developer's profit protects the fund's return and it is possible that the fund would agree to increase the developer's return by capitalising the developer's rental share at 7% rather than 8% (assumed to have been negotiated with the fund) so long as its priority yield is still achieved.

[2] The initial return to the fund is 7.5% per annum, which is 0.5% higher than the priority yield. By buying out the developer and capitalising the excess ground rent, the fund has improved its return.

Example 7.4 Ground rent with premium: Developer funded by profit erosion with priority yield

In this example the developer is assumed to agree to a 'package deal' with a fund that will provide both long- and short-term finance. This type of funding offers the developer an incentive. If the scheme is let and the sub-tenants pay

Example 7.4 Ground rent with premium: Developer funded by profit erosion with priority yield (*Continued*)

rent that is over the fund's priority yield, the extra rent is shared between developer and fund according to a pre-determined formula as described in Chapter 6. There is also the possibility that the local authority would be willing to accept part of its return as a capitalised top slice although both developer and local authority would have to be clearly encouraged to agree to this by the top slice being valued at a lower yield than would apply if the slice of income was valued in the market. This type of arrangement is only worthwhile when rents are rising and all parties can take advantage of the increased rent from the scheme during the development period compared with that stated in the business plan. A shopping centre project let to multiple tenants and centrally located with a prosperous catchment is particularly appropriate for this method. Although in the original example rental growth was assumed to be cooling, to illustrate this example, the rental income is assumed to increase to £4.25m per annum as a result of rental growth during the development period. Costs are assumed to remain as predicted in the basic appraisal given earlier.

	£	£
Rental income from scheme		4.25m pa
Costs		
Development cost	30m	
Premium	4.5m	
Total cost	34.5m	
Development yield @ 9% (as before)	0.09	
Initial return to fund and developer	3.105m	
Base ground rent	0.35m	
Total rent before incentive share	3.455m	3.455m pa
Residue to be shared as top slice		0.795m pa
Each party receives 33.33%		0.333
Rent as top slice to each party		0.265m pa

In Figure 7.3 the local authority receives £0.35m per annum as a 'base ground rent'. This rent would be paid as a minimum when the scheme is completed and all under-lettings have been finalised. Alternatively part of the base ground rent could be paid as a minimum of rent receivable expressed as a percentage of rack rent. The remainder of the base rent could be paid as a percentage of rents receivable above a stated minimum. There are many alternatives that a developer could consider when formulating a bid. If the local authority is strongly risk averse it could forgo the top slice in favour of a more secure base rent. The principle of higher risk, higher returns should govern the rationale behind the developer's bid for the site and any subsequent negotiation. The rent from the scheme up to the fund's priority yield, the developer's return and the local authority base rent amount to £3.455m per annum (£3.105m + £0.35m). Only if rental income from the scheme exceeds this level will the top slice profits be payable. The developer's share of rent up to this point and the top slice would be capitalised and paid as lump sums by the fund as would the local authority's top slice rent. Following this method the fund's final position is as follows:

Chapter 7

Example 7.4 Ground rent with premium: Developer funded by profit erosion with priority yield (*Continued*)

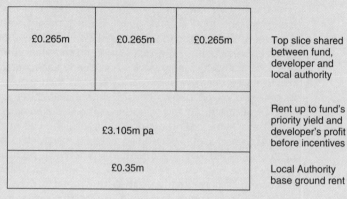

£0.265m	£0.265m	£0.265m	Top slice shared between fund, developer and local authority
£3.105m pa			Rent up to fund's priority yield and developer's profit before incentives
£0.35m			Local Authority base ground rent

Figure 7.3   Rental shares.

Fund's expenditure (assuming buyout of top slices to third parties)

	£	£	£
Cost of scheme		30m	
Premium		4.5m	
Buyout of developer's base profit			
£34.5m × 0.02 =	0.69m pa		
YP @ 7% perpetuity	14.29		
First payment to developer		9.86m	
Buyout of developer's top slice	0.265m pa		
YP @ 6% perpetuity	16.66		
Second payment to developer		4.41m	
Buyout of local authority top slice	0.265m pa		
YP @ 6% perpetuity	16.66		
		4.41m	
Total cost to fund		53.18m	
Rent from scheme			4.25m pa
Initial return to fund		4.25m	7.99%
		53.18m	

The developer's base profit represents 2% of the cost of the scheme capitalised at 7%. The rent up to the local authority's base ground rent, the fund's priority yield (7% of cost) and the developer's base return represent the returns from the three parties until the rental growth in the development period is taken into account. The developer's base rent is capitalised at the fund's priority yield as it has a similar risk profile but the top slice is capitalised at 1% lower to account for the risk accepted by the developer. Similarly, the local authority's top slice rent is capitalised at 6%. The developer's base slice rent (2% of cost) also includes a return on the premium, which is regarded as part of short-term cost. There are many other methods that could be considered and a developer could decide, in discussion with the fund, to offer the local authority a higher premium and keep the entire top slice if rents are rising very strongly.

Comments

The fund had achieved a return of 0.99% in excess of its priority yield although the capital package has risen to just under £50m. The developer receives £14.27m (£9.86m + £4.41m), which is effectively a project management fee with partial incentive. It amounts to 32.9% of the total scheme cost, including land value, predicted in the initial appraisal but if the new rental income of £4.25m is capitalised at 6% as used in the initial appraisal the GDV is £71m rather than £58m. The profit is therefore 20% of the new GDV, which is the standard figure used for the developer's profit in a conventional residual valuation (Darlow 1990, Dubben and Sayce 1991, Isaac 1996). Admittedly the developer is very much at risk in terms of the top slice rent and has a good case for additional profit as a result of this. The local authority receives premiums of £8.91m (£4.5m + £4.41m) and ground rent of £0.35m per annum. The initial premium will be paid at the end of the developer's licence period on site and the time will be defined in the ground lease. The top slice will be paid when the scheme is fully let. The ground rent is well secured as it amounts to 8.23% of the rack rent of £4.25m per annum. If capitalised at 5.5% (slightly under the all risks yield of 6%) the capital value that the authority has put into the scheme can be compared with the market value of the site as follows:

	£	£	£
Premiums received			4.50m
			4.41m
Ground rent		0.35m pa	
YP @ 5.50% in perpetuity		18.18	
Value of ground rent			6.36m
Total value of rent and premiums			15.27m
Outline Residual Valuation			
Rent from scheme		4.25m pa	
YP @ 6% in perpetuity		16.67	
GDV		70.85m	
Costs of disposal 5.5%		3.90m	
NDV		66.95m	
Expenditure costs			
Construction cost	£25m		
Other costs	£5m		
Total cost	30m		
Developer's profit 20% GDV	14.17m		
Total cost		44.17m	
Gross land value		22.78m	
PV £1 for 2 years at 9%		0.842	
Net land value			19.18m

Chapter 7

From the analysis given earlier, therefore, it would appear that the local authority has put £19.18m of land into the scheme for a capital return equivalent to £15.27m.

Comments

1. A residual valuation values a site by capitalising occupational rent at an all risks yield that would apply to the building if it existed today. Costs are then deducted including a standard 20% of GDV for developer's profit. When ground rents are capitalised to arrive at a land value, the valuation reflects the additional security where ground rent is well covered by rack rent. This should mean that cap- italising the local authority's ground rent should result in a higher site value than a residual valuation. In the calculation given earlier, the financial arrangements do not appear to favour the local author- ity unless there are additional unseen benefits such as Section 106 contributions.

2. The timing of the calculation of ground rent can disadvantage a local authority. The developer will tender for the scheme and may, as discussed earlier, become the preferred bidder for the scheme. Negotiations then take place to agree the details of the scheme. If the local authority agrees to ground rent and premiums too early, and the rental market is rising strongly, the avoidance of risk will come at a high cost as no benefit is received from the additional value created by higher rack rental levels. Example 7.3 does allow the local authority to benefit from rental growth but, on the figures as calculated, the benefits could be greater.

Example 7.5 Ground rent with premium and clawback above minimum returns to developer and fund

A variation of the arrangement described in Example 7.4 assumes full disclosure of development cost by the developer and fund and allows the authority to benefit from rises in site value. As part of the deal the parties would agree to a maximum development cost with the local authority receiving an additional capital sum on completion of the development should the level of rent exceed that predicted in the developer's bid for the site. It is assumed, as before, that the developer's bid for the site predicts occupational rents at £3.5 per annum. It is also assumed that the cost of £30m is that predicted at the time of the bid but both rent and cost in reality turn out at £4.25m and £32m, respectively. It would be necessary for a maximum cost to be agreed upon by the developer and local authority in addition to a formula for arriving at the authority's extra profit, related to increased land value, when the scheme is completed.

In Example 7.1 the land value, including interest and fees was £13.40m but we will make the assumption that developer and local authority have agreed that the bare land value at the time of the bid is £8.75m and the developer

Example 7.5 Ground rent with premium and clawback above minimum returns to developer and fund (*Continued*)

has agreed that the authority will receive 70% of any increase of land value over this figure up to the completion of the scheme. The maximum cost is agreed at £33m. The fund will receive its priority yield up to that level of cost and the developer its return before any top slice profit share. Any top slice income will be shared equally by fund and developer with the developer's slice being capitalised and paid by the fund allowing the developer to depart with a lump sum profit. The land value uplift will be arrived at by taking the proportional increase in occupational rent at first letting (using the definition in the development agreement) compared with that predicted in the developer's bid for the site.

	£	£
Rental income from scheme		4.25m
Development cost	32m	
Premium	4.5m	
Clawback		
$\underline{£4.25m} = (1.21 \times £8.75m) \times 0.7$	7.41m	
£3.5m		
Total cost	43.91m	
Development yield @ 9% (as before)	0.09	
Initial return to fund and developer		3.95m pa
Residue to be shared as top slice		0.30m pa
Developer and fund receive 50% each		× 0.50
Rent as top slice to developer and fund		0.15m pa

The deal is shown in diagrammatic form in Figure 7.4.

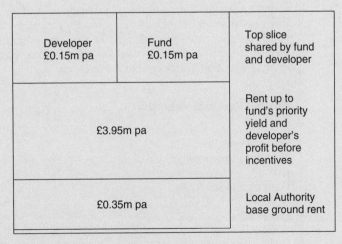

Figure 7.4 Rental shares with clawback.

Example 7.5 Ground rent with premium and clawback above minimum returns to developer and fund (*Continued*)

The fund's final position is as follows:

	£	£	£
Fund's expenditure (assuming buyout of developer's top slice)			
Cost of scheme			32m
Premium			4.5m
Clawback payment			7.41m
Buyout of developer's base profit			
£43.91m × 0.02	0.88m		
YP 7% perpetuity	14.29		
First payment to developer		12.58m	
Buyout of developer's top slice	0.15m		
YP @ 6% in perpetuity	16.66		
Second payment to developer		2.50m	
Total cost to fund of developer's capital profit			15.08
Total cost to the fund			58.99m
Rent from scheme			4.25m pa
Less ground rent			0.35m pa
			3.9m

Initial return to fund $\dfrac{£3.9m}{£58.99m}$ = 6.61%

By agreeing on the clawback arrangement the fund has reduced its initial return and is below the priority yield. However the initial ground rent at only 8.23% of the occupational rent at first letting is an acceptable gearing and allows the fund to enjoy most of the rental growth from the scheme in the future. The developer's profit amounts to £15.08m and if this is compared with the costs of £32m and the original land value, fees and interest at £10m, it is seen that the developer has earned a capital profit of 35.90% of cost, which appears more than acceptable for the developer. A slightly different picture emerges however if the land value is recalculated using the outline residual valuation from Example 7.4 updated.

Outline Residual Valuation

	£	£
Rent from scheme		4.25m pa
YP @ 6% in perpetuity		16.67
GDV		70.85m
Costs of disposal 5.5%		3.90m
NDV		66.95m
Expenditure		
Costs	32m	
Developer's profit 20% GDV	14.17m	
Total cost		46.17m
Gross land value		20.78m
PV £1 for 2 years at 9%		0.842
Net land value		17.49m

Example 7.5 Ground rent with premium and clawback above minimum returns to developer and fund (*Continued*)

The net land value of £17.49m can be compared with the value of the land that the authority has put into the scheme based on the financial arrangements with developer and fund. The authority has received a premium of £4.5m and a clawback payment of £7.41. The well-secured ground rent of £0.35m per annum can be capitalised in a valuation at 5.5%, slightly less than the all risks yield, to reflect the lack of risk in comparison with the fund's rental income. The value of the land in the scheme and that provided by the local authority is therefore the total capital sum of £11.91m (£4.5m + £7.41m) received from premium and clawback plus the capitalised ground rent of £6.36m (£0.35m capitalised at 5.5%: YP 18.18). The total site value derived from capitalising the local authority's various receipts is therefore £18.27m (£11.91m + £6.36m).

The financial arrangement with clawback appears to be a far more acceptable deal for the local authority and the developer's profit is also £0.91m (£15.08m–£14.17m) above the standard figure from the residual valuation. The local authority has achieved the equivalent of £0.6m above the value of the land based on rents of £4.25m per annum. However, the fund has seen its return reduced in comparison with the deal without clawback and has not achieved its priority yield.

Analysis of bids from the local authority's viewpoint

What appears to be an attractive bid from a developer may, on closer inspection, appear less attractive when future costs and income are considered. Example 7.1 will be used to illustrate the potential problem. It is assumed that the ground rent from the scheme is £0.35m per annum and the premium offered is £4.5m as in Example 7.2. Let us assume that the authority has received two bids for the opportunity outlined in Example 7.2.

Example 7.6 Bid from developer A

This bid assumes that rent and building cost will remain static during the development period.

	£	£
Estimated rental value		3.5m
Development cost	25m	
Other costs	5m	
Total cost	30m	
Development yield @ 9%	0.09	
Rent required by fund and developer		2.7m

Chapter 7

Example 7.6 Bid from developer A (*Continued*)

	£	£
Ground rent as residual		0.80m
Maximum ground rent acceptable to fund		
(£3.5m × 10%)		0.35m
Rent to be capitalised as premium		0.45m
Capitalisation rate YP 10% in perpetuity		10
Premium to local authority		4.5m
Local authority return to equity	0.8m =	22.86%
	3.5m	

This bid shows a 22.86% return to equity if the premium is decapitalised.

Example 7.7 Bid from developer B

This bid assumes that both building cost and estimated rental income will rise during the development period – rent by 10% and building cost also by 10%. This developer requires a higher development yield, 10%, than developer A.

	£	£
Estimated rental value (£3.50m × 1.10)		3.85m pa
Development and other cost (£30m × 1.10)	33m	
Development yield @ 10%	0.10	
Rent required by developer and fund		3.30m pa
Ground rent as residual		0.55m pa
Maximum ground rent acceptable to fund (£3.85m × 10%)		0.38m pa
Rent to be capitalised as premium		0.17m pa
Capitalisation rate. YP in perpetuity @ 10%		10
Premium to local authority		1.7m
Local authority return to equity	$\dfrac{0.55m}{3.85m}$ =	14.28%

Here again the bid shows a return to equity of 14.28% if the premium is decapitalised. The bid appears to be inferior to that made by developer A. The return to equity is lower and the premium and the ground rent are lower.

Example 7.8 Bid from developer A if rents and costs rise as predicted by developer B

	£	£
Rental income from scheme		3.85m pa
Development cost and other cost	33m	
Development yield @ 9%	0.09	
Rent required by developer and fund		2.97m pa
Ground rent as residual		0.88m pa
Maximum ground rent acceptable to fund		0.38m pa
(£3.85m × 10%)		
Rent to be capitalised as premium		0.50m pa
Capitalisation rate. YP in perpetuity @ 10%		10
Premium to local authority		5.0m pa
Local authority return to equity	$\dfrac{0.88m}{3.85m} =$	22.85%

If the bid from developer A is recalculated on the same assumptions made by developer B, it will be seen that the bid from A is even more attractive with a higher ground rent, premium and return to equity. In analysing bids from developers local authorities should ensure that the developer states assumptions regarding rent level and construction cost within the bid as what appears attractive at the initial bid stage might be less so when actual rents and costs are known. It would be usual for developers to state a building cost within the draft ground lease but if cost exceeds that limit, the development return will still be taken on the increased figure.

Refurbishment

Local authority ground leases are frequently granted on town centre retail developments and, as seen earlier, authorities have a number of options available in arranging for the development of their land. At some point into the life of the shopping centre, refurbishment will be required and this may be fairly frequent in the case of shopping centres where landlords have to be mindful of the need to continue to attract tenants in rapidly changing tenant markets. Sometimes refurbishments will be more extensive where a centre, for example, has been constructed to cater to tenants requiring small units just as the tenant market starts demanding larger areas in excess of the standard shop unit. Where refurbishment is required both fund and authority will benefit from the increased rent roll but only one of the parties, the fund, is able to contribute to the cost. Rental shares have to be recalculated at that time. The examples given later set out the type of arrangement that will allow a refurbishment to take place where a local authority holds the freehold interest in a shopping centre and a fund has a long leasehold interest. In the examples given later, it is assumed that a local authority receives a fixed ground rent of £500 000 per annum in respect of a shopping centre and in addition, 5% of any rent above £500 000 per annum (equity rent). This equity rent is assumed to be received on a side-by-side basis and is therefore a percentage of rent received by the fund, not the rent receivable. The full rental value is assumed to be £10m. The authority would have received a substantial premium when the ground lease was originally granted. The calculations show an equitable solution to the need for refurbishment expenditure when rents are also rising.

Example 7.9

	£	£
Authority receives fixed rent		0.500m pa
Equity rent (10m−0.5m)	9.5m	
Take 5%		0.475m pa
Total rent received by local authority		0.975m pa
Rental shares		

Local authority receives $\dfrac{0.975m}{10m}$ = 9.75%

Fund receives $\dfrac{9.025m}{10m}$ = 90.25%

Example 7.10

Assume income from the centre rises to £15m pa. As income rises, so does the fund's share of the rent.

	£	£
Authority receives fixed rent		0.500m pa
Equity rent (15m−0.5m)	14.5m	
Take 5%		0.725m pa
Total rent received by local authority		1.225m pa

Local authority receives $\dfrac{1.225m}{15m}$ = 8.17%

Fund receives $\dfrac{13.775m}{15m}$ = 91.83%

Example 7.11

Assume a refurbishment scheme costing £5m and paid by the fund results in additional income of £0.5m per annum.

	£	£
Authority receives fixed rent		0.500m pa
Equity rent (15.5m−0.5m)	15m	
Take 5%		0.750m pa

Example 7.11   (*Continued*)

	£	£
Total rent received by local authority		1.250m pa
Local authority receives	$\dfrac{1.25m}{15.50m}$	8.06%
Fund receives	$\dfrac{14.25m}{15.50m}$	91.93%

The authority's share of the rent has fallen in percentage terms but has increased in money terms by £0.025m per annum with no capital outlay. The refurbishment has returned 10% but the fund's return on the money expended is only 9.5%. The solution to this anomaly is for the fund to pay for all the refurbishment costs but for the income sharing proportions to be recalculated.

Example 7.12

The fund pays for all the refurbishment costs of £5m and receives all the extra income of £0.5m per annum. The income sharing proportions are recalculated accordingly.

Authority receives fixed rent	0.500m pa
Equity rent (15.0m–0.5m)	£14.5m pa
Take 5%	0.725m pa
Total rent received by local authority	1.225m pa
Local authority receives $\dfrac{£1.225m}{£15.50m}$	= 7.90%
Fund receives $\dfrac{£14.275m}{£15.50m}$	= 92.10%

The new proportion will apply to future rents received from the centre although the authority's ground rent of £0.5m per annum will always be paid in cash terms.

Refurbishment – overall appraisal

Whether or not the refurbishment itself is viable will depend on an appraisal of the centre before and after the proposed refurbishment. The problem here is the necessity to predict a new rack rental value for the refurbished centre as, without this, the expenditure cannot be justified. In the appraisal to justify the refurbishment a higher rental value must be predicted and possibly a shading down of the all risks yield. The calculations given earlier concerning the local authority will come to fruition when the extra rental income is generated and the fund will then see the benefit of the extra expenditure. It may take some time for the new rental value to be established if there are no voids to let and no rent reviews to agree. An investor faced with such a situation may rely on evidence from nearby lettings outside of the centre or in a nearby refurbished scheme for evidence of probable rental growth or may cite rental growth in a refurbished centre in a town of similar socio-economic profile. Perhaps the best way is to deliberately leave one unit empty during the course of the refurbishment and let it some months after the refurbishment is complete. The resulting evidence will be far more valuable in establishing rental evidence than an agreed rent review based on more tenuous evidence. To a large extent, however, because direct evidence is unavailable at the time, the decision to refurbish requires a belief in the health of the retail market and an awareness that unless refurbishment is undertaken rents will probably decline. Any refurbishment will be a project management challenge as firstly the major anchor tenants, the local authority landlord, and the multiples that make up the majority of tenants will have to enthusiastically approve the proposals. This will require persuasive material produced by the investor's architect and publicity consultant as well as an understandable programme showing minimal disruption to trading. Tenants will also wish to be informed of any increase in service charge that may result from the refurbishment, the investor's projected trading figures and footfall for the improved centre. In some cases, it may be possible to link the refurbishment with the launch of a business improvement district (BID) to regenerate the town centre as a whole. The refurbishment project will be appraised by adding the original value of the fund's interest in the centre to the proposed building cost and deducting the resulting figure from the new value of the centre. This is shown in Example 7.13 given later in outline although, in practice, the most accurate method of preparing a financial appraisal of this type is by a discounted cash flow. This would take account of the timing of both the expenditure and the newly assumed rental income as new lettings and rent reviews take place. In the calculation, the value of the improved centre takes into account the deferral of the increased income by a notional 2-year period as it is assumed that existing voids and rent reviews would increase the rent to the new level within a 2-year period. Also to give a true return, any increase in income that would have resulted from market rental increases without the refurbishment should be discounted; but it is assumed that the centre without the works taking place would not experience any significant rental growth. Other figures are taken from Examples 7.11 and 7.12.

Example 7.13 Refurbishment outline appraisal

Pre-refurbishment

	£	£	£
Centre income	15.00m pa		
Rent to local authority			
Base rent	0.50m pa		
Equity rent	0.725m pa		
Total	1.225m pa		

Example 7.13 Refurbishment outline appraisal (*Continued*)

	£	£	£
Profit rent		13.775m pa	
YP @ 6.75% in perpetuity		14.81[1]	
Value of head lease		204.00m	
Add cost of refurbishment		5.00m	
Value + cost			209.00m
Post-refurbishment			
Centre income		15.00m pa	
Rent to local authority			
Base rent	0.50m pa		
Equity rent	0.72m pa		
Total		1.225m pa	
Profit rent		13.775	
YP for 2 years @ 6.50%		1.820[1]	
Term value			25.07m
Reversion to FRV		15.50m pa	
YP reversion to perpetuity			
Deferred 2 years @ 6.50%		13.56	
Reversion value			210.18m
Value of head lease after			235.25m
refurbishment			
Increase in value			26.25m
Return on original value and cost	$\dfrac{26.25m}{209}$	12.559%	

[1] The head lease in the unrefurbished centre is valued at 6.75%, which compares with the fund's priority yield of 7% and this seems appropriate as the priority yield states the value of the income to the fund taking into account the risk associated with the development scheme. The lower yield is used to value the reversion as it is assumed that there is a slight decrease in risk associated with the additional rental income. The return of 12.559% takes into account the original capital value but the return looks far more profitable when compared with expenditure of only £5m.

The problem of high gearing

The various calculations given earlier assume that the fund will find a ground rent that is over 10% of occupational rack rent unacceptable, and this appears to be a truism in the current funding market. Some historic arrangements do however display higher gearing arrangements and this can lead to problems as the investment matures. If voids occur later or rents fall in the future, there can be problems if the local authority's ground rent is reviewable in an upwards-only direction. Where the original grant of the ground lease establishes high gearing, it is prudent for the fund to seek to renegotiate and perhaps pay a lump sum to the local authority, rather than be left with a declining top slice income (Darlow *et al.* 1994). Figure 7.5 illustrates the potential problem.

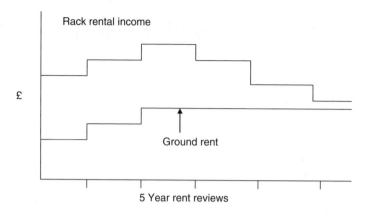

Source: Adapted from Darlow et al. 1994.

Figure 7.5   High gearing.

Examples of partnerships based on clawback and overage

Clawback and overage are methods of paying additional monies to original landowners when a development scheme has been completed. Rather than buy land outright, developers can enter into an arrangement to pay additional profits to original landowners based on either rises in land values (clawback), as a result of the development scheme, or development profits based on an agreed formula (overage). These methods should not be defined too precisely as there are many examples of innovative arrangements with landowners that fall between the two or use one method with some other arrangement in addition. The two examples used later are based on real projects and there are conclusions to be drawn from each. Both involve a department store operator owning the freehold interest in a site and store where the potential exists to build a shopping centre and a new store for the operator. In both cases the operator stands to benefit from future development profit or rises in land value. For reasons of commercial confidentiality the two projects cannot be identified.

Project A

Project A is based on a site currently occupied by an obsolescent department store owned freehold by the occupier. The site is capable of accommodating a new department store and a new shopping centre as it is currently occupied only by the department store, loading yards and outbuildings. The project is located in a prime retail location and at the time the development was agreed, retail rents were rising strongly. The department store company was concerned to complete any new development speedily as it had ambitions to restructure and wished to boost the value of its balance sheet.

Development arrangements

The department store owner resolved to sell the freehold interest in the site to an experienced retail development company. The original owner would then contract to take a lease on the shell of a new department store, which would become the anchor tenant for the new shopping centre that was to be built on the site. When all the shop units in the new development had been let extra profits would be paid to the original owner based on a pre-agreed formula that effectively revalued the site and deducted the original land price paid by the developer. The rent agreed for the shell of the new department store would be part of the rent from the new shopping centre in this formula. The arrangement is a clawback deal with the added complication of the retailer remaining on site as an anchor tenant. The structure of the development arrangements is summarised in Figure 7.6.

Contracts and documents

The main contractual documents were a development agreement between the retailer and developer and an agreement to lease for the new department store. An important part of the development agreement was the specification for the new department store and the new shopping centre. The new department store to be built by the developer was reasonably easy to specify as it was only being built to shell standard but the shopping centre itself proved too complicated to specify in detail in the time scale required, bearing in mind the overall necessity for speed. The department store owner wanted a quick completion of the development as it wished to boost its balance sheet and the developer did not want to miss a buoyant letting market. There was therefore a procedure in the agreement for the department store owner's

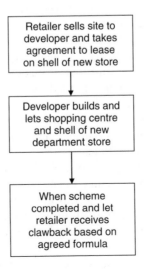

Figure 7.6 Clawback.

Chapter 7

surveyor to approve the details of the specification as these were known. An added complication was that the department store owner's contractor would be on site at the same time as the developer's contractor for the main scheme. As both the main scheme and the fit out of the department store were procured by the management contracting route, it meant that the department store's surveyor had to approve design packages as they were produced by the architect before they were provided to the management contractor. The fit out of the new store had to be coordinated with the main work on site and there had to be a procedure for any variations to be costed and approved. All of these matters were covered in the development agreement and other agreed procedures between the parties.

The development agreement

The development agreement is a lengthy document designed to give the required rights and impose agreed responsibilities on the parties. It is summarised as follows:

1. The sale of the site is specified at a specific date with time being of the essence.
2. The works to be undertaken by the contractor are defined as the plans that formed the planning approval and the agreed specification.
3. The development allowed the department store owner to continue trading on site throughout. There was therefore a time when the store decanted from its original premises into an interim store and then into the new store when the fit out was complete.
4. The net square footage of the new store was specified in the agreement.
5. The net income, which was to be capitalised at completion as part of the clawback calculation, was defined as the income payable from the scheme, including the rent from the new department store, ignoring any rent-free periods or recoverable expenses. Open market rent was to be applied to any voids.
6. The total development cost was defined as the price paid for the land, all building costs, fees, servicing equipment, alterations at the behest of a pre-let tenant and loss of income for any rent-free periods. Interest was added as part of the development cost at a specified rate and at quarterly rests.
7. Those parts of the specification that had not been agreed upon were to be submitted to the store's surveyor for approval, which was not to be unreasonably withheld.
8. The developer had to seek the approval of the store's surveyor in respect of any change in the specification that would cost more than £10 000 but approval was not to be unreasonably withheld.
9. Unreserved rights of approval were given to the store's surveyor in respect of any changes to the specification of the interim store or the new store.
10. Regular statements of account regarding the total development cost were sent to the store's surveyor as the works proceeded.

11. The developer contracted to use 'best endeavours' to complete the works by a stated date and there was also a 'long stop' date when the works must be completed unless the contractor was able to substantiate a claim for additional time under the form of building contract.

12. The certificate of practical completion for both the interim store and the shell of the new store was to be issued jointly by the developer's architect and the store's surveyor.

13. Any dispute in respect of practical completion was referred to a third party acting as expert not arbitrator.

14. The developer agreed to use 'all reasonable endeavours' to give the store's fitting out contractor access to the interim store and the new store when required.

15. The lease term and rent for the new store were stated in the agreement.

16. The clawback payable to the store owners was calculated by capitalising the net income (as defined) from the centre, including the rent from the department store, at a figure that was stated in the agreement. From this figure all of the development cost (as defined) plus the amount the developer has paid the store owner for the land was deducted. The residual figure was paid to the store owner as a clawback lump sum. The clawback calculation is summarised in Example 7.14.

Example 7.14 Clawback payment

	£
Rent from shopping centre when fully let (based on rents receivable with assumed lettings for any voids and including rent paid by new department store)	15m
Capitalised at figure stated in development agreement	12.5
Notional centre value	187.5m
Development cost including shell of new department store, original site cost, all fees, costs of all descriptions, and short-term interest	150m
Clawback payable to original site owner	37.5m

The deal described here can be defined as a clawback arrangement but as the amount of clawback depends on the development profits (rents) achieved by the developer, the clawback can also be seen as a share of development profit that would be classified as overage. There are various disadvantages and advantages in the arrangement from the point of view of the department store owner.

Advantages

1. A new department store is available and money received from the site sale is available for its fit out.

2. The store owner does not have its finance tied up in under-performing property but in its core business where returns should be maximised.

Chapter 7

Example 7.14 Clawback payment (*Continued*)

3. The store owner is able to keep trading throughout the development period and has the benefit of being the anchor tenant in a new (assumed successful) shopping centre.
4. The store owner can (theoretically) quickly agree to the development deal while retaining the right to receive additional land value later.
5. The new department store boosts the balance sheet of the store owner's company.

Disadvantages

1. There is little duality of interest between the parties. The developer will have an incentive to spend as much as possible on the shopping centre until the predicted clawback is used up. Money expended on the centre may have the effect of increasing the centre's value or rental levels, which is only of marginal benefit to the store owner.
2. With a broad-brush specification, and most approvals subject to a reasonableness test, the store owner's surveyor has little power to keep development cost down. The form of procurement, management contracting, allows for design to proceed in parallel with construction, which gives ample scope for the developer's design team to enhance the specification.
3. The store owner has no powers to prevent the developer from selling its interest to an unsuitable third party.

Overage/lease and leaseback

Overage deals allow a landowner to benefit from future development profits. Usually the original landowner will receive rental income above a certain level of return to the developer and this will be on a side-by-side or top slice basis. The example discussed once again involves a department store freehold owner of a large obsolescent store on a site in a prime shopping location. The opportunity to become the tenant of a new store as the anchor tenant of a new shopping centre to be constructed by a developer was available. In this case, a long lease (99 years with an option to extend by another 36 years) was granted to a developer for a premium and when the scheme was completed the store owner received a percentage of rents received by the developer from the scheme, including the rent received from the store owner as anchor tenant. The arrangement can therefore be described as a side-by-side lease and partial leaseback. Although the store owner benefits from the developer's profits in terms of rent, a true overage deal would allow extra payments to the original landowner when rents exceeded a certain return to the developer.

Development agreement

A ground lease and a development agreement together with an occupational lease were the main documents agreed by the parties. The store owner, while retaining the freehold of the whole site, would also sign an agreement to lease in respect of the new department store to be built on site. In this case the developer undertook to provide the store owner with a fully fitted out unit although the retailer would be responsible for a final finishing contract. The cost of the fitting out works carried out by the developer would be reimbursed by the store owner. The agreement provided for the following matters:

1. The developer took possession of the site on licence during the development period and the ground lease was not executed until completion of the centre.
2. A phasing programme was agreed between store owner and developer to allow trading to continue on site during the development.
3. Base plans and specifications were agreed between the parties when the developer took possession of the site. The store owner had rights to approve any variation but this was not to be unreasonably withheld where the proposed variation did not adversely affect the store owner's intended use and occupation of its store and its interest in the scheme as a whole.
4. The store owner was given 20 days to approve any variation or consent was assumed to have been given. If the store owner 'commented' on any variation the developer was to have 'proper regard' to the comment but the words 'and act upon such comments' were not surprisingly deleted from the agreement by the developer's solicitors.
5. Any minor variations were to be given verbal approval.
6. The store owner was given 10 working days to approve any tender packages, drawings or specifications.
7. The ground lease reserved a rent for the department store owner, which was a percentage of rents received by the developer thus making it a side-by-side deal with no income guaranteed for the store owner. There was, however, a minimum rent stated and this is payable from the completion of the scheme when the ground lease is executed.
8. The developer retained the right to assign the leasehold interest but the store owner's right to do the same provided the developer with an ability of first refusal.
9. Little thought was given to the future need to refurbish the centre – only a statement that the parties would seek to agree what to do based on their respective interests.
10. The developer, in making the financial offer for the ground lease, projected rents by 5% pa compound and this reflects the confidence of the developer when dealing with a prime site in benign economic conditions where rental growth seems assured. In fact the projected rents were very soon exceeded by the actual rental values in the centre.
11. Minimum net areas for the new department store in terms of sales areas, storage and office areas were stated in the agreement.

The deal described earlier had advantages and disadvantages for the original landowner.

Advantages

1. There was a clear duality of interest. Both parties benefit from rental growth in the centre and both have an interest in letting to quality tenants.
2. Expenditure on the centre will benefit both parties – the retailer in terms of trading and the developer in terms of value.
3. A minimum rent is received on completion. If required, the side-by-side rent can be sold back to the developer as the monies realised may be better invested in the retailer's core business.

Disadvantages

1. The developer has absolute freedom to assign and this may mean that the store owner has an unsuitable partner in the future.
2. Refurbishment, a frequent necessity for shopping centres, is not dealt with adequately in the agreement.
3. The store owner's freedom to assign is restricted.
4. The store owner has little control over the costs of the new store fit out that have to be reimbursed to the developer.

Figure 7.7 summarises the arrangement agreed upon.

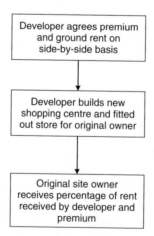

Figure 7.7   Lease and leaseback with rent share.

Equalisation agreements

Equalisation agreements are only usually relevant for large residential development sites with a number of landowners. There has to be a need for the landowners to cooperate and this will be proven by the presence of marriage value, which is present if the combined value of the landowners' individual holdings is exceeded by the value of the site as a whole. A large residential site will have to provide at least 20% of the dwellings as 'affordable' and the local authority's Local Development Framework may require an even higher percentage. The equalisation agreement proposes a method of equalising development revenue and development cost where landowners will benefit from marrying their sites together. There are many factors that have to be overcome in finalising an equalisation agreement. Typically costs and revenues must be applied to the following:

1. type and location of affordable/social housing;
2. location of water treatment plant;
3. location of foul water pumping station;
4. location of electricity sub-station;
5. areas of the site that are sterilised as a result of, for example, flood plain or overhead cables;
6. areas that cannot be built on as a result of house buyer resistance – areas very close to communication masts or main distributor roads;
7. areas suitable for supporting mixed uses such as a neighbourhood centre, doctor's surgery, school, playing fields and play areas;
8. main access and egress points;
9. location of public transport hub and associated buildings;
10. location of any community facilities that may be required in excess of affordable housing in the Section 106 agreement;
11. areas of filled, contaminated or made-up ground where exceptional foundations will be required or extensive site decontamination works carried out;
12. areas of archaeological interest that may not be developed until investigations have been carried out;
13. areas of established woodland with tree preservation orders in place;
14. areas where the topography makes development unlikely to achieve planning consent (e.g. skyline development) or where the slope of the land makes development very expensive;
15. programme and phasing issues.

Types of agreement

There are four basic methods of formulating an equalisation agreement. Firstly, gross rate per acre will base costs and revenues on the landownership areas of each of the parties. This is only likely to be acceptable if the landowners own a site with very few infrastructure problems and established services with no necessity for elaborate infrastructure on site such as water treatment plants. The second method is by pro rata square footage of development to be built on the respective sites. This would need agreement between the parties in respect of the planning application and the master plan for the whole site. The third method is to apportion costs and revenues to different uses and areas. This is unlikely to result in agreement without a watertight master plan as each party would attempt to locate the low value

Chapter 7

uses onto other land holdings. The fourth method is firstly to agree to a robust master plan based on planning policy, eventual planning consent and the most profitable method of phasing and types of housing. Those areas of the site that add value to the whole site would be identified (such as the site for the foul water pumping station) and apportioned equally for all parties and it would be assumed that the land area is also shared between the parties. The remaining land would be valued pro rata to land holdings when the cost of the common infrastructure has been deducted.

Deals with landowners

Increasing development density

Minimum residential development densities of 30 houses per hectare have been promoted through PPS3 (para 47, Communities and Local Government 2006). There is also an emphasis on affordable housing provision (PPS 3 para 22) for development in excess of 15 dwellings and the stated requirement is that 60% of new housing should be built on brownfield sites (PPS 3 para 41). Coupled with a booming housing market over the period 1996–2007, this has led to developers identifying opportunities to redevelop existing housing stock to higher densities. Both house owners and developers can benefit from this feature of the housing market. Example 7.15 below sets out how a residential development to provide higher density housing might work.

The calculation is based on an actual housing scheme that is typical of this type of redevelopment and frequently seen in today's market. A developer has the opportunity to acquire seven detached houses that stand on large plots. Planning consent is likely to be forthcoming for a total of 47 dwellings including 13 affordable homes, which will be sold to a housing association.

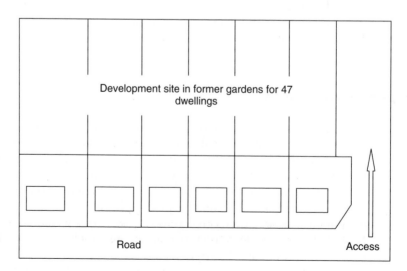

Figure 7.8   Schematic site plan for Example 7.15.

The development site will be the rear gardens of the existing houses, with one house demolished for access, and when the development is completed these houses will be resold with reduced back gardens. The market value of the houses before the development is £600 000 per house and this will fall to £480 000 per house with smaller gardens. A sketch scheme of the development is provided in Figure 7.8.

Example 7.15 Increased site density

	£
GDV	
34 dwellings sold for average price of £465 000 per dwelling	15.81m
34 × £465 000	
13 affordable homes sold to housing association 13 ×	2.34m
£180 000	
GDV	18.15m
Disposal costs @ 1%	0.18m
NDV	17.97m
Expenditure	
47 dwellings at average build cost of £150 000 per dwelling	7.050m
including ancillaries, road and infrastructure. 47 × £150 000	
Architects and QS fees @ 7%	0.493m
Developer's profit @ 20% GDV	3.630m
Brochure, marketing, etc.	0.200m
Interest on construction and fees $\frac{1}{2}$ × (£7.050m + £0.493m) @	0.396m
7% for 18 months	
Total cost	11.77m
Gross land value (£17.97m–£11.77m)	6.20m
PV £1 for 18 months @7%	0.904
Net land value	5.60m
To buy seven houses developer can offer $\dfrac{£5.60m}{7}$ per house	= £800 000
Developer offers £60 000 over the market value of the houses (note 1)	
Land price is 7 × £660 000	4.620m
Then sells six houses with smaller gardens early in development	2.88m
period: six houses @ £480 000 per house	
Net land price (£4.620–£2.88)	1.74m
Add interest @ 7% for 18 months	0.183m
Gross land price	1.920m
Development cost as above	11.77m
Total cost including net land cost (£11.77m + £1.920m)	13.69m
Deduct from NDV £17.97m–£13.69m	4.28m
Profit return on cost $\dfrac{£4.28m}{£13.69m} =$	31.26%

[1] The charge to interest throughout this calculation is not compounded in view of the short periods. It should be compounded quarterly to be accurate.

Example 7.15 Increased site density (*Continued*)

[2] The developer is able to offer 10% over the market value for the houses in view of the value of the houses when the gardens are truncated. This might be attractive to the house owners and this is assumed to be the case. However, if the owners are professionally represented, a less favourable deal might be struck (from the developer's viewpoint) or a clawback arrangement agreed. In practice it is difficult to agree on this type of deal as every owner has to agree for the development to work. Again, professional advice might emphasise the value that the dwellings collectively possess in allowing access to a development site as well as providing the land. The margins between the value of the houses with large back gardens and with smaller gardens will not have to be too large as reselling the houses amounts to a substantial portion of the developer's profit. The developer does, of course, have the option, if the house owners are willing, to take just the rear gardens rather than purchase all the dwellings outright. Some developers will consider offering the householders the freehold interest in one of the dwellings to be built rather than a cash sum for the houses.

[3] Disposal costs are included at 1% as it is assumed that a volume housebuilder would negotiate very favourable fees with selling agents and solicitors.

Crystallising Section 106 costs

Section 106 of the Town and Country Planning Act 1990 gives local authorities the power to make agreements with developers for contributions for, typically, public facilities, which are often referred to as planning gain.

Government circular 05/05 encourages local authorities to prepare standard legal agreements setting out clear formulae for situations where planning obligation contributions may be sought. Many authorities have responded to this by applying a standard charge for social, physical and economic infrastructure costs and these are applied per square metre of development. It therefore becomes important for landowners and developers to be aware of the maximum planning gain commitment that can be borne by a scheme if they are to work together to complete the development. Example 7.13 shows how a maximum Section 106 contribution may be calculated.

Example 7.16 Planning gain contribution

This calculation assumes that a mixed-use building of restaurant and office use is to be redeveloped with a restaurant and residential scheme. The building value as it stands is first calculated and then the residual value of the site assuming a new development. The existing use value is then deducted from the residual value to arrive at a maximum Section 106 contribution.

Example 7.16 Planning gain contribution (*Continued*)

Existing Use

	£
600 m² A3 use @ £130 per m²	78 000 pa
YP @ 8% in perpetuity	12.5
Capital value	975 000
3000 m² offices @ £145 per m²	435 000 pa
YP @ 7.5% in perpetuity	13.33
Capital value	5 798 550

Development value

650 m² A3 use @ £150 per m²	97 500
YP @ 7% in perpetuity	14.29
Capital value	1 393 275
6000 m² (87 units) @ 3500 per m²	21 000 000
Total GDV	22 393 275

Development costs

Construction 7980 m² @ 1200 per m²	9 576 000
Architects and QS fees @ 12.5%	1 197 000
Finance $\frac{1}{2}$ × 10 773 000 @ 10% for 1 year	538 650
Marketing	100 000
Developer's profit 20% on cost	2 282 330
Total	13 693 980

Residual to crystallise maximum Section 106 contribution

GDV	22 393 275
Development costs	13 693 980
Residual value	8 699 295
Existing use value	6 773 550
Balance for Section 106 costs	1 925 745

The calculation shows that if the owner of the property is going to be reimbursed for its current value, the Section 106 contribution must be £1 925 745 or less. The standard charge by the local authority will probably be a lot less than this figure and the development is highly profitable. Clearly if the landowner is reluctant to sell, the developer is able to make an increased offer for the site and still show an acceptable profit.

Joint ventures

In the broadest sense any relationship between two companies to complete a property development can be called a joint venture. This section, however, is confined to the activities of joint venture companies in terms of structure and methods used.

Chapter 7

Structures

The simplest form of joint venture company is where two companies own half the shares each in a joint venture company, which itself then can own the freehold of a development site or other property (Figure 7.9). Alternatively two major companies can set up two wholly owned subsidiaries (Figure 7.10). This structure allows increased flexibility as the original partners can sell their shares in the subsidiaries to show a profit on the original share provision or the two subsidiary companies can sell the shares they hold in the joint venture company itself. With this structure it would be possible for the joint venture company to issue debenture stock to secure the loan made to it by the two wholly owned subsidiaries. As this stock will be secured on the joint venture company's sole asset, a property development project that will become a property investment it can be used to secure the loan made to the two subsidiaries by the parent companies.

Management of the joint venture company

If it is assumed that the joint venture has been set up to carry out a property development there are a multiplicity of matters that have to be resolved to ensure that roles and responsibilities are clear and unequivocal. These include the following:

1. Key terms agreed together with agreement for non-disclosure/confidentiality.

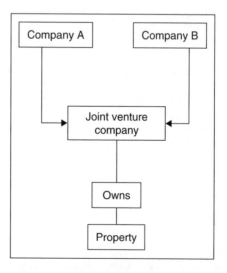

Source: Adapted from Darlow *et al.* 1994

Figure 7.9   Simple joint venture.

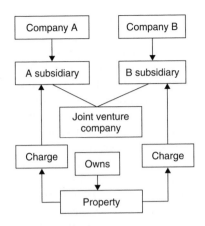

Figure 7.10   Subsidiary companies.

2.   Roles and responsibilities of principals and consultants including a programme and fee cost estimates.
3.   Which party takes on the project management role for the project? How is progress to be reported and to whom?
4.   Conditions of finance, tax implications.
5.   How is land title held?
6.   The joint venture company will be off balance sheet for both parents so long as the provisions of the Companies Act 1989 are satisfied. No one party must be able to take action without the other party either agreeing to it in the articles of association or by board resolution. If the joint venture company is set up in such a way that either of the parents can be shown to have overriding powers, the Customs and Excise Inland Revenue may seek to treat it as part of one of the parent companies and thus on balance sheet.
7.   Preparation and provision of accounts including VAT (value added tax).
8.   Provision of future finance and funding.
9.   Agreed roles and responsibilities of landowner, occupier, developer, long- and short-term funders and contractor.
10. Action if one party has problems in funding.
11. Extraction of value and profits.
12. Use of guarantors.
13. Resolution routes in the case of failure to commence work on time, failure to let buildings, increased project costs, lack of finance or finance at too high an interest rate, insolvency of joint venture partner or third party.

Step in rights and joint venture termination

Should a joint venture partner default, it is important that action be taken by the aggrieved party without the joint venture agreement being terminated or the project for which the venture was set up being jeopardised. The right to step in will normally be either a right to buy out the defaulting party (should the defaulting partner be unwilling) or a right of first refusal (a pre-emption right). As this type of joint venture will involve a building contractor and design consultants there must be a clause inserted into the building contract and the consultants' appointments to allow the step in to occur within a stated period. If the defaulting party is in financial difficulties it may be that an obligation to meet all costs will be irrelevant and if the building contract is novated to a new employer, it may also be necessary to renew warranties from the design team and others, which may entail a cost.

The joint venture company exists as a separate legal entity and therefore, as with any company, any termination of the joint venture will involve disposal of shares and a reorganisation of the company. For a company to be regarded as a joint venture there has to be no overall control either practically or in the case of the shareholding. Therefore there is no obvious solution if the board should find itself deadlocked on a decision or if one of the partners is unable to continue for financial or other reasons. One method is well known by its jargon name. The 'Texas shoot out', as it is described, involves one of the shareholders 'putting on' to the remaining partner his shareholding at a stated price or alternatively buying the partner's shares at the same price. The other shareholder can accept or refuse the offer during a stated time period. If the second shareholder does not agree to buy the first shareholder's shares at the stated price the first shareholder may dispose of his shares at the price stated to a third party or purchase the shares of the second shareholder.

Example of joint venture with syndicated funding package

A syndicated loan is one where a group of lenders each contributes to a loan package to an investor or developer, thus reducing the risk to the individual lenders (Isaac 2003). One example where a syndicated loan commitment was arranged by a joint venture company occurred with an office development at 1 Finsbury Pavement in the City of London. The joint venture company, which acted as developer, was Rosehaugh Greycoat (R+G), which was set up and financed by two successful (at the time) property development companies from which the name of the joint venture was derived. The two parents were run by two well-known and respected developers, Godfrey Bradman and Stuart Lipton. It was important for the success of the venture that the two principals had a high profile and enviable reputations in business circles.

The joint venture company was created to carry out the development of an office building at 1 Finsbury Pavement, which had attracted pre-let interest for a first phase of approximately 23 000m^2 of offices at £5m per annum. The problem faced by the company was that with a risky venture, finance was not available at an acceptable rate of interest. The solution adopted by the developer was ingenious.

The joint venture principals contacted five major 'blue chip' industrial companies and persuaded them to subscribe to £33.8m of nil paid first mortgage debenture stock in the joint venture company with an obligation to pay in 2 years' time. The developer paid no interest on this commitment in the first instance and no money was lent immediately by the five companies; they only made a commitment to do so in 2 years' time. In consideration of the commitment the five companies became entitled to receive class B ordinary shares (equity voting) in R+G for 28% of the asset value of the company. As the joint venture company had as yet no assets, the five companies acquired a 28% share in an office investment (initially a site) that was not yet built but when it was, would offer an attractive investment.

In effect R+G now had a promissory note that it could use as security for a loan. Offering the note as security, R+G then borrowed £33m from Chase Manhattan Bank at the advantageous rate (at the time) of 5/8% above LIBOR (London Inter Bank Offered Rate). With this funding in place, R+G was able to buy the site, construct the first phase of the development scheme and let it to the pre-let tenant at £5m per annum. On completion of the scheme, R+G released the loan stock holders from their obligations to pay the £33.8m price for the debenture stock and successfully issued a £40m, 11% debenture issue secured on the investment that had been created. This issue produced a rental surplus (effectively a profit rent) of £600 000 per annum excluding any reversion.

Comments

The R+G joint venture shows how a risky project can still be funded by offsetting the risk among a number of parties. The crucial factor in the project was the presence of the pre-let tenant as without this commitment, the project could not have succeeded. This project was negotiated shortly before the property crash of the early 1990s and it is sobering to think what the fate of the joint venture company would have been if the timing of the project had been slightly later. R+G fortunately avoided being a late cycle developer. The project also depended on the credibility of the principal players, Bradman and Lipton, who were able to achieve a commitment from

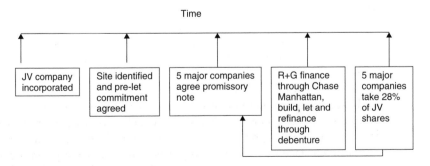

Figure 7.11 Syndicated loan commitment.

five major companies to an unfunded project and a company with no assets. The project was completed to the satisfaction of all the participants – R+G became a viable company, the bank earned interest on its loan that was repaid on time and the five major companies acquired a 28% interest in a major office building by taking a risk but not by expending money. Figure 7.11 summarises the way the project was financed.

References

Cushman and Wakefield, Healey and Baker (2004) *The Financing of Retail Property Development in the UK*. Report prepared for The Department of Trade and Industry, Cushman and Wakefield, Healey and Baker, European Research Group, Department for Business and Regulatory Reform, London.

Darlow (ed) (1990) *Valuation and Development Appraisal*, Estates Gazette, London.

Darlow *et al.* (1994) *Property Development Partnerships*, Longman, London.

Department of Communities and Local Government (1997). *Planning and Development Briefs, A Guide to Better Practice*, office for Public Sector Information, London.

Dubben N and Sayce S (1991) *Property Portfolio Management, An Introduction*, Routledge, London.

Fisher P, Robson S and Todd S (2006) The disposal of public sector sites by "development competition". *Property Management*, **25**, (4), 381–399.

Fraser W (1993) *Principles of Property Investment and Pricing*, Macmillan, Basingstoke.

Isaac D (2003) *Property Finance*, Palgrave Macmillan, Basingstoke.

Planning and Development Briefs, a Guide to Better Practice (1998), Department for Communities and Local Government, Communities and Local Government Publications, London.

Planning Policy Statement 3, Department for Communities and Local Government, the Stationery Office, Norwich.

Chapter 8
International Trends in Public–Private Partnerships

Evolving PPP programmes internationally

In essence many of the issues raised in the debate on public–private partnerships (PPPs) internationally resemble the preceding debate on privatisation in many developed economies of the world from the 1970s onwards. The assumption that dominated this debate was that increased efficiencies in resource use could be gained through changing ownership and control of public assets. The perception that public ownership in itself was a cause of inefficiency was developed in debates that divided public opinion internationally. The poor record of the public sector in terms of profitability and returns on capital invested and its lack of market and service innovation were an indication of the poor performance of public sector asset ownership. Many aspects of the public sector's operations including incentive systems, control mechanisms, resource allocation mechanisms and financial and regulatory constraints were discussed in this period in relation to their contribution to such outcomes (Convery and McDowell 1990).

Effective long-term performance monitoring has often been viewed as a key challenge for both public and private sector organisations. The private sector along with any public sector organisation will experience organisational problems and become inefficient. However, if they are subject to market pressures and have the flexibility to respond, such organisations can change and improve often due to competitive pressure. For the public sector, the absence of and protection from competition are therefore standard arguments favouring privatisation or commercialisation. Equally valid may be issues such as government policies, regulatory controls and especially price control, which can hamper the efficiency of either a public or private sector organisation. The conclusion of many such debates has been that privatisation can achieve efficient economic outcomes when there is a contestable market rather than in a transfer from a public to private monopoly. In such monopoly situations clear benefits can accrue to the new owners; for consumers, however, the transfer of assets from public to private monopoly bears less benefits. Better management and capacities to innovate have been seen positively in privatised areas of the international economy including examples such as cellular phone services where competing services are present. The unpopularity of privatisation in many countries has been seen as resulting from the fact that in many instances public monopolies were transformed into poorly regulated private monopolies (IMF 2004, p. 4).

A major issue that influenced both public and government attitudes to traditional procurement approaches was the rapid and often unexpected cost escalations in public building projects and infrastructure over the period from the 1970s to 2000. Altshuler and Luberoff (2003, p. 245) discuss the results of several international studies over periods from 1927 to 1998 covering expected and actual costs of major infrastructure projects. The results show consistent overruns in costs, routinely over 40% and often substantially greater or a multiple of the original cost. The same authors have cited the description of the two cost phases in certain public contracts as being: too early to tell and too late to stop (Altshuler and Luberoff 2003, p. 246). The consistency of such overruns over both time and countries leads to mistrust of public financing systems and the seeking of alternative solutions. Lower cost estimates may often be used as a tactic in the public debate that surrounds the planning, approval and adoption of major projects along with other causes such as project alterations and unforeseen changes. There is no guarantee, however, that policy alternatives including PPPs will not be subject to similar pressures.

One of the reasons for the popularity of PPPs with governments in Europe and internationally is the fact that under Eurostat guidance and other national/regional accounting rules, PPP transactions can be claimed or classified as off the public sector's balance sheet in any given year. This means a public agency or government authority may only need to account in a given year for the annual payments it makes to the PPP organisation or company, and not for the total capitalised present or future cost of the assets and liabilities of the project, including its financial cost or debt. This off-balance sheet treatment of PPPs is attractive in the short term for governments or administrations, as long-term obligations under PPPs are not obliged to be stated within the current budgets. For many European Union (EU) members, for example, the annual government budgets only need to show the PPP annual payments for the agreed services received, thereby helping to keep government deficits within the limit or reference value of 3% of gross domestic product (GDP). This helps such countries comply with the Stability and Growth Pact adopted in 1997 to strengthen the EU Maastricht Treaty provisions.

A less benign consequence of this is that the public may lack a clear picture of, or not be adequately informed of, the full condition of the state's finances including such legally agreed obligations. This obviously could lead to a lack of accountability and ill-informed decision-making. Critics of the PPP approach contend that governments are creating markets in public services such as education, health and social care, housing, planning, urban regeneration and the criminal justice system. Such commentators contend that in doing so, the post World War II welfare/social state services created and sustained over decades are all being marketised, their role reduced and even marginalised. In the end such contributors contend that this represents a desire to move much of what was the public sector into the hands of the private market (Harvey 2005; Whitfield 2006). Perhaps surprisingly the promotion of PPPs, which was part of liberal or market economy political agendas, is now part of the major changes in the public sector in a wide range of countries ruled by governments of a wide variety of political perspectives.

A more positive view is that the value of PPPs in terms of financial relief to the exchequer is more than just an accountancy exercise and that it can yield real benefits. In this case, it is argued that PPPs can relieve exchequer spending not just in nominal terms, but also in real terms, by balancing the present budget and reducing overall public debt (Government of Ireland 1999, 2007). Proponents of PPPs argue that in many European economies public sector investment has been dominating and substituting for private sector investment for many years. PPP is a means of substituting private sector investment for public sector investment in a manner that is still directed by central government. The EU Commissioner responsible for internal markets and services (McCreevy 2005), in addressing the issue of PPPs and their role in ensuring effective competition, stated that in terms of public procurement there is enormous untapped potential across Europe, not least in those member states with large public sector deficits. The example of the United Kingdom with up to 20% of public financing stated as being provided by PPPs was cited by the commissioner. A general additional assumption promoting the PPP concept is that by introducing the link of consumers paying to use a service, the quality of the service will affect profitability, making the operator automatically accountable to the service users by means of the profit motive.

In countries such as Ireland, the national Public Accounts Committee (PAC) has considered the issue of financial relief to the exchequer and whether this should be taken into account in making cross-country comparisons involving different states. For example, Ireland may have a lower level of public debt-to-GDP than France and, at the same time, a higher level of private debt than many other states. Thus a reason for preferring PPP in countries that have high levels of public debt may not apply in countries such as Ireland and raises questions about the increasing use of financially driven PPPs across the broad range of EU states with their differing states of public and private debt positions (PAC 2007). A problem for the promotion of PPPs has been the central argument that provision of infrastructure and services funded by private debt inevitably leads to higher costs as private borrowing is more expensive than a government bond rate, and the private interest requires an additional rate of return. This has led to a shift in emphasis on PPP policy internationally with the emphasis on the achievement of value for money through the altered allocation of risk and management responsibilities. It is significant that despite many countries having adopted PPP programmes, the IMF (2004, p. 6) reports that it is too early to draw meaningful general lessons from their experience. However, in terms of intentions, procedures and outcomes, useful comparisons can be made.

Use of PPP internationally

It is not possible to apply models directly from a range of jurisdictions, as the administrative, legal and other contexts can be substantially different. The standard term PPP has been, in general, used internationally since the 1990s. There is no single definition or model of a PPP. In an international context, the term PPP covers a range of different structures where the private sector delivers a public project or service. Concession-based road transport and utilities projects have existed in EU member countries for many years, particularly in France, Italy and Spain, where major inter-city motorways were built with tolls or revenues derived from payments by road users (PAC 2007). The Private Finance Initiative (PFI) in the United Kingdom expanded this concept to a broader range of public infrastructure and combined it with the concept and practice of services being paid for by the public sector directly rather than end-users. The use of PPPs has now spread to many EU member countries as is illustrated in Figure 8.1. The term can cover a spectrum of models from relatively short-term management contracts involving limited capital expenditure, concession contracts involving the design and build of capital assets along with the provision of services and the financing of the project construction and operation. It can also include joint ventures and partial privatisations with a sharing of ownership and responsibilities between the public and private sectors. Internationally an emerging policy shift has evolved towards inclusion of PPP, particularly for ambitious infrastructure undertakings that present difficulties for public funding sources (IMF 2005). This International Monetary Fund (IMF) report identified the successful examples of PPP as being in the procurement rather than the financing of transport infrastructure and cited the weakness of many PPP programmes as being the poor degree of project transparency and ex post evaluation of project performance. The fundamental rationale provided for the involvement of the private sector in the provision of transport infrastructure is stated as the betterment of society in the form of reduced costs from allocative and productive efficiencies, and increased benefits from the accelerated provision of cost-beneficial infrastructure and services (IMF 2005, p.17). The case made for accepting the PPP option is that the relative efficiency of the private sector will make a shared public–private service or infrastructure delivery inherently more efficient.

An earlier study by the IMF based on analysis of established PPP programmes in countries such as the United Kingdom, Ireland, Chile and Mexico in 2004 identified key issues in the international debate on PPPs as follows:

1. Although the inclusion of private capital and management can ease fiscal constraints and increase efficiency, it cannot be taken for granted that it

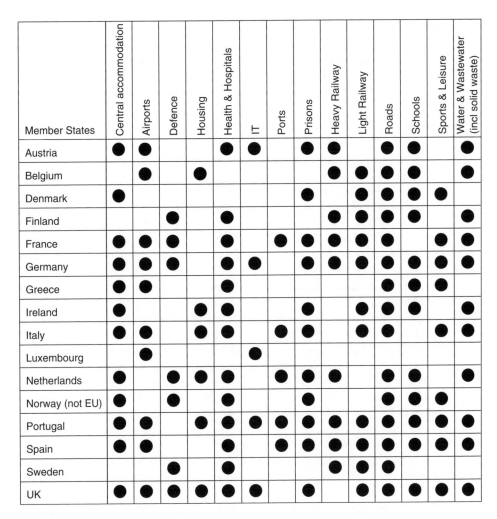

Figure 8.1 PPP in 15 EU countries. *Source*: Adapted from PAC (2007) and PWC (2005).

will be more efficient than public investment and government supply of services. A particular concern in the IMF report was that PPP should not be used to bypass spending controls by moving debt off the government balance sheet while governments still held most of the final risk and potentially large fiscal costs.

2. The adequacy of risk transfer from the government to the private sector requires an appropriate institutional framework, good governance and clear political commitment along with supporting legislation. Either competition or incentive-based regulation is essential if efficiency is to be maintained over time.

3. Significant difficulties arise in assessing risk transfer due to the complexity of many PPP contracts. Disclosure of PPP contracts is regarded as necessary to assess risk transfer.

Chapter 8

4. Given the absence of internationally agreed guidance on the known and future potential costs of PPP, disclosure of contractual obligations regarding government purchase agreements and guarantees should be standard in order to assess the fiscal consequences of such programmes in an appropriate and transparent manner (IMF 2004, p. 3).

There is an increasing use of PPP across the world in the delivery of infrastructure and services arising initially from concerns regarding public debt as governments tried to encourage private investment in infrastructure, services or operations that can be run jointly with the private sector or contracted out. Other variations include the private sector making a capital investment in the development of a specific project, such as hospital facilities on the basis of a financial package/contract, with a government agency to provide the agreed services. The government's financial payment may be in terms of an annual payment, transfers of existing assets or a combination of contribution types. The PPP programmes established by a high number of OECD countries in the past 20 years have been well documented in studies such as IMF (2004), PricewaterhouseCoopers (PWC 2005) and PAC (2007). Analysis of these reports indicates that the trend has grown in recent years, and in 2004 and 2005, around 206 PPP deals worth approximately US$52bn (€42bn) were closed in the world, of which 152 projects with a value of US$26bn (€21bn) were located in Europe, referring to the EU member states and the EU acceding countries (Bulgaria, Romania, Turkey and Norway). From January 1994 to September 2005, it was estimated that PPP deals with a value of approximately US$120bn (€100bn) were closed across Europe. It is estimated that two-thirds of these arrangements were closed in the United Kingdom, with Spain and Portugal accounting for 9–10% each. The United Kingdom showed substantially more PPP activity than the rest of Europe with 118 deals closed in 2004 and 2005, with the next most active PPP market being Spain, which experienced the closing of 12 PPP contracts during the same period (PAC 2007). The United Kingdom stands out as the country most reliant on its PPP programme or PFI, which commenced in 1992. By 2004, PFI was responsible for 14% of public investment with key projects throughout the infrastructure and service areas.

The first chart shows the state of PPP development in 15 EU countries. Many countries start using PPPs in the provision of road infrastructure, moving on to their use in other sectors, such as water and waste treatment, education, health and energy. The chart shows that roads and water and wastewater were the most frequently used sectors across the sample of countries. Many continental EU countries including the Netherlands, Germany, Italy, Greece and Portugal have PPP projects although with some exceptions their share of total public investment is small. A number of central and eastern European countries are embarking on future PPP programmes in attempting to deal with their need for large-scale infrastructure investment with a relatively weak fiscal position. In addition, the EU Growth Initiative includes the use of PPPs as a primary component in the development of new trans-European road networks. There is also a trend for PPPs in Europe to grow at sub-national level with regional and large city administrations

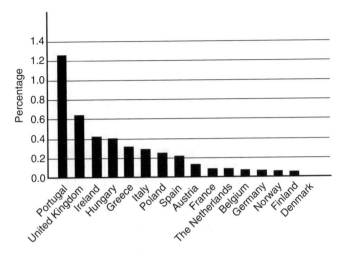

Figure 8.2 Average 2000–2005 PPP activity as a percentage of mean GDP. *Source:* Adapted from PAC (2007) and PWC (2005).

turning to PPPs for delivery of services (IMF 2004, p. 5). The United Kingdom remains the most advanced country with respect to PPP (PFI) use, having substantial numbers of closed projects across a wide variety of services and infrastructure by 2007, with a majority of them in operation.

While the United Kingdom closed the greatest number of PPP deals in 2000–2005, if PPP activity is considered as a percentage of GDP, Portugal has the greatest involvement with PPPs relative to its GDP, with Ireland ranking third. Other countries including Hungary and Greece also have high levels of PPP usage relative to GDP as shown in Figure 8.2, which illustrates the average 2000–2005 PPP activity as a percentage of mean GDP.

In areas outside of Europe, PPP experience in Australia, United States and, to a lesser degree, Canada and Japan has relatively advanced in the current decade (IMF 2004). Figure 8.3 shows that Australia, particularly the state of Victoria, is one of the most advanced countries with respect to the use of PPPs, having a substantial number of closed and 12 operational projects in the airports, ports and roads sectors. Prisons and water and wastewater projects are also very advanced. Japan has concentrated its PPP projects in the sectors of government offices and schools. Mexico and Chile have advanced the use of PPPs to promote private investment in public development projects. The United States had reached procurement stage in the prisons, light railway and water and wastewater sectors, with most other sectors at the stage of ongoing discussions. PPPs were first used to finance road development in Mexico in the 1990s and subsequently, projects in the energy sector.

In Chile, PPP programmes have been used in the development of transport, airports and prisons with successful completion of 24 projects by 2004 (IMF 2004, p. 35). This process was reported as involving foreign exchange and demand risk being shared with the government while construction and performance risks are borne by the private sector. The

Chapter 8

Country	Central accommodation	Airports	Defence	Housing	Health & Hospitals	IT	Ports	Prisons	Heavy Railway	Light Railway	Roads	Schools	Sports & Leisure	Water & Wastewater (incl solid waste)
Australia	●	●	●	●	●	●	●	●	●	●	●	●	●	●
Canada	●				●			●		●	●	●	●	●
Japan	●	●	●	●	●	●	●		●	●	●	●	●	●
Mexico		●			●		●		●	●	●			●
Singapore	●		●		●						●	●	●	●
South Africa	●	●			●	●		●	●		●	●	●	●
United States		●	●	●	●			●	●	●	●	●	●	●

Figure 8.3 PPPs for selected non-EU countries. *Source*: Adapted from PAC (2007) and PWC (2005).

government has assumed significant fiscal commitments under such contracts but as full disclosure and reporting requirements were not in place, these are difficult to quantify. The World Bank was assisting in defining and calculating future budgetary requirements in terms of maximum payments that could occur, revenue guarantees and expected payments over the period 2003–2020. Asian experience was more limited and proposals were at feasibility stages in other countries such as South Africa (IMF 2004, pp. 5–6). Data on PPPs for selected non-EU countries is illustrated in Figure 8.3.

Accountability issues

The monitoring of PPPs takes place at several levels. The first level is the relationship between the public sector's operational team, often a government agency, and the private interest involved in the project. Secondly, at the parliamentary level, there is a need for both government and parliaments to be able to access information on what are important and far-reaching financial and budgetary decisions. Lastly, for European countries, there are important guidelines that must be observed to ensure compliance with EU budgetary commitments by national governments and to ensure compliance with EU directives on public procurement. National/regional operational relationships were discussed in previous chapters on operational PPPs and PFIs indicating that public authorities were required to give a significant amount of inputs in contract monitoring which was greater than had originally been anticipated. Internationally PPPs provide public infrastructure in many areas of life, from schools to roads and prisons raising important issues of public accountability.

In their examination of PPPs internationally, the Irish government's PAC (2007) found that the mechanisms of market accountability and public accountability can to some extent be mutually compatible although monopoly PPPs require specific public accountability approaches because in these cases markets do not function. In such situations there is less justification for commercial confidentiality clauses to be used, which seeks to protect market-sensitive data from competitors. It is found that with PPPs in the competitive sectors there may be a requirement for commercial confidentiality, but at least such cases can offer market accountability through the operations of the market. Two citations from this report present differing perspectives on the issue of accountability. First the report cited George Monbiot, a critic of PFIs in the United Kingdom (Monbiot 2000) as stating: 'Poor visibility corrupts; invisibility corrupts absolutely'. The PFI, which is the means by which billions of pounds of new public projects in the United Kingdom are now being funded, is doubly obscure: first because it is so complicated and appears so boring that few people have grasped its implications; secondly, because so many of the crucial details are hidden from public view by the blanket ban on disclosure known as 'commercial confidentiality' (PAC 2007, S. 1). The report also cited the former auditor general of the State of Victoria in Australia who indicated that he was concerned about the ongoing oversight and monitoring arrangements for PPPs and the potential to lose corporate memory over the life of the contract: 'Typically . . . project teams are established . . . However, once the arrangements are established and operating, these teams generally are dispersed, with a resultant loss of detailed knowledge of the arrangements. This represents a major issue impacting on the effective ongoing oversight of the arrangements . . . A further issue that emerges from these long-term "outsourcing" arrangements is that, over time, there is a loss of expertise in the effective oversight of these arrangements given that the State may no longer be involved in areas similar to those subject to PPPs, and therefore individuals responsible for oversight functions may not fully appreciate the associated management issues. Therefore, it is important that effective strategies are developed by the public sector to mitigate these risks. This is particularly important given the public sector's ongoing duty of care associated with key aspects of public sector service delivery' (PAC 2007, S. 3).

Political accountability

It is clear from the analysis of the reports and websites of various jurisdictions (Websites accessed 2007/2008) that common themes emerge in attempts to oversee the PPP process by elected politicians. Parties in government are anxious to achieve as much progress in infrastructure and services as is possible. Cross party committees involving both government and opposition parties with a responsibility or input into overseeing public expenditures on such schemes are often in a difficult position to carry out such functions due to the restricted information available. The pattern of issues arising may be summarised as follows:

1. Are members of the public and politicians entitled to know what contracts are entered into on their behalf, and on what terms and conditions were such agreements signed? If they are entitled to know clearly what is required in terms of public monies spent and in turn what precisely is to be delivered under the terms of the contract? They would need to know how legal and financial risks are allocated between the contracting parties. Also they would need to be aware of guarantees, monitoring and enforcement procedures existing in the event of contractual default. Much of this information may not be available or can be subject to commercial confidentiality restrictions but is necessary if processes are to be in place to ensure public accountability and value for money.

2. Local communities are often concerned about the lack of transparency and accountability of PPP projects despite most governments over time strengthening governance processes and systems for evaluation and review.

3. Conflicts of interest involving consultancy advice and the numbers, timing and arrangements of any staff being transferred or seconded from a public agency involved in negotiating a contract to the private consortium chosen after such negotiations are to be avoided.

4. In a review or enquiry situation, what are the obligations of the parties involved to disclose details relating to such arrangements where the public interest is in question? Do such obligations extend to information held by private interests? Can disclosure of information be unnecessarily restricted because of commercial confidentiality issues?

5. At what stage and at what level of detail should public–private partnerships be made available to the public? Should disclosure of information be scaled according to the scale of the contract or universally applied?

6. Which elements of a contract are legitimately commercially sensitive? Do these elements include elements such as financing arrangements, cost structure or profit margins, issues where disclosure might place the contractor at a commercial disadvantage with its competitors?

7. In many jurisdictions there is a reliance on an auditor general system to review such schemes. Information and evidence taken in this process may not be publicly available. Is this an adequate level of review and are resources of such offices sufficient for their tasks?

8. Should the complete future liabilities associated with individual PPPs be computed and a transparent means of accounting for them developed in line with best international practice? Would such computations be publicly available?

9. Value for money should be the justification for the consideration of PPPs. A policy bias for or against particular procurement approaches should be avoided.

10. Provision for periodic review and measurement of the performance of a PPP should be built into such agreements.

National and international accountability

For public projects including PPPs, national and international accountability issues exist along with other responsibilities. One of the main driving forces for PPP programmes in Europe was the desire to decrease dependence on public finances and to avail of private investment and management. This engagement of private investment was greatly facilitated by the low interest rates and easy availability of credit in the past decade. For EU member states, national law is supplemented by European Community regulations, which are of special importance in the negotiation and creation of PPPs. At EU level, a public consultation process was held on the PPP Green Paper on Public–Private Partnerships and Community Law on Public Contracts and Concessions (EC 2005). Following consultations and review, the European Commission (EC) adopted an interpretative communication on the application of European community law to institutionalised PPPs on 05/02/2008. This process presents policy options with a view to ensuring effective competition for PPPs without unduly restricting or limiting the flexibility to design innovative and often complex projects in member states. In this report, it is stated that the term public–private partnership is not defined at community level and the term is taken to refer to forms of cooperation between public authorities and business interests that aim to ensure the funding, construction, renovation, management or maintenance of an infrastructure or the provision of a service.

The Green Paper (EC 2005) analyses the issue of PPPs with regard to community law on public procurement and concessions. Under community law, there is no specific system governing such PPPs. In general terms, PPPs, which qualify as public contracts under the coordinating procedures directives for the award of public contracts, must comply with the detailed provisions of those directives. Other PPPs that qualify as work concessions are covered only by secondary legislation and those PPPs qualifying as service concessions are not covered by the public contracts directives (EC 2004). Nevertheless, any contract, in which a public body awards work involving an area of economic activity to a third party, whether covered by secondary legislation or not, must be examined in the light of the standard rules and principles of the EC Treaty including in particular the principles of transparency, equal treatment, proportionality and mutual recognition. The aim of the Green Paper was to explore how procurement law applies to the different forms of PPP developing in the various member states, in order to assess whether there was a need to clarify or improve the current legal framework at the European level. The prime objective of any community initiative in this area is stated to be the provision to both the public and the private sides of such contracts with legal certainty to facilitate a framework within which PPPs can work most efficiently.

Guidance on setting up institutionalised public–private partnerships

On 05/02/2008, the commission adopted an Interpretative Communication on the application of Community Law on Public Procurement and Concessions to Institutionalised Public–Private Partnerships (IPPP). The communication (EC 2008) explains compliance with EC rules when private partners are chosen for an IPPP. Depending on the nature of the task (public contract or concession) to be attributed to the IPPP, either the Public Procurement Directives or the general EC Treaty principles apply to the legal standards involved in selection procedures of the private partner. The view of the commission is that under community law on tendering procedure one process is sufficient when an IPPP is set up. Community law does not require double tendering such as one for selecting the private partner to the IPPP and another for the award of public contracts or concessions to the public–private entity when the IPPP is established. The communication also states that the IPPP must remain within the scope of their initial object and cannot obtain further or subsequent public contracts or concessions without a procedure respecting community law on public contracts and concessions. It is acknowledged that an IPPP is usually set up to provide services over a long time and must be able to adjust to change in the economic, legal or technical environments.

Risk transfer

Eurostat, the Statistical Office of the European Communities, provides specific guidance on the classification of PPP assets based on risk transfer. This decision on the accounting treatment in national accounts of contracts undertaken by government units in the framework of partnerships with non-government units specifies the impact on government deficit/surplus and debt of such projects. Key extracts require consideration.

Importantly, Eurostat (2004) recommended that the assets involved in a public–private partnership should be classified as non-government assets, and therefore recorded off balance sheet for government, if both of the following conditions are met:

1. the private partner bears the construction risk; and
2. the private partner bears at least one of either availability or demand risk.

The decision states that if the construction risk is borne by government, or if the private partner bears only the construction risk and no other risks, the assets are classified as government assets. In such cases, the initial capital expenditure relating to the assets will be recorded as government fixed capital formation, with a negative impact on government deficit/surplus. Commenting on this definition the IMF suggested that despite efforts at specifying risk categories, many projects are effectively too big or important to actually allow risk transfer. In such cases, it suggested that government in fact bears more of the risk than suggested in the contract as effectively it will be obliged as the last resort to bail out such projects (IMF 2004, p. 22).

It is clear that the application of such guidelines as detailed in Box 8.1 leads many international PPP contracts to be classified as government assets. This may be regarded as appropriate given that the government guarantees provided to PPPs and the continued calls for full disclosure of contingent liabilities are a major source of fiscal risk (IMF 2004, p. 27).

In conclusion, many OECD countries have now advanced PPP programmes with infrastructure and service provision assisted by a range of innovative approaches. The principal benefit of such approaches is the accelerated delivery of public sector development. Improvements regarding transparency, risk transfer and accountability are the focus of policy-making initiatives in many jurisdictions. The focus for governments in a wide range of European countries and in other parts of the world is on exchanging experiences and best practices and raising awareness of key drivers in successful PPPs. The inception of many programmes was driven by the desire to move public development projects away from dependence on public finance and towards the engagement of private sector investment and management. The changing nature of public and private debt positions in many countries in the period from 2009 onwards may impact negatively on PPP programmes in the coming years.

Box 8.1 Key Features and Extracts of Eurostat Decision on Treatment of PPPS

Recognising that many risks are involved in practice in such PPP arrangements and that wordings used may be confusing, Eurostat identified three main categories of generic risks.

The first category is defined as 'construction risk' covering notably events like late delivery, non-respect of specified standards, additional costs, technical deficiency and external negative effects. Government's obligation to start making regular payments to a partner without taking into account the effective state of the assets would be evidence that government bears the majority of the construction risks.

The second category is 'availability risk'. This can be related to the private partner's ability to deliver the volume that was contractually agreed on or to meet safety or public certification standards relating to the provision of services to final users, as specified in the contract. It also applies where the partner does not meet the required quality standards relating to the delivery of the service, as stated in the contract, and resulting from an evident lack of 'performance' of the partner. It states that government payments must depend on the effective degree of availability supplied by the partner during a given time. Application of penalties where the partner is defaulting on its service obligations should be automatic and should also have a significant effect on the partner's revenue/profit, and must not be purely 'cosmetic' or symbolic.

The third category listed by Eurostat is 'demand risk' covering variability of demand (higher or lower than expected when the contract was signed) irrespective of the behaviour (management) of the private partner. This risk should only cover a shift of demand not resulting from inadequate or low

Chapter 8

> ## Box 8.1 Key Features and Extracts of Eurostat Decision on Treatment of PPPS (*Continued*)
>
> quality of the services provided by the partner or any action that changes the quantity/quality of services provided. It can result from other factors, such as the business cycle, new market trends, direct competition or technological obsolescence. Government will be assumed to bear the risk where it is obliged to ensure a given level of payment to the partner independently of the effective level of demand expressed by the final user, rendering the fluctuations in level of demand on the partner's profitability irrelevant. However, this statement does not apply where the shift in demand results from an obvious government action, such as decisions of units of general government (and thus not just the unit(s) directly involved in the contract) that represent a significant policy change, or the development of directly competing infrastructure built under government mandate.
>
> The analysis of the risks in such partnerships will be carried out in all member states and acceding countries under the responsibility of the National Statistical Offices.
>
> In this respect, if the assets remain the property of the partner at the end of the project, and if they still have a significant economic value, it is normally classified on the partner's balance sheet. This also includes contracts where government has merely an option to buy the asset at the current market value. On the other hand, if the government has a firm obligation to acquire the assets at the end of the contract at a pre-determined price that does not reflect the economic value of the assets at that time (such as expected on the basis of conservative hypothesis at the time the contract was signed), or has paid for the right to acquire the assets throughout the contract through regular payments that were higher than they would have been without that right, then there can be a reason to record the assets as government assets if the other tests do not give a clear answer.
>
> *Source*: Extracts adapted from Eurostat (2004) Decision of Eurostat on deficit and debt treatment of public–private partnerships.

References

Altshuler A and Luberoff D (2003) *Mega-Projects. The Changing Politics of Urban Public Investment*, Lincoln Institute of Land Policy, Cambridge, USA.

Convery F and McDowell M (1990) *Privatisation Issues of Principle and Implementation in Ireland*, Gill and MacMillan, Dublin.

European Commission (EC) (2004) *Community Directives Coordinating the Procedures for the Award of Public Contracts*, Directives 2004/17/EC and 2004/18/EC, available at www.europa.eu.

European Commission (EC) (2005) *Report on the Public Consultation on the Green Paper on Public–Private Partnerships and Community Law on Public Contracts and Concessions – SEC (2005) 629*, available at http://www.europa.eu.

European Commission (EC) (2008) *Interpretative Communication on the Application of Community Law on Public Procurement and Concessions to Institutionalised Public–Private Partnerships (IPPP)*, available at http://www.europa.eu.

Eurostat (2004) *Treatment of Public Private Partnerships*, available at http://www. Epp.eurostat.ec.europa.eu.

Government of Ireland (1999) *National Development Plan 2000–2006*, The Stationery Office, Dublin.

Government of Ireland (2007) *National Development Plan 2007–2013*, The Stationery Office, Dublin.

Harvey D (2005) *A Brief History of Neo-liberalism*, Oxford University Press, Oxford.

International Monetary Fund (IMF) (2004) *Public Private Partnerships*, International Monetary Fund, Fiscal Affairs Department, Washington, USA.

International Monetary Fund (IMF) (2005) *Development of Public Private Partnerships in Infrastructure. Successful Examples of Public Private Partnerships and Private Sector Involvement in Transport Infrastructure Development, Final Report.* Washington, USA.

McCreevy C (2005) *European Commissioner for Internal Market and Services. Public – Private Partnerships – Options to Ensure Effective Competition.* Speech to PPP Global Summit *The 6th Annual Government – Industry Forum on Public – Private – Partnership*, 17 November 2005, Copenhagen.

Monbiot G (2000) *Captive State, the Corporate Takeover of Britain*, MacMillan, London.

PricewaterhouseCoopers (2005) *Delivering the PPP Promise: A Review of PPP Issues and Activity*, PricewaterhouseCoopers, London.

Public Accounts Committee, First Interim Report (PAC) (2007) *Access to the Private Element of Public Private Partnerships – An International Comparison, available on web at* http://www.irl.gov.ie.

Whitfield D (2006) *New Labour's Attack on Public Services*, Spokesman Books, Nottingham.

Websites accessed 2007/2008

www.audgen.gov.ie
www.irl.gov.ie
www.parliament.nsw.gov.au.publicacounts
www.europa.eu
www.partnerships.vic.gov.au
www.auditoffice.gov.uk

Chapter 8

Chapter 9
Economic Background and Future Trends

At the time of writing this book, the property market is experiencing one of its regular, but unwelcome, readjustments. Commercial property yields have moved out dramatically and the forecasts from commentators are not encouraging. The Investment Property Forum (IPF 2008) reports that the total return forecast for 2008 for all property is −5.2% with confidence in the City and West End office markets badly affected by the weakening financial services sector. These two sectors are also predicted to show returns below inflation and negative total returns for 2009 (IPF 2008).

As can be seen from the IPF's forecasts in Figures 9.1 and 9.2, returns are not expected to recover until 2010 and these estimates have been revised downwards from previous predictions.

Returns from property development and investment are derived from the value of the utility offered by property to the end-user, freehold owner or tenant. This is represented by the level of rent received and the subsequent rental growth. Capital growth is achieved through a fall in the all risks yield applied when the property is valued as an investment. When investors believe that rents will rise in the future and if a property is believed to offer returns over and above inflation, the all risks yield will be driven downwards as investors compete to own the investment. In a boom time for property, when rents are rising strongly, falls in yield may reflect investors sentiment in seeking property investments in competition with others rather than cold analysis of the probability of the level of future rental growth. The behaviour of investors in an economic boom reflects what John Maynard Keynes described as 'animal spirits'.

It is clear that the animal spirits referred to earlier have increasingly been at work in the long boom in property rental and capital growth from 1995 until 2007. Apart from minor periods of slowdown in 2000 and 2001 when the dot com boom ended, the period has been one of property rental and capital growth, noticeably in the housing markets, and many successful development schemes have been completed with developers, public authorities, other landowners, banks and institutions working in various types of partnership

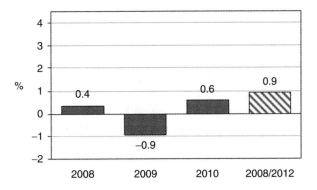

Figure 9.1 All property rental value growth forecasts. Averages shown in right hand column. *Source* : Investment Property Forum 2008 (with permission).

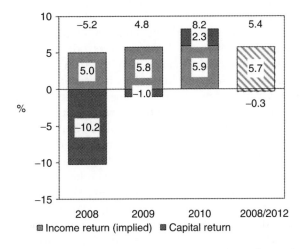

Figure 9.2 All property total return forecasts. Averages shown in right hand column. *Source* : Investment Property Forum 2008 (with permission).

arrangements. The degree of utility offered to occupiers has been reflected in rental and capital growth driving successful schemes in the retail and leisure fields particularly. Growth may not necessarily depend upon the actual occupier of a property and the example may be taken of a shopping centre where the level of rent at rent review is determined by a new letting to a company not trading in the centre.

The economic factors that influence the activities of property developers and investors are the balance of payments current account, the level of aggregate demand, the level of money supply (M3), the exchange rate (£ to € and $), the rates of unemployment and inflation and the Minimum Lending Rate (MLR) and the London Inter Bank Offered Rate (LIBOR) which itself is derived, in normal times, from the MLR. Statistically all these translate into key economic indicators. Other key indicators are all risks yields for

Chapter 9

commercial property and gross redemption yields on medium- and long-term government stock (gilts).

The IPF (2008) report lists the continuing concerns for the economy. GDP growth was 0.4% in the first quarter of 2008 compared with 0.7% in the fourth quarter of 2007. Economic forecasts collated by the Treasury show the economy growing by 1.7% for 2008 and 1.5% for 2009. Production industry output shows a similar decline with growth in the service sector down from 0.7 to 0.5% in the fourth quarter of 2007. Retail sales recently showed a remarkable monthly growth against trend but in the current quarter (second 2008), slower growth is noted particularly in household goods although growth held up in the sales of mobile phones, games and sports goods. For the present, unemployment is not rising as a result of economic problems and the unemployment rate of 74.9% shows an increase in numbers employed with the number of job vacancies increasing. Anecdotal evidence suggests that these figures will be badly affected by employment in property related professions caused by the rapid decline in transactional business. The Bank of England cut its base rate to 5% in April 2008 and consumer price inflation was 3% at that time with the Treasury forecasting the same figure for the remainder of 2008 and 2.25 for 2009 (all statistics from IPF 2008; The Treasury 2008). Fears remain that the rising price of oil as a result of a speculative boom on world markets (caused itself by the decline in the value of the dollar as the reserve currency of choice) and the increasing price of food and commodities worldwide will result in inflationary pressures that will force interest rate rises in the United Kingdom just as economic activity is falling. The resulting 'stagflation', not experienced in the United Kingdom since the 1970s, is an outcome feared by many commentators.

Rising inflation is sometimes seen as a benefit for property investors and developers as it may signify rising rents and values. This has been shown to be a fallacy in a paper written by David Miles (admittedly in 1996): 'in the short run commercial property returns do not respond at all to unexpected inflation... but even after 24 months nominal returns are only slightly higher; barely 50% of the increase in inflation is matched by higher commercial property return even in the very long run' (Miles 1996, p. 24). Inflationary pressures may cause the Bank of England Monetary Policy Committee to raise interest rates in order to prevent a run on the currency and a dramatic fall in monetary deposits in UK banks. The rise in interest rates will trigger a rise in gilt yields as money is withdrawn from gilts to take advantage of higher rates available in banks. This in turn will tend to pull all risks yields upwards, which will have a corresponding effect on the property investment market to which development activity is highly sensitive. With higher interest rates development schemes become more expensive and developer's profit margins are squeezed. The tenant market will be affected as expansion becomes more expensive although there will be differences between sectors.

Figure 9.3 shows the effect of interest rate movements (represented here by the 5-year swap rate) on gilt yields and property yields. It is noticeable that gilt yields are fairly well correlated with interest rate movements. There will never be perfect correlation as the market will tend to act on predictions of

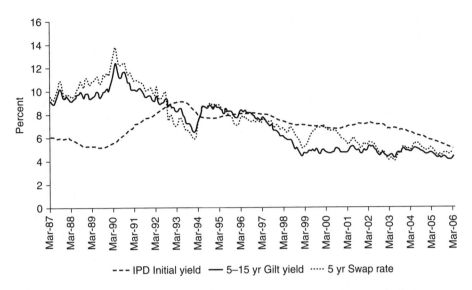

Figure 9.3 Property yield and financial rates. *Source*: Bloomberg, IPD, DTZ Research.

interest rate movements before they happen. As interest rates and gilt yields rose from March 1988 until early 1990 property yields continued to fall, and as interest rates and gilt yields fell from March 1990 onwards property yields rose strongly. This counter cyclical feature of property yields is caused by the particular features of the property cycle especially the development lag caused by price inelasticity in the supply of commercial property. A similar feature is seen in 1993 and 1994 but after 1994 interest rates, property yields and gilt yields display a steady downward trend until 2006. It is noticeable that when interest rates rose temporarily in 2000, largely due to a fallout of the dot com boom, markets believed that they would quickly fall and this is evidenced by the lack of movement in the gilt markets at this time although property yields showed a slight upward trend. This would be expected as property yields are countercyclical for a time.

The attraction of debt finance for developers is that as debt increases as a proportion of total finance so the return to equity increases. In benign economic conditions developers will increase their indebtedness both with corporate and project finance. The problem arises when economic conditions worsen quickly. This happened in the 1970s with the Yom Kippur war leading to a 400% rise in the price of oil in the West. The subsequent cost push inflation led to high interest rates and a collapse in demand for commercial property from investors and tenants. The 1990s boom was caused by unsustainable consumer spending encouraged by government fiscal policy. A collapse in world oil prices in 1986 led to a depreciation of sterling and the decision by the then Chancellor to shadow the DM resulted in the money supply expanding rapidly. Excessive aggregate demand led to demand pull inflation and increasing deficits on the Balance of Payments current account resulted in interest rate rises, fall in tenant demand, yields

Chapter 9

moving out and a deep recession. Both booms, the 1970s and the 1980s, were characterised by imprudent bank lending based on expectations of continued rental growth. These factors can be seen in the chart below.

Figure 9.4 shows private debt, mainly bank debt, outstanding to United Kingdom based property companies from 1970 until 2006 and it can be seen that the two property booms referred to earlier were both supported by increases in bank lending. However the scale of current indebtedness is unprecedented and reflects the growing confidence during the long period of steady growth since 1996. Inflationary pressures have been contained by growing competition and downward pressures on prices worldwide resulting from increased globalisation. The UK government would claim that Bank of England independence and a flexible labour market have also contributed. However, it has now emerged that bank lending had become very sophisticated with debt of various types and risk profiles being packaged for onward transmission. Loans were secured against property in the US sub-prime market based on the belief that if the borrower defaulted the loan would be covered by the value of the property. The result is that many lenders found themselves with worthless securities when continued growth faltered and borrowers defaulted. The resulting losses resulted in Bear Stearns bank failing in the United States with a similar fate befalling Northern Rock in the United Kingdom. A rash of successful and unsuccessful rights issues represent attempts by banks to stay viable in the face of expensive or non-existent borrowing opportunities. Initially, the Bank of England made a £50bn rescue package available by swapping government bonds or bills for mortgage bonds held by banks. The banks could then trade the government bonds for cash. Recent evidence suggests that this action was insufficient to persuade banks to start to lend to each other again and the markets appear to believe that more debt defaults may yet result in further bank failures and the necessity for government action to prevent a deep recession. The *Financial Times* reported

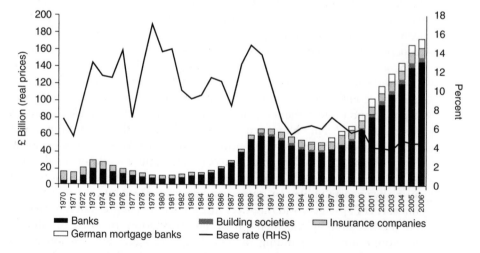

Figure 9.4 Private debt outstanding to UK property companies. *Source*: Bank of England, ONS, VDH, DTZ Research.

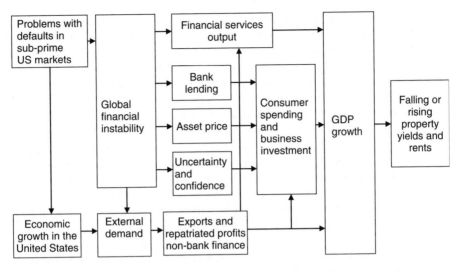

Figure 9.5 The link from sub-prime defaults to property yields. Adapted from PricewaterhouseCoopers (2008).

on 15/05/2008 that global banks had written off 80% of their losses against assets linked to the sub-prime mortgage market, which is considered to be an encouraging sign although 'crucial parts of the financial system remain fairly clogged up' (Citigroup quoted in Sakoui, *FT* 15/5/08). The problems in the sub-prime markets in the United States transmit themselves into the UK economy as described in Figure 9.5. It would be expected that rising GDP growth would support continued growth in all sectors of the property market as a healthy business environment worked through into continued demand for property. PricewaterhouseCoopers (2008) identify four main drivers for GDP growth, namely, domestic demand, the trade deficit and current account balance, inflation and the labour market and monetary and fiscal policy developments. The indicators from these four factors are not encouraging in the short term. It is reported that the underlying trend in retail growth is 'well below the rapid pace of growth seen in the first half of 2007' with reduced consumer confidence as a result of a lowering of the spendable income. The trade deficit expanded to £20bn in 2007 and this was mainly due to rising oil prices and the weakness of sterling against the euro. Consumer price inflation has been above the government's target level of 2% per annum but not by a great deal reaching 2.2% in January 2007, before rising to over 3% in April 2007 before falling back and then rising slightly to 2.1% in January 2008. Higher oil and food prices working through into domestic energy bills have caused this rise and the RPIX (retail prices index excluding mortgage payments) has also risen to over 4% through 2007 and into 2008. The Bank of England remains in something of a dilemma with the threat of inflation and a recession at the same time. There is also a budget deficit in the year to January 2008 of £8.5bn and the public sector finances are described as being in a 'relatively fragile state'. The bank has little room to manoeuvre with deficits of this magnitude.

A recession, generally taken to mean negative economic growth for two quarters is now a virtual certainty for most Western economies. The rapid downturn in property markets and the link with the continuing credit crisis is immediately evident in the United Kingdom, Ireland and across all the Western market economies. Taking the United Kingdom as an example the implications of these trends can be seen. It is clear that imprudent lending through complex financial packages combined with weak regulation has resulted in bank lending being secured on assets that are falling in value or people who are unable to meet debt repayments. This lending was predicated on the assumption that asset prices would continue to rise so that any default could be reimbursed by selling the asset. If this was ever the case it no longer is and banks are exposed and, in many cases, unviable. In an attempt to stabilise their economies and protect their populations from the appalling results of a general collapse of the banking system, Western governments have taken action by what is in effect partial nationalisation. The dangers of an unsustainable boom have long been known: 'All assets become overvalued in a speculative bubble. The readjustment that is inevitable and which everyone knows is coming sooner rather than later, typically occurs in one dramatic collapse...the reality is that the prices of speculative assets repeatedly diverge from their underlying values, financial intermediaries can provoke rather than contain binge buying, unrestricted monetary flows add to the pressure and, when sentiments change, sudden price adjustment can be catastrophic' (Cleaver 2004). The catastrophe has now arrived and, at the time of writing, it is unclear whether government or IMF (International Monetary Fund) action will be effective in reducing its worst effects.

The Bank of England Monetary Policy Committee recently cut minimum lending rate to 4.5%, a reduction of a full 50 basis points. Although lower interest rates may help the housing market and High Street spending they may also fuel inflation. It may be that policy instruments, which government has deliberately restricted to monetary policy, are ineffective in current economic circumstances. Keynes described attempts by government to use monetary policy to control the economy at times such as these as 'pushing on a piece of string'. The prospects for successful property partnerships do not look hopeful with falling rents and the prospects of rising yields, and it is probable that apart from the largest schemes such as Grosvenor's Paradise Street regeneration in Liverpool, values will continue to fall until confidence returns and economic growth resumes at some point in the future. It is to be hoped that the collapse of property values in virtually all sectors, unprecedented in modern times, will not fatally damage any potential recovery.

References

Cleaver T (2004) *Economics, the Basics*, Routledge, Abingdon.
Investment Property Forum (IPF) (2008) *Summary Report*, IPF, London.
Miles D (1996) *Property and Inflation*, Merrill Lynch, London.
PricewaterhouseCoopers (PWC) (2008) *UK Economic Outlook*, PWC, London.
The Treasury (2008) *Forecasts for the UK Economy*, The Treasury, London.

Index